Buffy the vampire slayer™

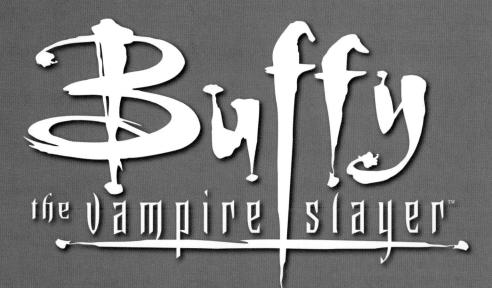

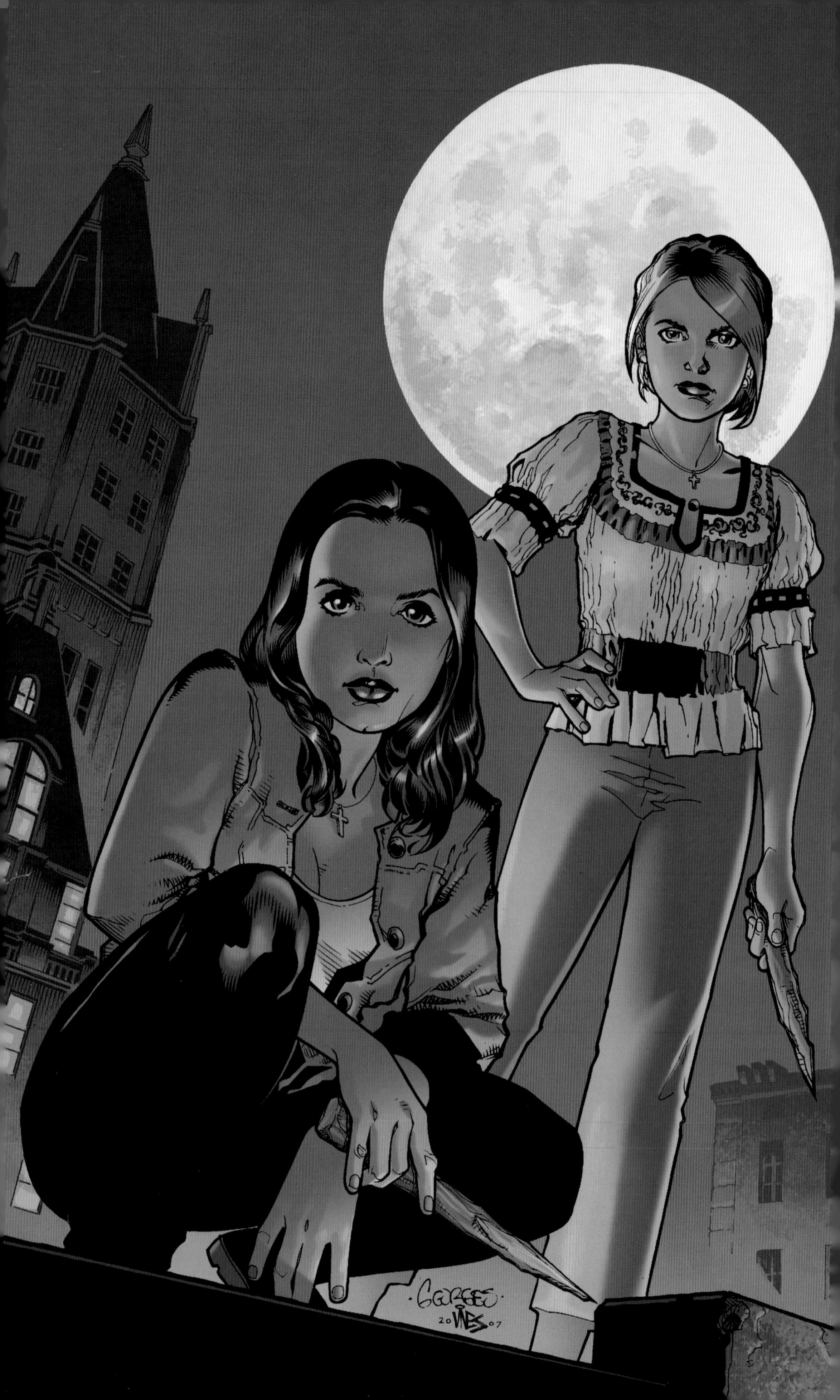

Buffy the Vampire Slayer

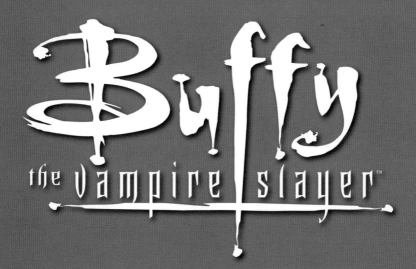

SEASON EIGHT VOLUME 2

NO FUTURE FOR YOU

Script BRIAN K. VAUGHAN

Pencils GEORGES JEANTY

Inks ANDY OWENS

Colors DAVE STEWART

Letters RICHARD STARKINGS
& COMICRAFT'S JIMMY & ALBERT

Cover Art JO CHEN

"Anywhere But Here"
Script JOSS WHEDON
Pencils CLIFF RICHARDS

Executive Producer JOSS WHEDON

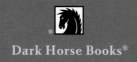

Dark Horse Books®

Publisher MIKE RICHARDSON

Editor SCOTT ALLIE

Assistant Editors SIERRA HAHN & KATIE MOODY

Collection Designer HEIDI WHITCOMB

This story takes place after the end of the
television series *Buffy the Vampire Slayer*
created by Joss Whedon.

Special thanks to Debbie Olshan at Twentieth Century Fox and Michael Boretz.
Thanks also to Jarrod and Robin Balzer

BUFFY THE VAMPIRE SLAYER™ VOLUME TWO: NO FUTURE FOR YOU

This volume reprints the comic-book series *Buffy the Vampire Slayer* Season Eight #6–10 from Dark Horse Comics.

Published by
Dark Horse Books
A division of
Dark Horse Comics, Inc.
10956 SE Main Street
Milwaukie, OR 97222

darkhorse.com

To find a comics shop in your area,
call the Comic Shop Locator Service toll-free at (888) 266-4226.

First edition: June 2008
ISBN 978-1-59307-963-5

1 3 5 7 9 10 8 6 4 2

Printed in China

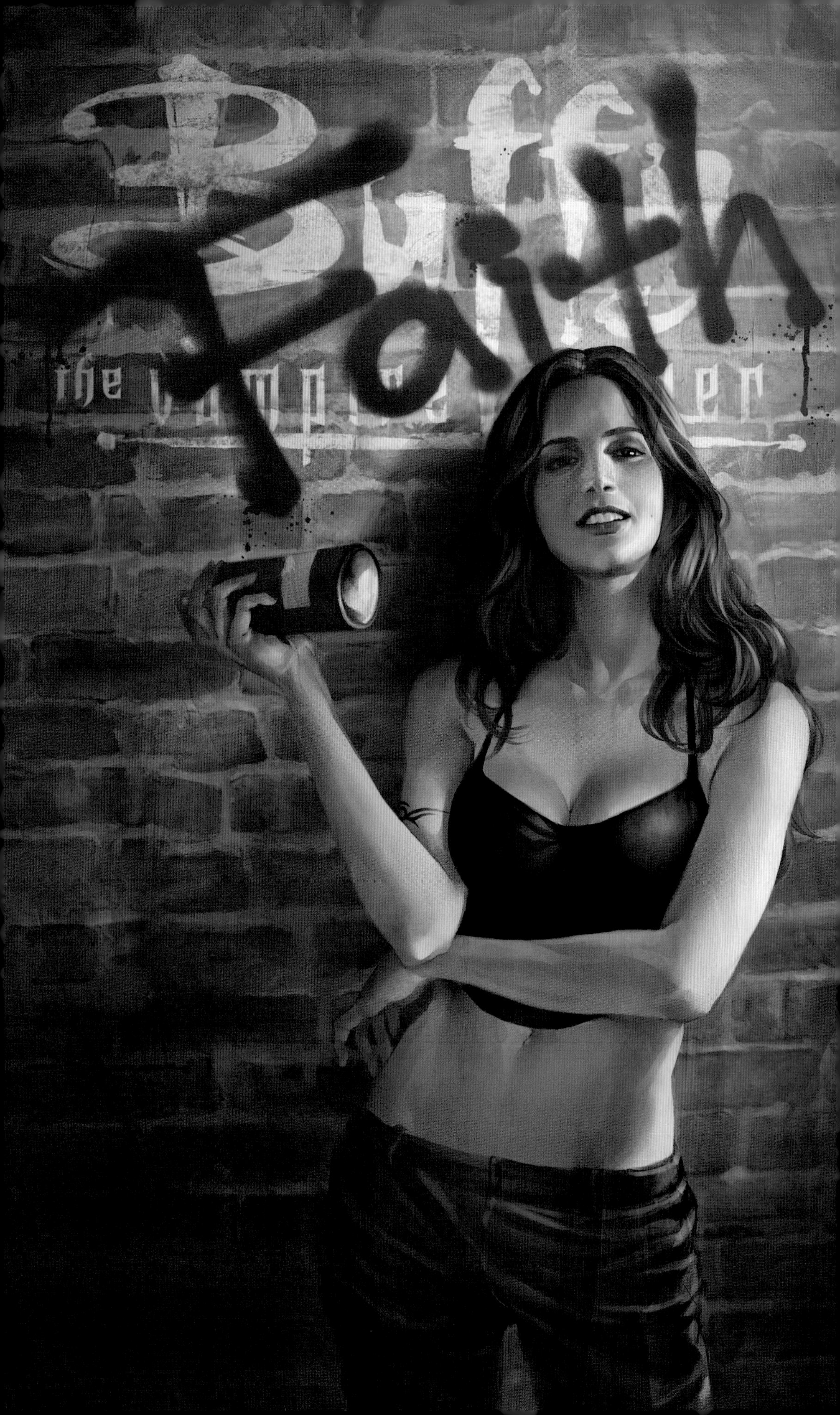
Faith

NO FUTURE FOR YOU

PART ONE

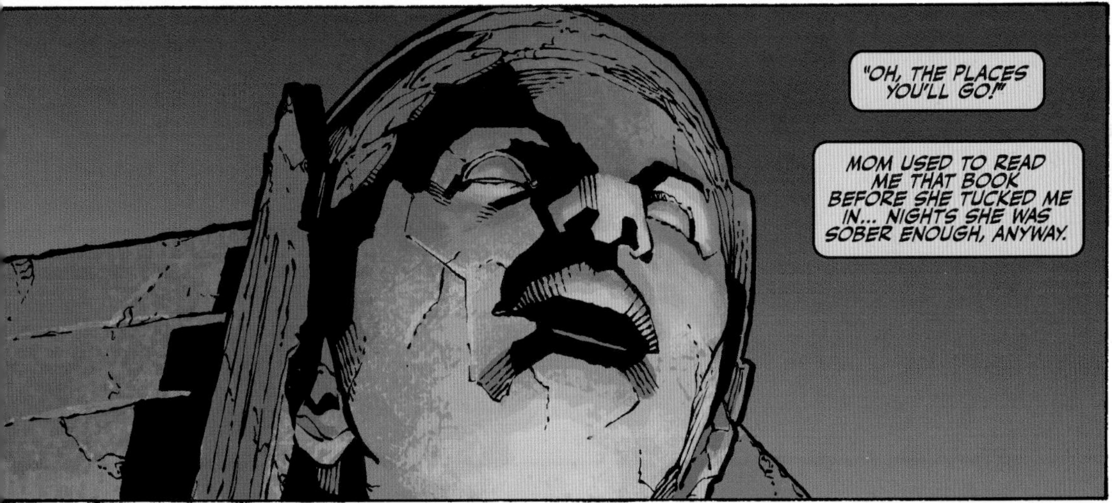
"OH, THE PLACES YOU'LL GO!"
MOM USED TO READ ME THAT BOOK BEFORE SHE TUCKED ME IN... NIGHTS SHE WAS SOBER ENOUGH, ANYWAY.

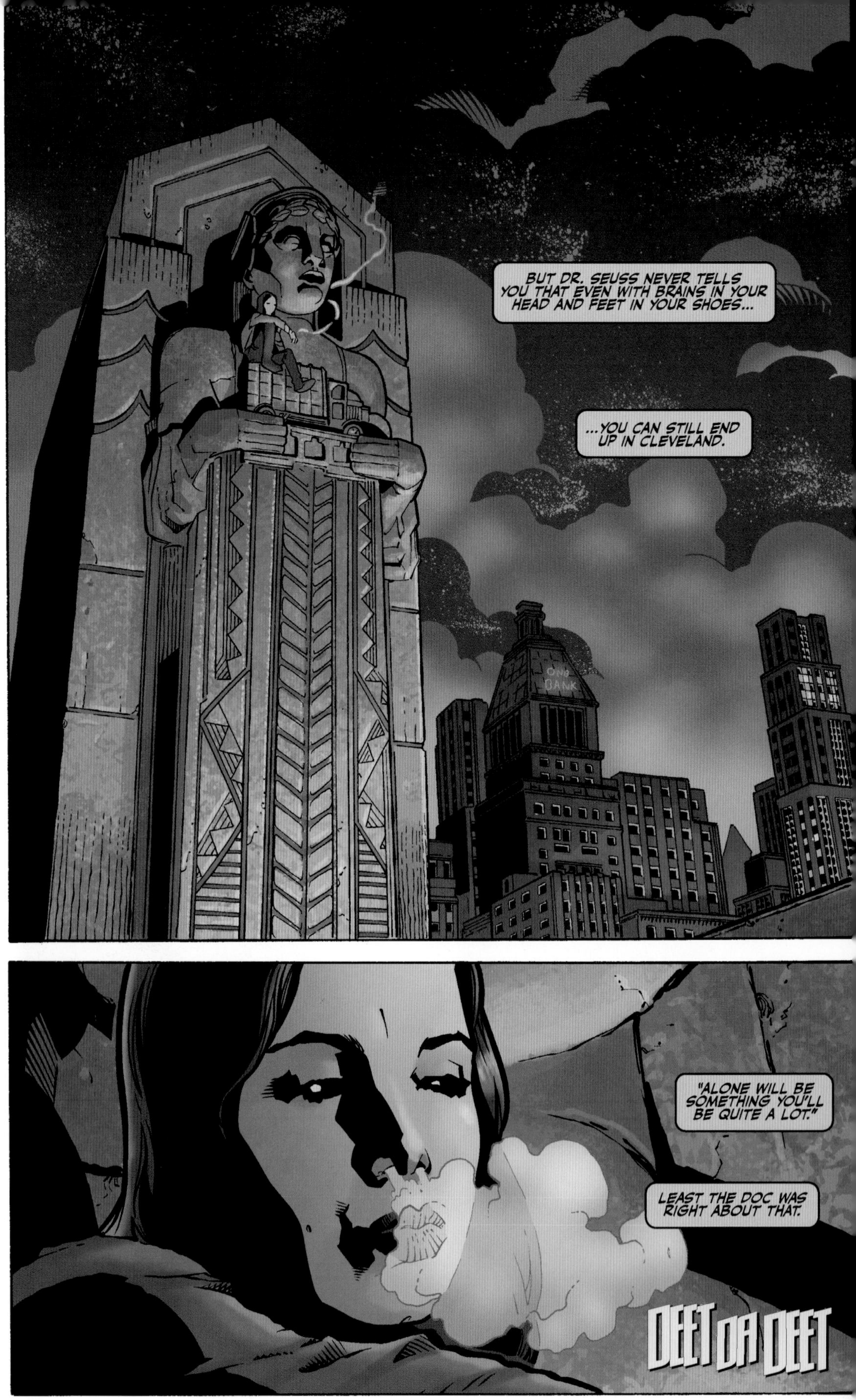

BUT DR. SEUSS NEVER TELLS YOU THAT EVEN WITH BRAINS IN YOUR HEAD AND FEET IN YOUR SHOES...
...YOU CAN STILL END UP IN CLEVELAND.
"ALONE WILL BE SOMETHING YOU'LL BE QUITE A LOT."
LEAST THE DOC WAS RIGHT ABOUT THAT.
DEET DA DEET

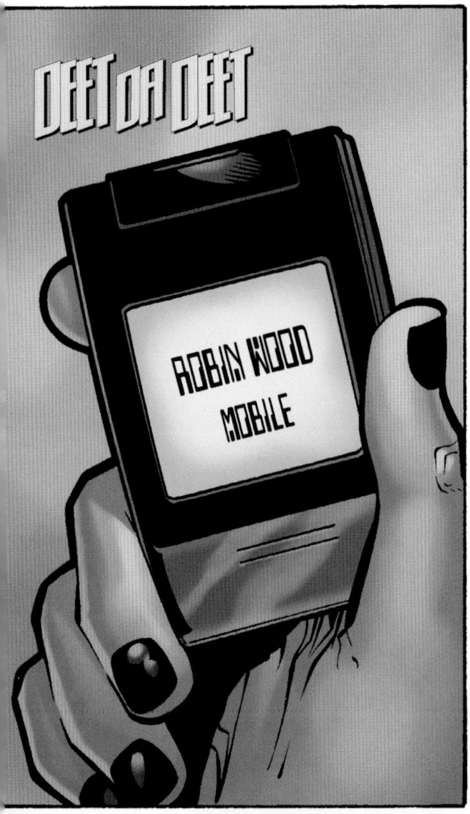
DEET DA DEET
ROBIN WOOD
MOBILE

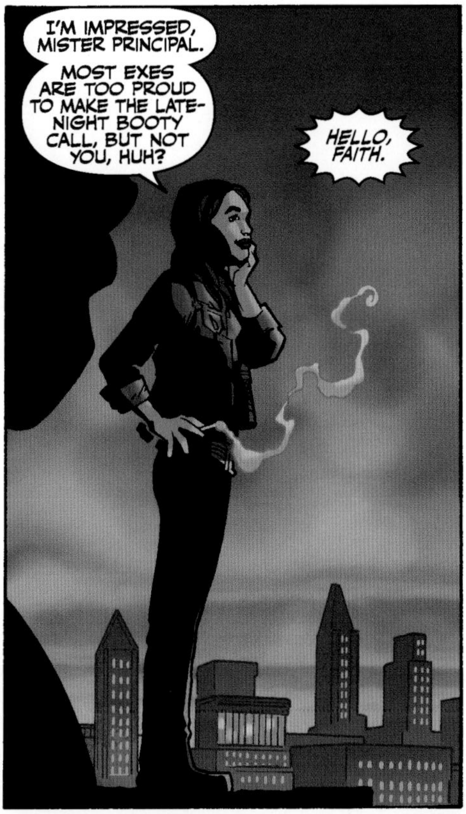
I'M IMPRESSED, MISTER PRINCIPAL.
MOST EXES ARE TOO PROUD TO MAKE THE LATE-NIGHT BOOTY CALL, BUT NOT YOU, HUH?
HELLO, FAITH.

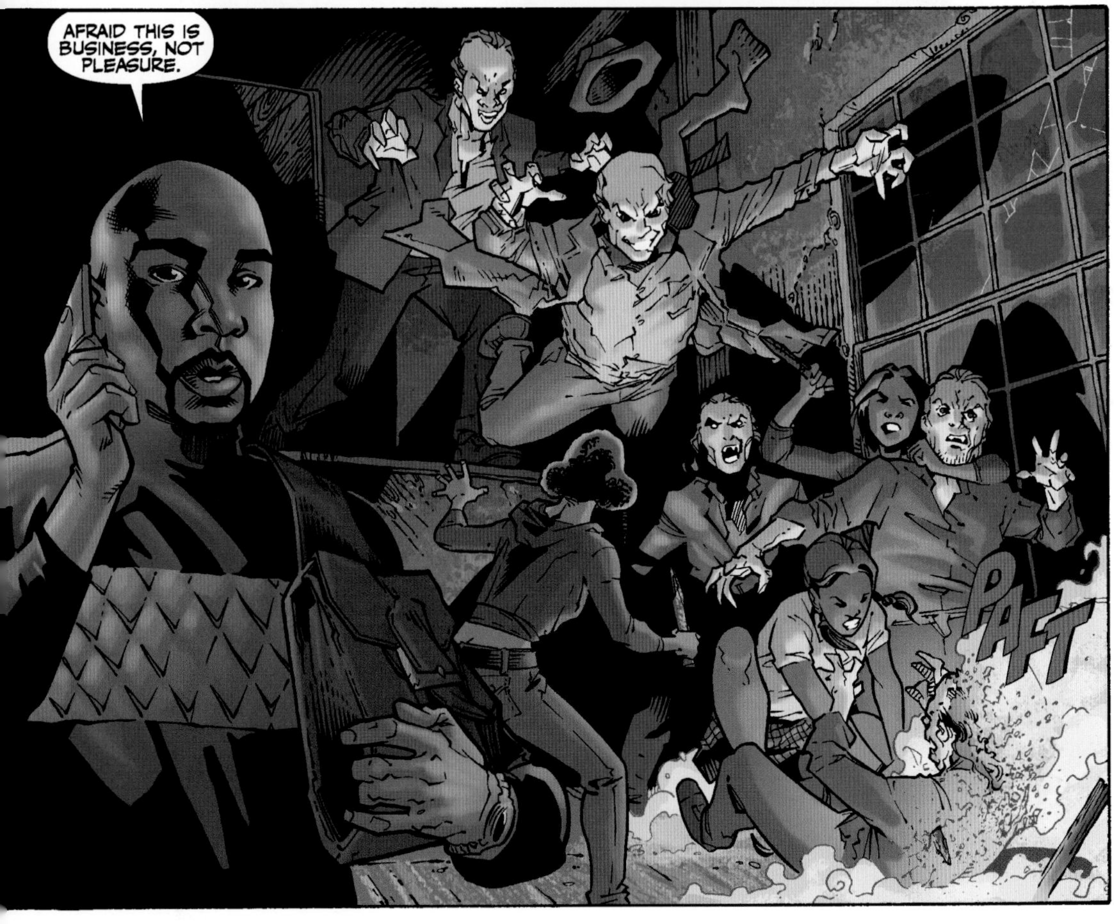
AFRAID THIS IS BUSINESS, NOT PLEASURE.
PAFT

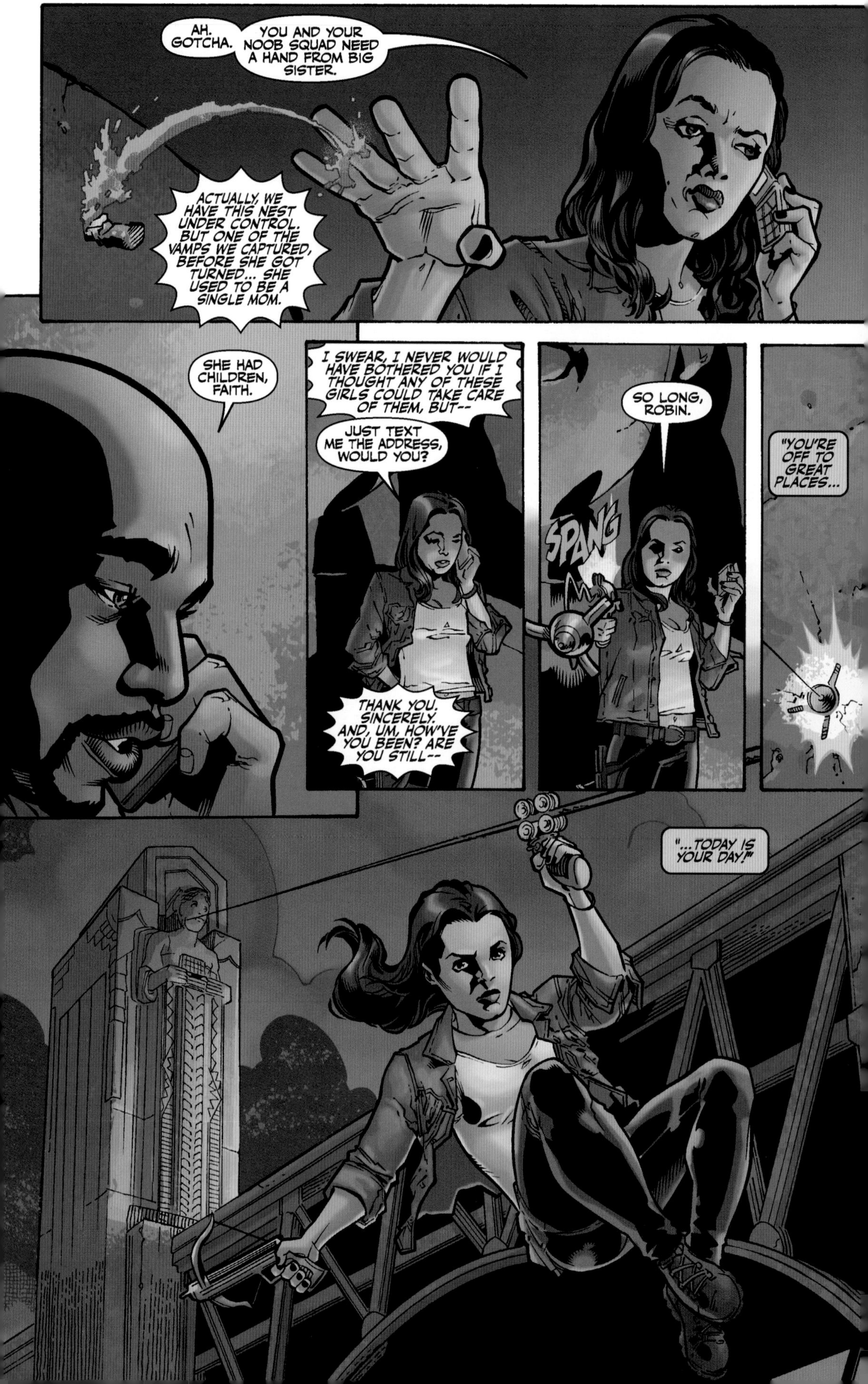
AH. GOTCHA.
YOU AND YOUR NOOB SQUAD NEED A HAND FROM BIG SISTER.
ACTUALLY, WE HAVE THIS NEST UNDER CONTROL. BUT ONE OF THE VAMPS WE CAPTURED, BEFORE SHE GOT TURNED... SHE USED TO BE A SINGLE MOM.
SHE HAD CHILDREN, FAITH.
I SWEAR, I NEVER WOULD HAVE BOTHERED YOU IF I THOUGHT ANY OF THESE GIRLS COULD TAKE CARE OF THEM, BUT--
JUST TEXT ME THE ADDRESS, WOULD YOU?
THANK YOU. SINCERELY. AND, UM, HOW'VE YOU BEEN? ARE YOU STILL--
SO LONG, ROBIN.
SPANG
"YOU'RE OFF TO GREAT PLACES...
"...TODAY IS YOUR DAY!"

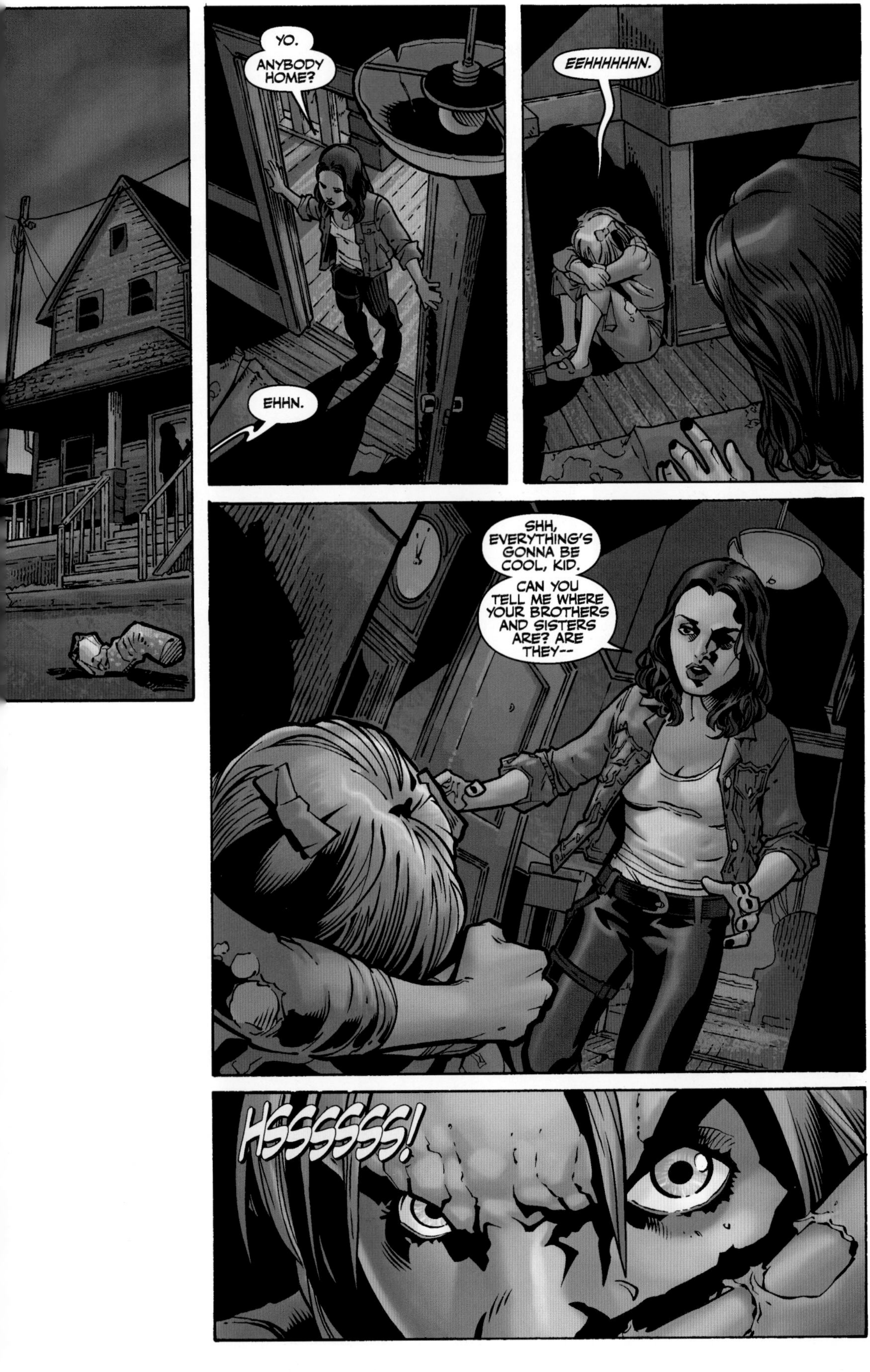
YO. ANYBODY HOME?
EHHN.
EEHHHHHHN.
SHH, EVERYTHING'S GONNA BE COOL, KID.
CAN YOU TELL ME WHERE YOUR BROTHERS AND SISTERS ARE? ARE THEY--
HSSSSSS!

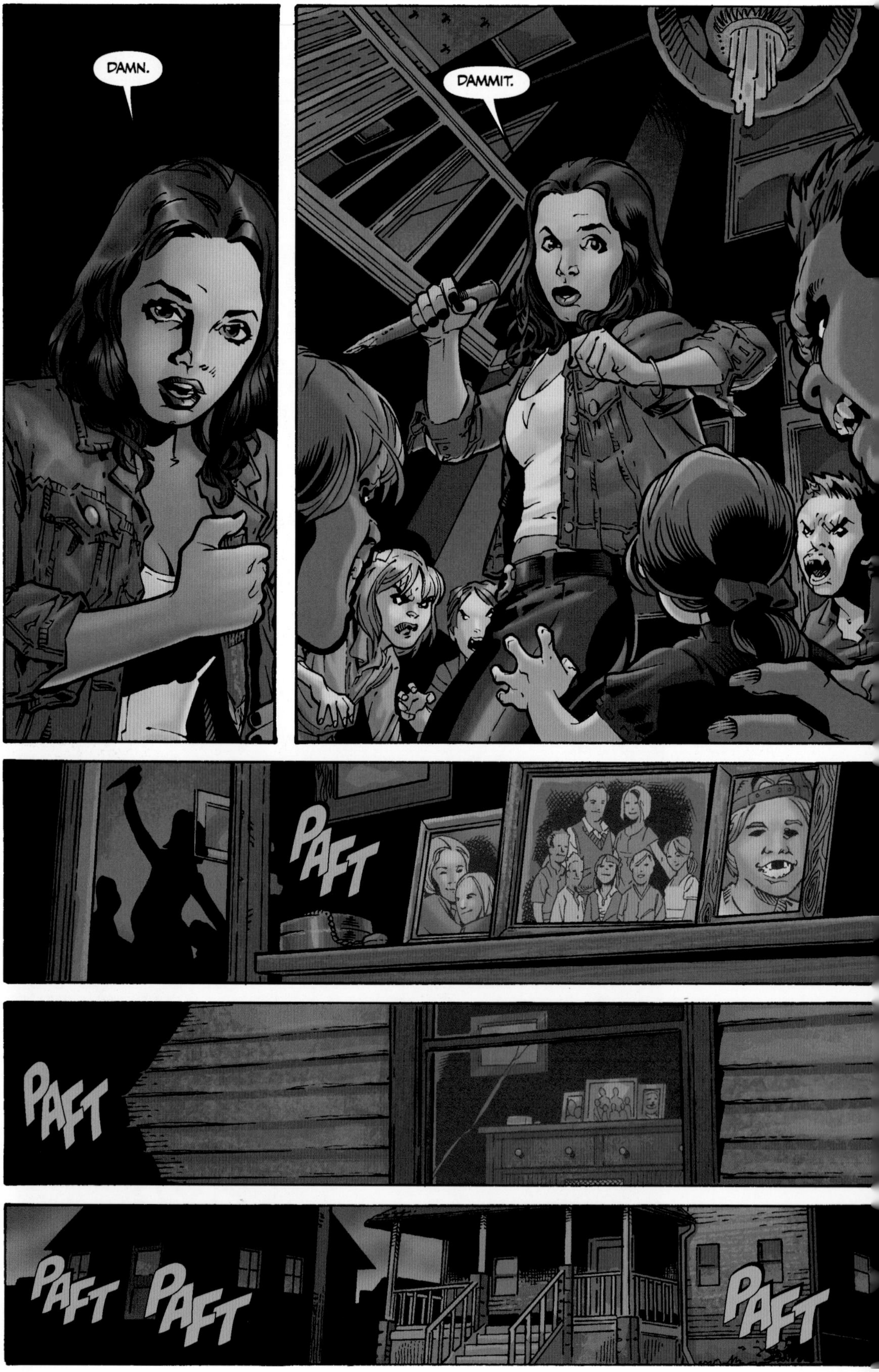
DAMN.
DAMMIT.
PAFT
PAFT
PAFT
PAFT
PAFT

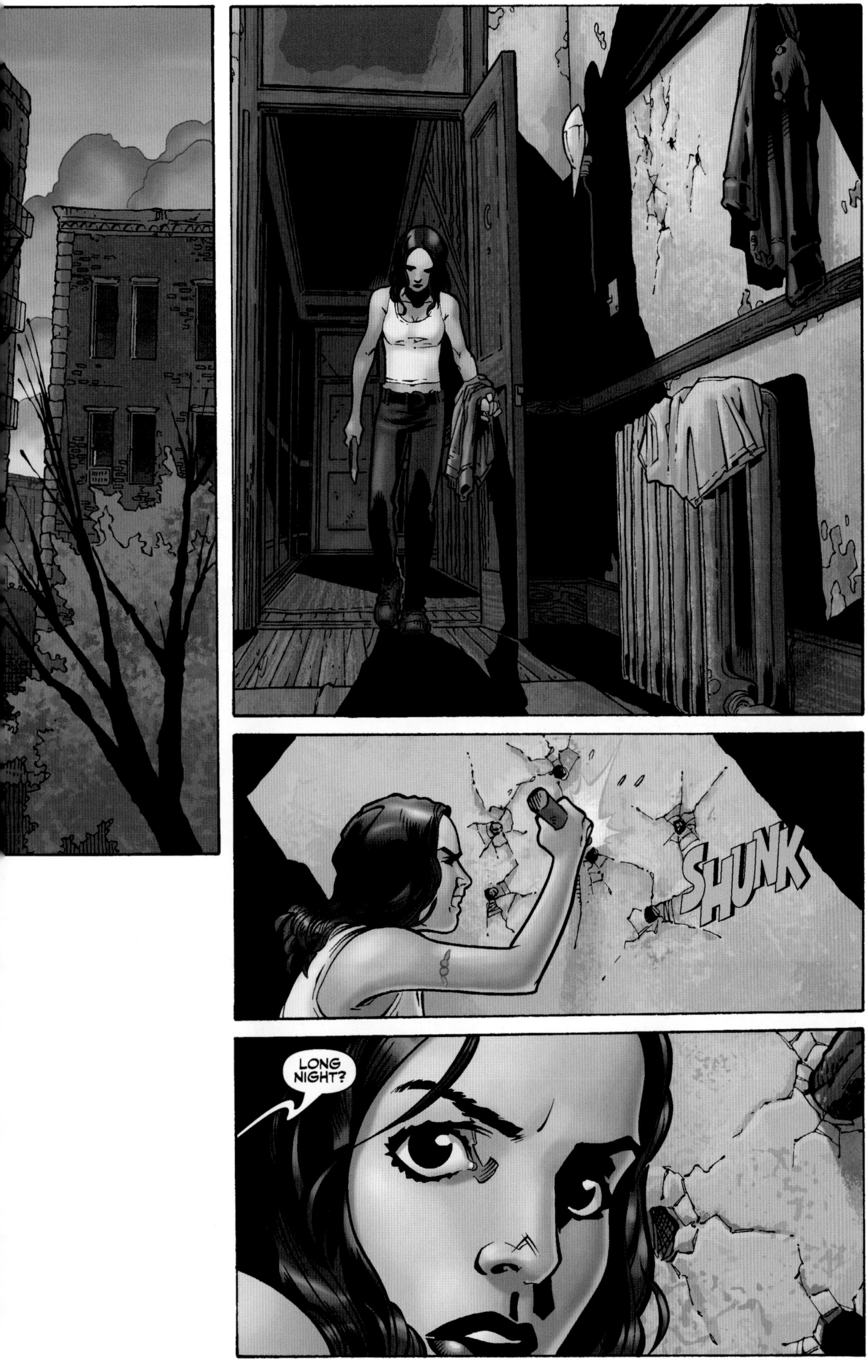
SHUNK
LONG NIGHT?

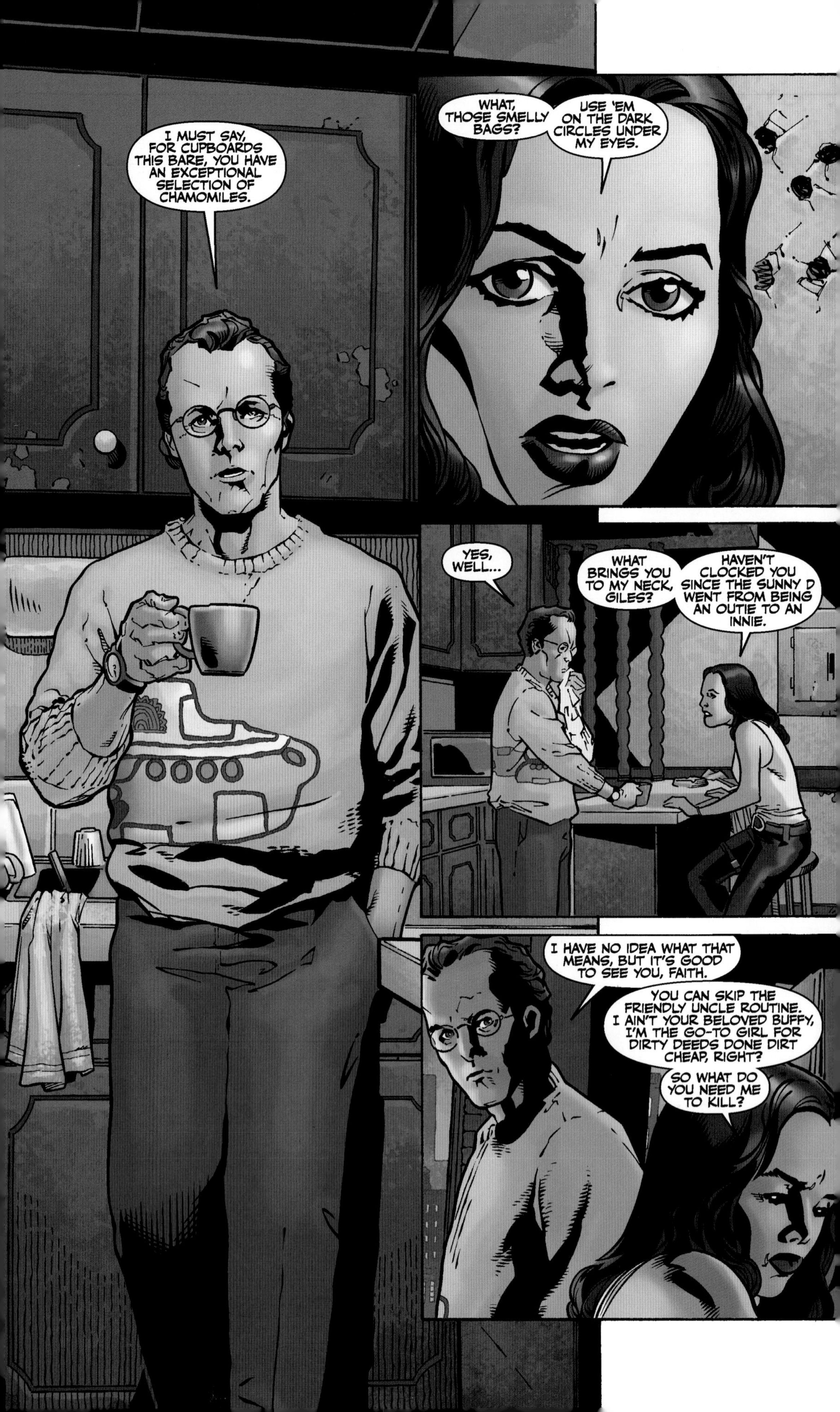
I MUST SAY, FOR CUPBOARDS THIS BARE, YOU HAVE AN EXCEPTIONAL SELECTION OF CHAMOMILES.
WHAT, THOSE SMELLY BAGS?
USE 'EM ON THE DARK CIRCLES UNDER MY EYES.
YES, WELL...
WHAT BRINGS YOU TO MY NECK, GILES?
HAVEN'T CLOCKED YOU SINCE THE SUNNY D WENT FROM BEING AN OUTIE TO AN INNIE.
I HAVE NO IDEA WHAT THAT MEANS, BUT IT'S GOOD TO SEE YOU, FAITH.
YOU CAN SKIP THE FRIENDLY UNCLE ROUTINE. I AIN'T YOUR BELOVED BUFFY, I'M THE GO-TO GIRL FOR DIRTY DEEDS DONE DIRT CHEAP, RIGHT?
SO WHAT DO YOU NEED ME TO KILL?

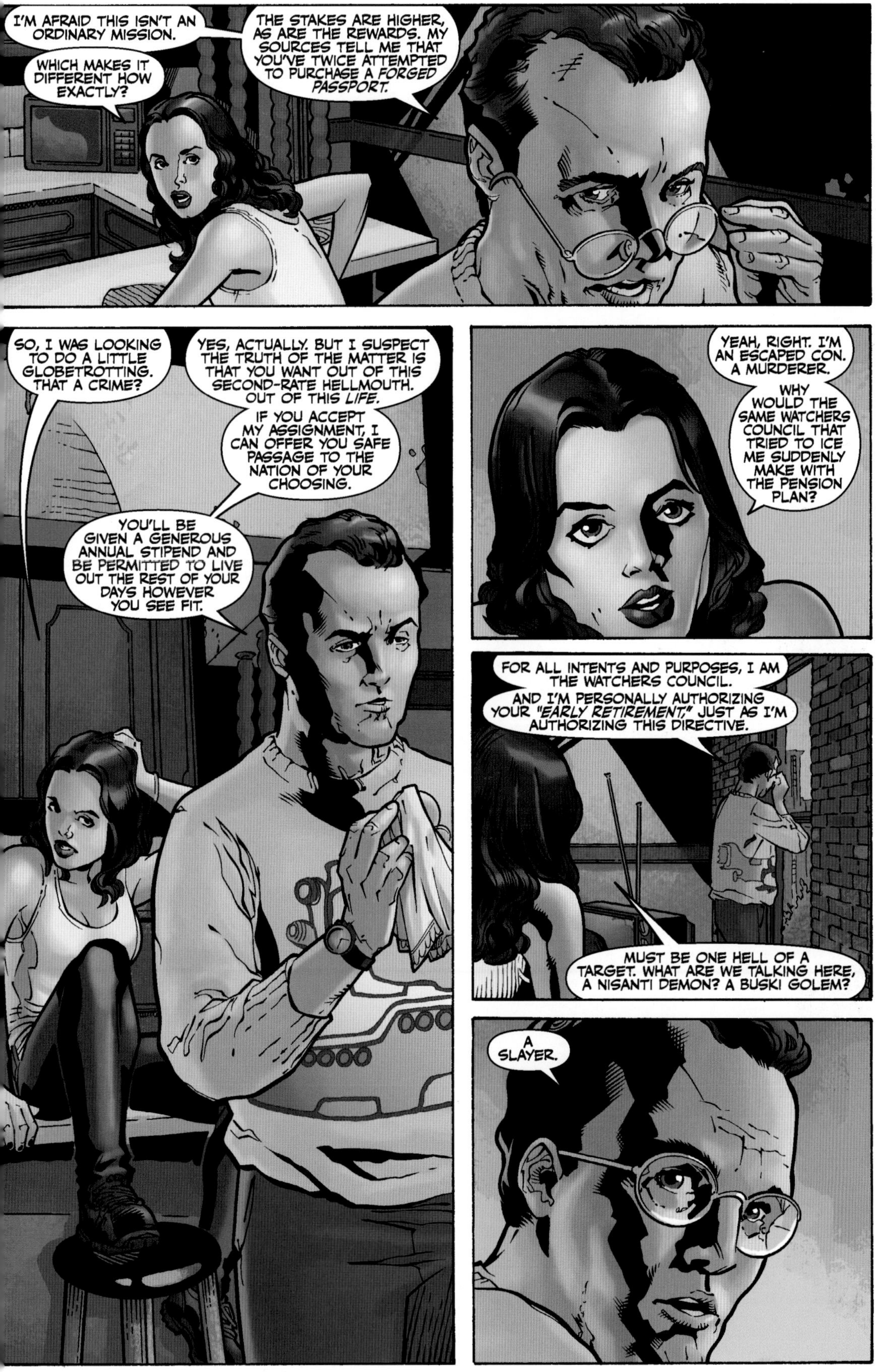
I'M AFRAID THIS ISN'T AN ORDINARY MISSION.
WHICH MAKES IT DIFFERENT HOW EXACTLY?
THE STAKES ARE HIGHER, AS ARE THE REWARDS. MY SOURCES TELL ME THAT YOU'VE TWICE ATTEMPTED TO PURCHASE A *FORGED PASSPORT.*
SO, I WAS LOOKING TO DO A LITTLE GLOBETROTTING. THAT A CRIME?
YES, ACTUALLY. BUT I SUSPECT THE TRUTH OF THE MATTER IS THAT YOU WANT OUT OF THIS SECOND-RATE HELLMOUTH. OUT OF THIS *LIFE.*
IF YOU ACCEPT MY ASSIGNMENT, I CAN OFFER YOU SAFE PASSAGE TO THE NATION OF YOUR CHOOSING.
YOU'LL BE GIVEN A GENEROUS ANNUAL STIPEND AND BE PERMITTED TO LIVE OUT THE REST OF YOUR DAYS HOWEVER YOU SEE FIT.
YEAH, RIGHT. I'M AN ESCAPED CON. A MURDERER.
WHY WOULD THE SAME WATCHERS COUNCIL THAT TRIED TO ICE ME SUDDENLY MAKE WITH THE PENSION PLAN?
FOR ALL INTENTS AND PURPOSES, I AM THE WATCHERS COUNCIL.
AND I'M PERSONALLY AUTHORIZING YOUR *"EARLY RETIREMENT,"* JUST AS I'M AUTHORIZING THIS DIRECTIVE.
MUST BE ONE HELL OF A TARGET. WHAT ARE WE TALKING HERE, A NISANTI DEMON? A BUSKI GOLEM?
A SLAYER.

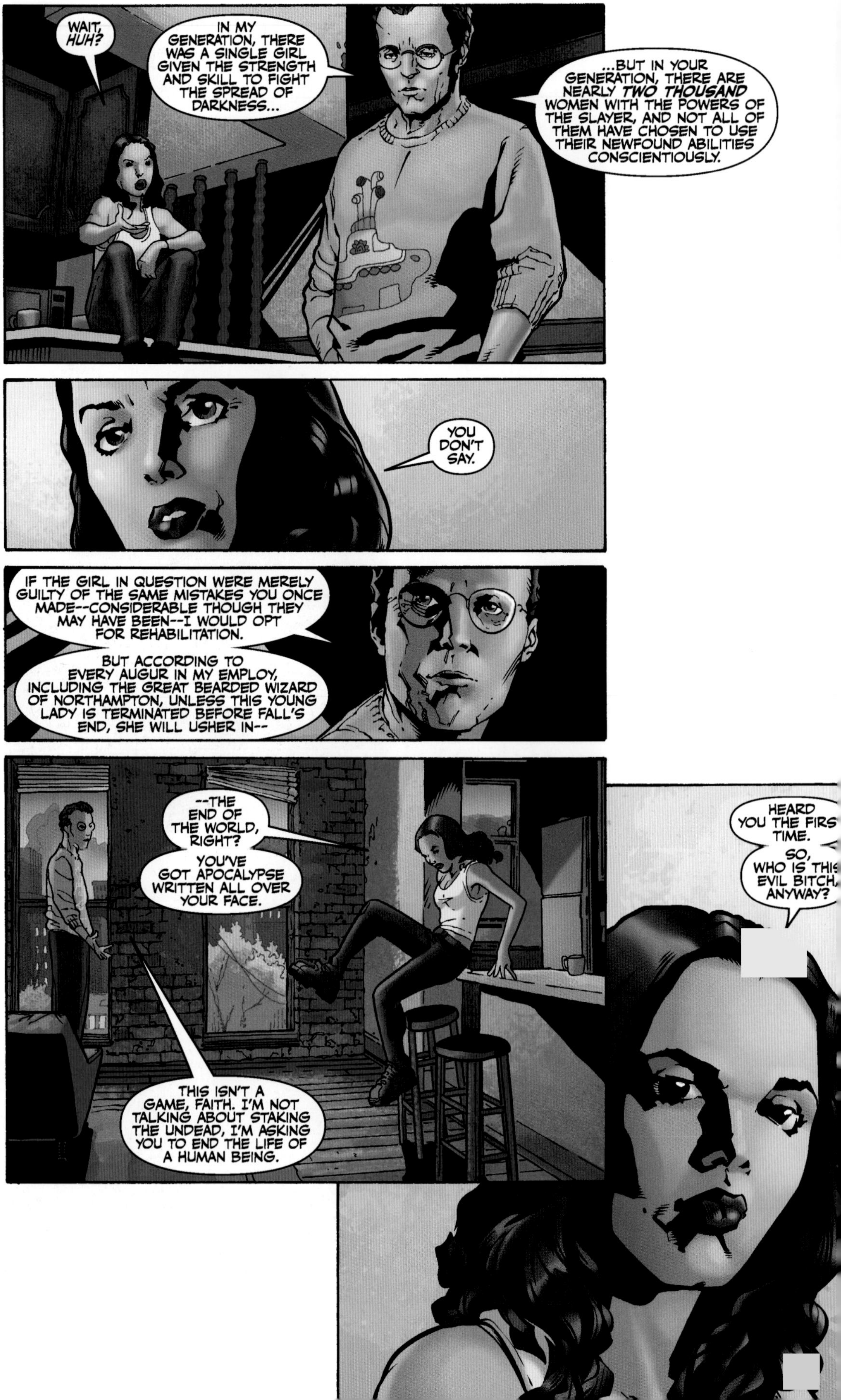
WAIT, HUH?
IN MY GENERATION, THERE WAS A SINGLE GIRL GIVEN THE STRENGTH AND SKILL TO FIGHT THE SPREAD OF DARKNESS...
...BUT IN YOUR GENERATION, THERE ARE NEARLY TWO THOUSAND WOMEN WITH THE POWERS OF THE SLAYER, AND NOT ALL OF THEM HAVE CHOSEN TO USE THEIR NEWFOUND ABILITIES CONSCIENTIOUSLY.
YOU DON'T SAY.
IF THE GIRL IN QUESTION WERE MERELY GUILTY OF THE SAME MISTAKES YOU ONCE MADE--CONSIDERABLE THOUGH THEY MAY HAVE BEEN--I WOULD OPT FOR REHABILITATION.
BUT ACCORDING TO EVERY AUGUR IN MY EMPLOY, INCLUDING THE GREAT BEARDED WIZARD OF NORTHAMPTON, UNLESS THIS YOUNG LADY IS TERMINATED BEFORE FALL'S END, SHE WILL USHER IN--
--THE END OF THE WORLD, RIGHT?
YOU'VE GOT APOCALYPSE WRITTEN ALL OVER YOUR FACE.
THIS ISN'T A GAME, FAITH. I'M NOT TALKING ABOUT STAKING THE UNDEAD, I'M ASKING YOU TO END THE LIFE OF A HUMAN BEING.
HEARD YOU THE FIRS TIME.
SO, WHO IS THIS EVIL BITCH, ANYWAY?

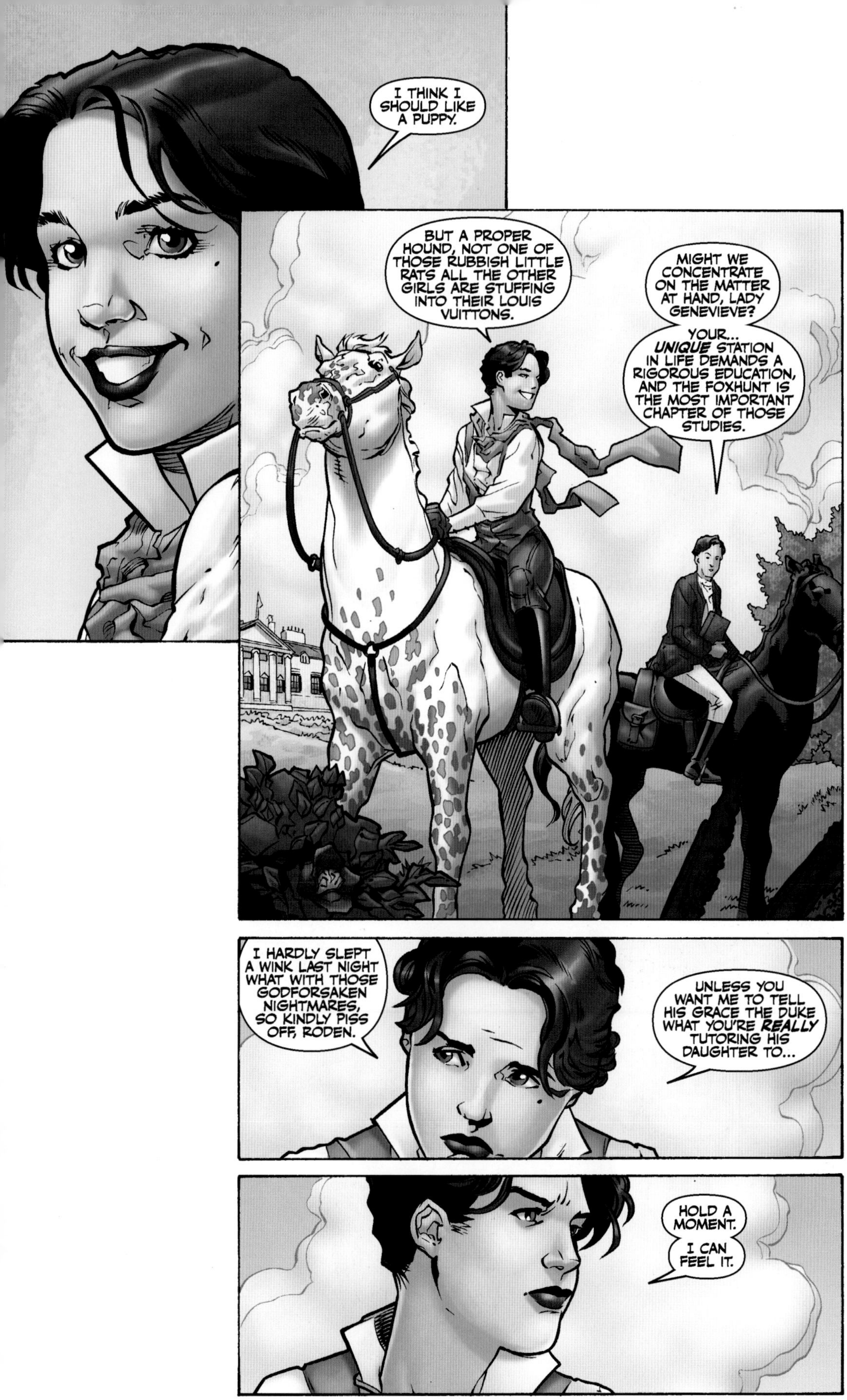
I THINK I SHOULD LIKE A PUPPY.
BUT A PROPER HOUND, NOT ONE OF THOSE RUBBISH LITTLE RATS ALL THE OTHER GIRLS ARE STUFFING INTO THEIR LOUIS VUITTONS.
MIGHT WE CONCENTRATE ON THE MATTER AT HAND, LADY GENEVIEVE?
YOUR... *UNIQUE* STATION IN LIFE DEMANDS A RIGOROUS EDUCATION, AND THE FOXHUNT IS THE MOST IMPORTANT CHAPTER OF THOSE STUDIES.
I HARDLY SLEPT A WINK LAST NIGHT WHAT WITH THOSE GODFORSAKEN NIGHTMARES, SO KINDLY PISS OFF, RODEN.
UNLESS YOU WANT ME TO TELL HIS GRACE THE DUKE WHAT YOU'RE *REALLY* TUTORING HIS DAUGHTER TO...
HOLD A MOMENT.
I CAN FEEL IT.

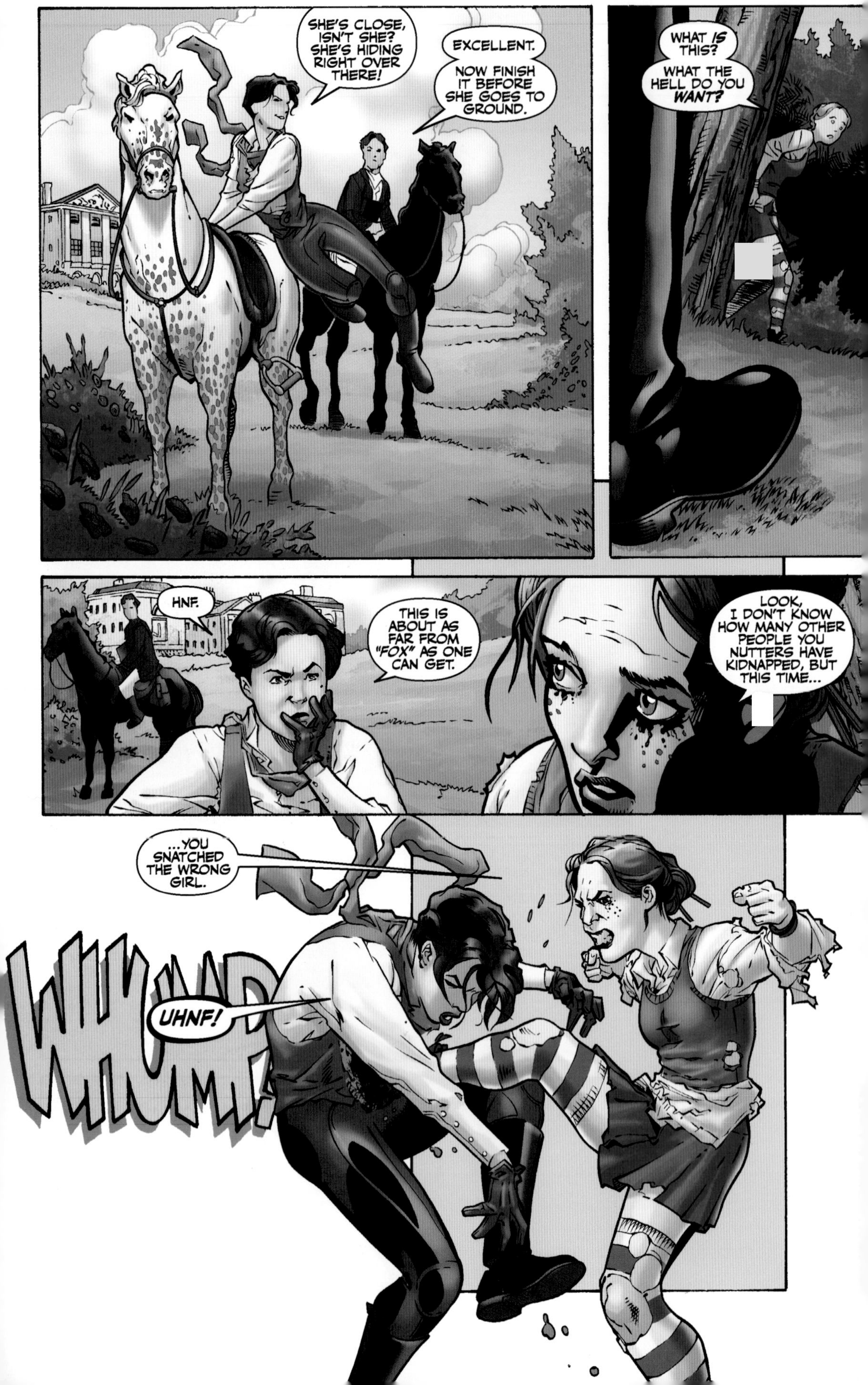
SHE'S CLOSE, ISN'T SHE? SHE'S HIDING RIGHT OVER THERE!
EXCELLENT.
NOW FINISH IT BEFORE SHE GOES TO GROUND.
WHAT *IS* THIS?
WHAT THE HELL DO YOU *WANT?*
HNF.
THIS IS ABOUT AS FAR FROM "*FOX*" AS ONE CAN GET.
LOOK, I DON'T KNOW HOW MANY OTHER PEOPLE YOU NUTTERS HAVE KIDNAPPED, BUT THIS TIME...
...YOU SNATCHED THE WRONG GIRL.
WHUMP!
UHNF!

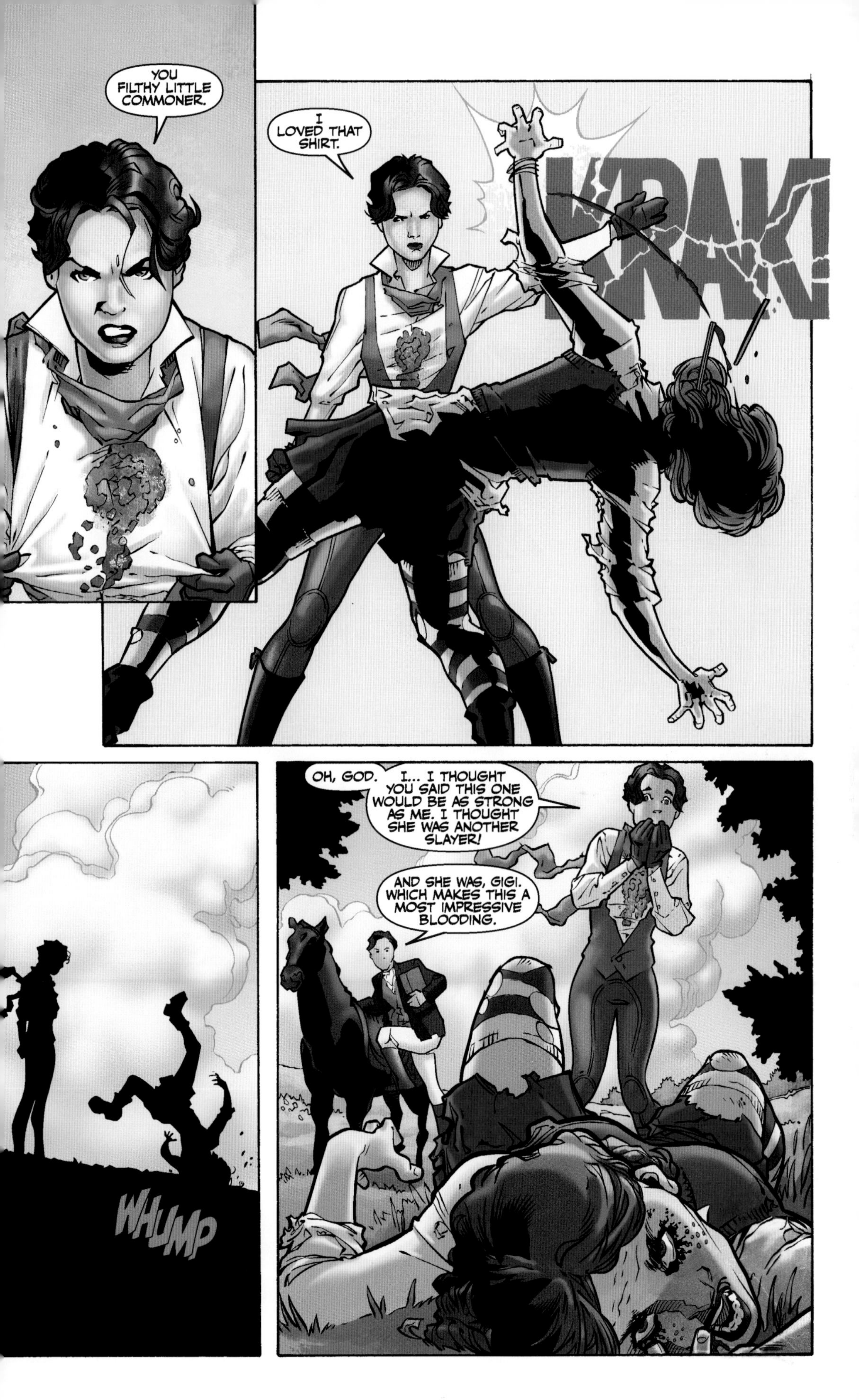
YOU FILTHY LITTLE COMMONER.
I LOVED THAT SHIRT.
KRAK!
WHUMP
OH, GOD.
I... I THOUGHT YOU SAID THIS ONE WOULD BE AS STRONG AS ME. I THOUGHT SHE WAS ANOTHER SLAYER!
AND SHE WAS, GIGI. WHICH MAKES THIS A MOST IMPRESSIVE BLOODING.

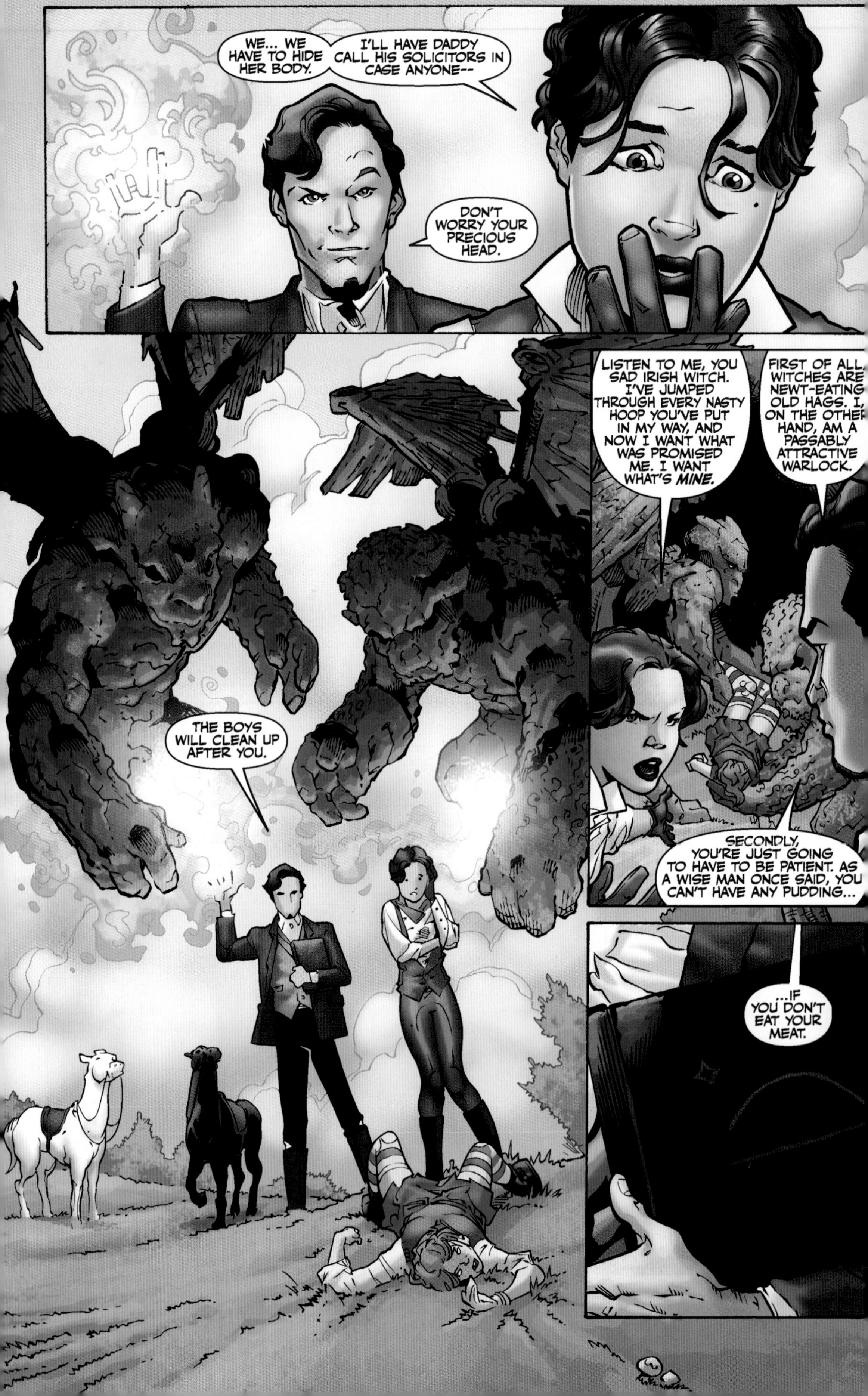

WE... WE HAVE TO HIDE HER BODY.
I'LL HAVE DADDY CALL HIS SOLICITORS IN CASE ANYONE--
DON'T WORRY YOUR PRECIOUS HEAD.
THE BOYS WILL CLEAN UP AFTER YOU.
LISTEN TO ME, YOU SAD IRISH WITCH. I'VE JUMPED THROUGH EVERY NASTY HOOP YOU'VE PUT IN MY WAY, AND NOW I WANT WHAT WAS PROMISED ME. I WANT WHAT'S *MINE.*
FIRST OF ALL, WITCHES ARE NEWT-EATING OLD HAGS. I, ON THE OTHER HAND, AM A PASSABLY ATTRACTIVE WARLOCK.
SECONDLY, YOU'RE JUST GOING TO HAVE TO BE PATIENT. AS A WISE MAN ONCE SAID, YOU CAN'T HAVE ANY PUDDING...
...IF YOU DON'T EAT YOUR MEAT.

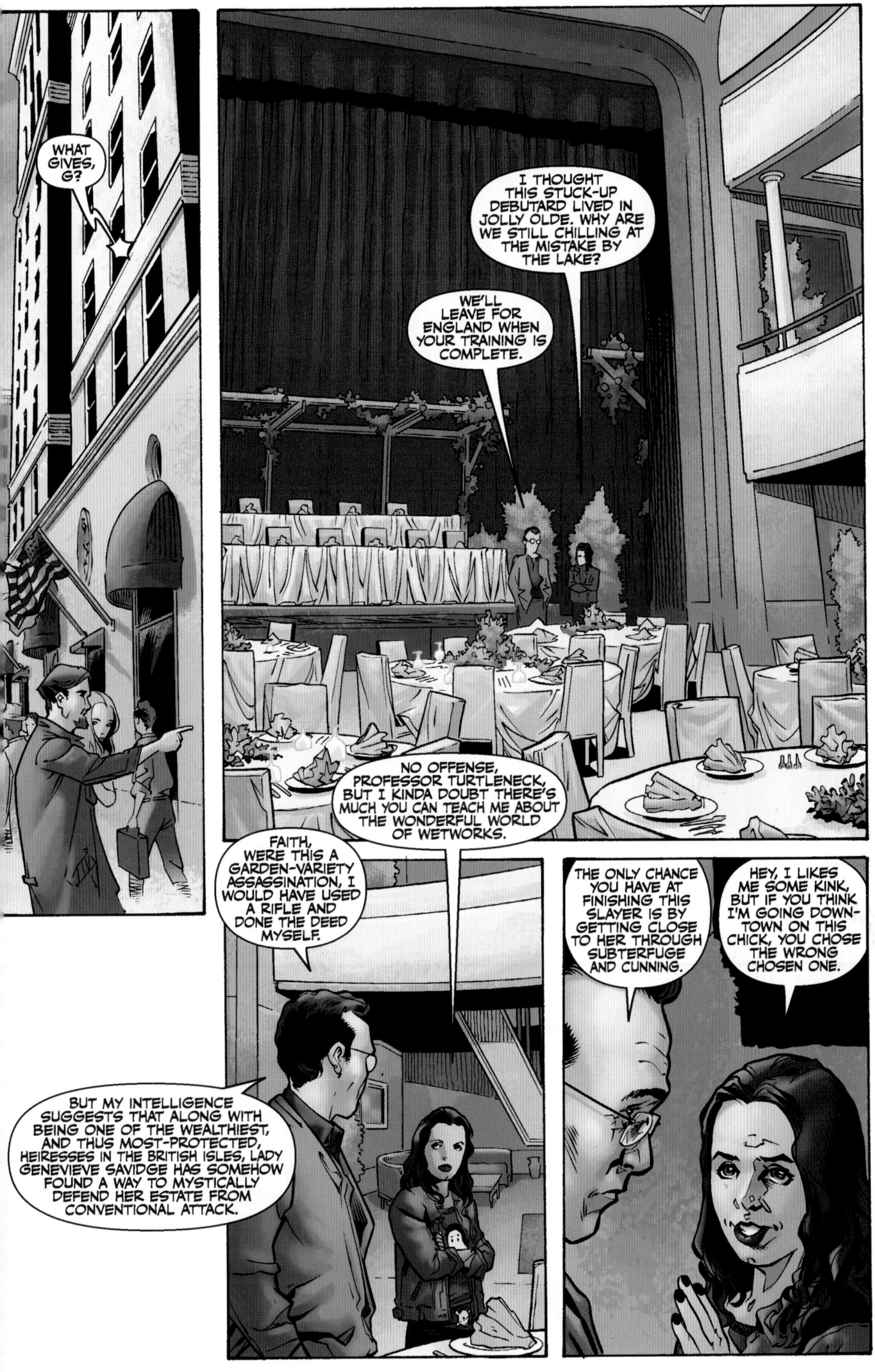
WHAT GIVES, G?
I THOUGHT THIS STUCK-UP DEBUTARD LIVED IN JOLLY OLDE. WHY ARE WE STILL CHILLING AT THE MISTAKE BY THE LAKE?
WE'LL LEAVE FOR ENGLAND WHEN YOUR TRAINING IS COMPLETE.
NO OFFENSE, PROFESSOR TURTLENECK, BUT I KINDA DOUBT THERE'S MUCH YOU CAN TEACH ME ABOUT THE WONDERFUL WORLD OF WETWORKS.
FAITH, WERE THIS A GARDEN-VARIETY ASSASSINATION, I WOULD HAVE USED A RIFLE AND DONE THE DEED MYSELF.
BUT MY INTELLIGENCE SUGGESTS THAT ALONG WITH BEING ONE OF THE WEALTHIEST, AND THUS MOST-PROTECTED, HEIRESSES IN THE BRITISH ISLES, LADY GENEVIEVE SAVIDGE HAS SOMEHOW FOUND A WAY TO MYSTICALLY DEFEND HER ESTATE FROM CONVENTIONAL ATTACK.
THE ONLY CHANCE YOU HAVE AT FINISHING THIS SLAYER IS BY GETTING CLOSE TO HER THROUGH SUBTERFUGE AND CUNNING.
HEY, I LIKES ME SOME KINK, BUT IF YOU THINK I'M GOING DOWN-TOWN ON THIS CHICK, YOU CHOSE THE WRONG CHOSEN ONE.

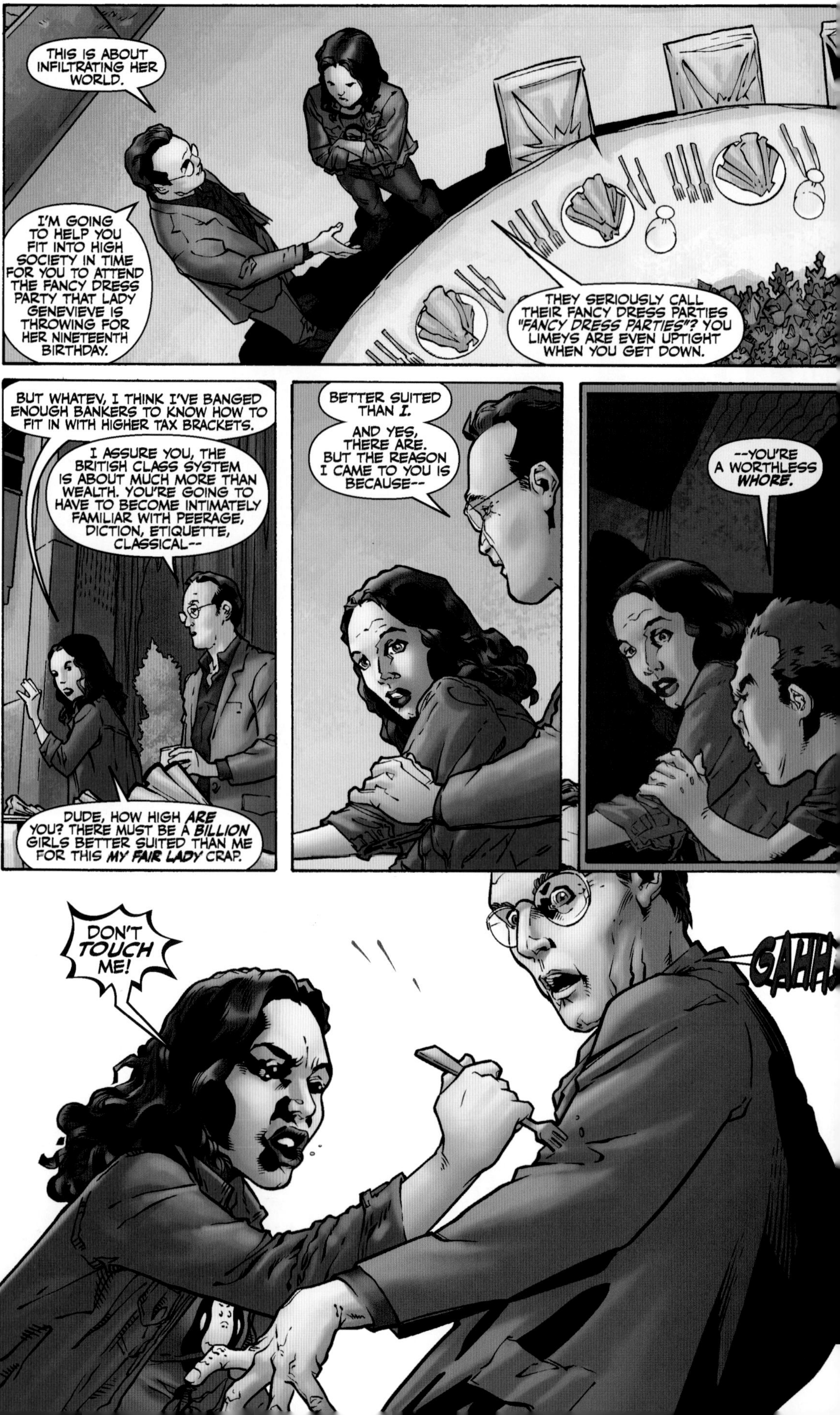
THIS IS ABOUT INFILTRATING HER WORLD.
I'M GOING TO HELP YOU FIT INTO HIGH SOCIETY IN TIME FOR YOU TO ATTEND THE FANCY DRESS PARTY THAT LADY GENEVIEVE IS THROWING FOR HER NINETEENTH BIRTHDAY.
THEY SERIOUSLY CALL THEIR FANCY DRESS PARTIES "FANCY DRESS PARTIES"? YOU LIMEYS ARE EVEN UPTIGHT WHEN YOU GET DOWN.
BUT WHATEV, I THINK I'VE BANGED ENOUGH BANKERS TO KNOW HOW TO FIT IN WITH HIGHER TAX BRACKETS.
I ASSURE YOU, THE BRITISH CLASS SYSTEM IS ABOUT MUCH MORE THAN WEALTH. YOU'RE GOING TO HAVE TO BECOME INTIMATELY FAMILIAR WITH PEERAGE, DICTION, ETIQUETTE, CLASSICAL--
DUDE, HOW HIGH ARE YOU? THERE MUST BE A BILLION GIRLS BETTER SUITED THAN ME FOR THIS MY FAIR LADY CRAP.
BETTER SUITED THAN I.
AND YES, THERE ARE. BUT THE REASON I CAME TO YOU IS BECAUSE--
--YOU'RE A WORTHLESS WHORE.
DON'T TOUCH ME!
GAHH

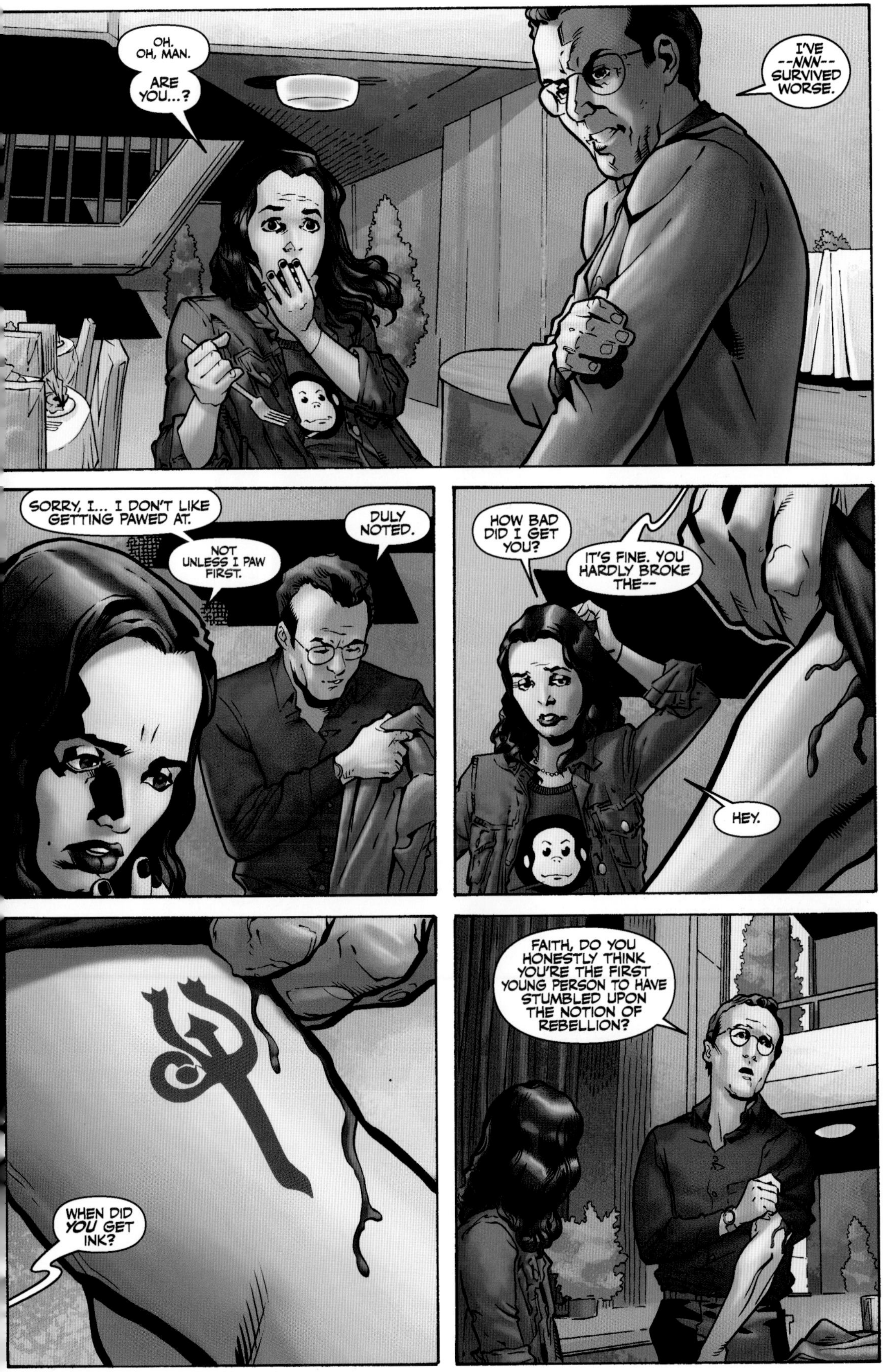
OH.
OH, MAN.
ARE YOU...?
I'VE --NNN-- SURVIVED WORSE.
SORRY, I... I DON'T LIKE GETTING PAWED AT.
NOT UNLESS I PAW FIRST.
DULY NOTED.
HOW BAD DID I GET YOU?
IT'S FINE. YOU HARDLY BROKE THE--
HEY.
WHEN DID YOU GET INK?
FAITH, DO YOU HONESTLY THINK YOU'RE THE FIRST YOUNG PERSON TO HAVE STUMBLED UPON THE NOTION OF REBELLION?

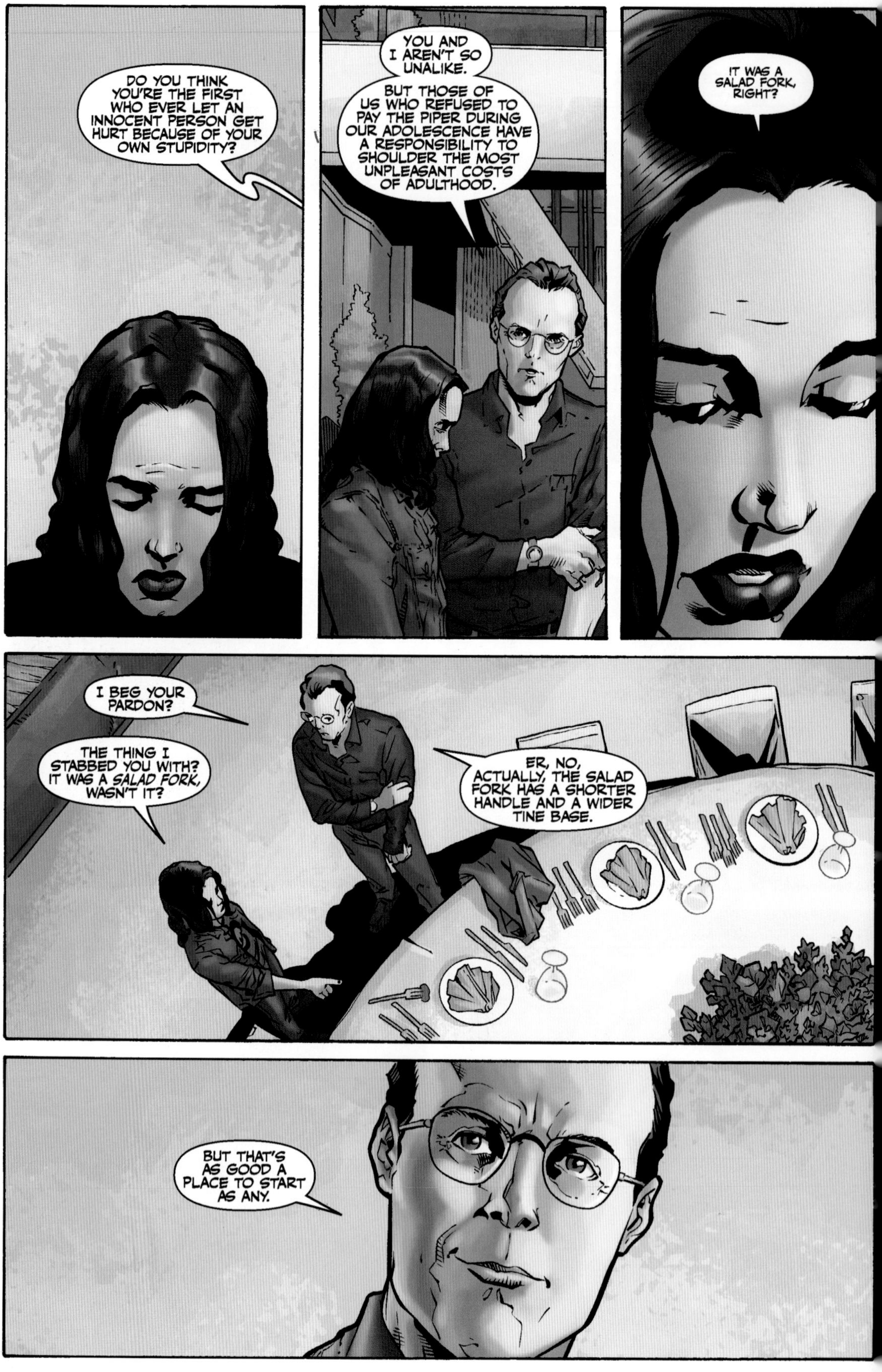
DO YOU THINK YOU'RE THE FIRST WHO EVER LET AN INNOCENT PERSON GET HURT BECAUSE OF YOUR OWN STUPIDITY?
YOU AND I AREN'T SO UNALIKE.
BUT THOSE OF US WHO REFUSED TO PAY THE PIPER DURING OUR ADOLESCENCE HAVE A RESPONSIBILITY TO SHOULDER THE MOST UNPLEASANT COSTS OF ADULTHOOD.
IT WAS A SALAD FORK, RIGHT?
I BEG YOUR PARDON?
THE THING I STABBED YOU WITH? IT WAS A *SALAD FORK,* WASN'T IT?
ER, NO, ACTUALLY, THE SALAD FORK HAS A SHORTER HANDLE AND A WIDER TINE BASE.
BUT THAT'S AS GOOD A PLACE TO START AS ANY.

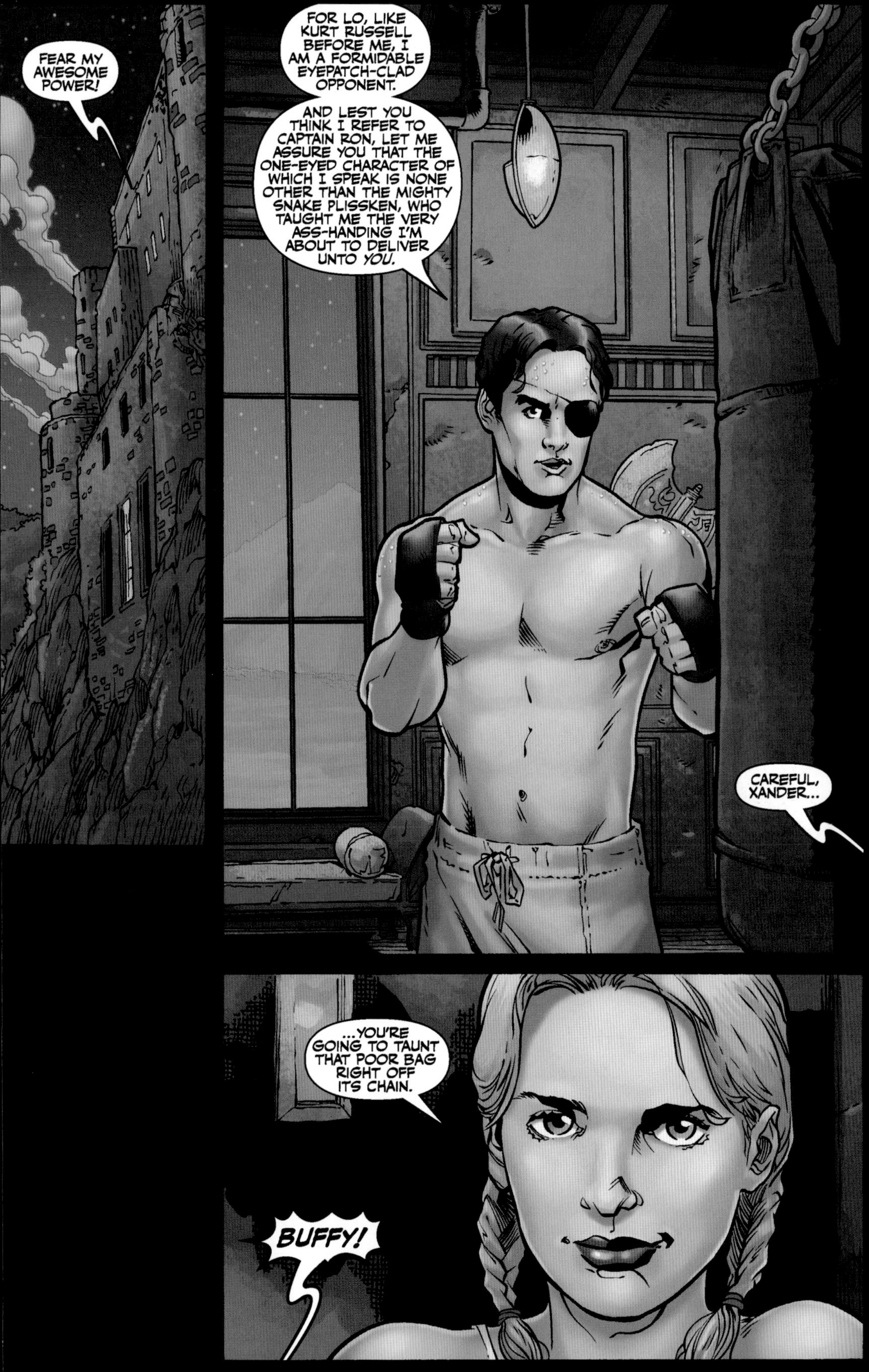
FEAR MY AWESOME POWER!
FOR LO, LIKE KURT RUSSELL BEFORE ME, I AM A FORMIDABLE EYEPATCH-CLAD OPPONENT.
AND LEST YOU THINK I REFER TO CAPTAIN RON, LET ME ASSURE YOU THAT THE ONE-EYED CHARACTER OF WHICH I SPEAK IS NONE OTHER THAN THE MIGHTY SNAKE PLISSKEN, WHO TAUGHT ME THE VERY ASS-HANDING I'M ABOUT TO DELIVER UNTO *YOU*.
CAREFUL, XANDER...
...YOU'RE GOING TO TAUNT THAT POOR BAG RIGHT OFF ITS CHAIN.
BUFFY!

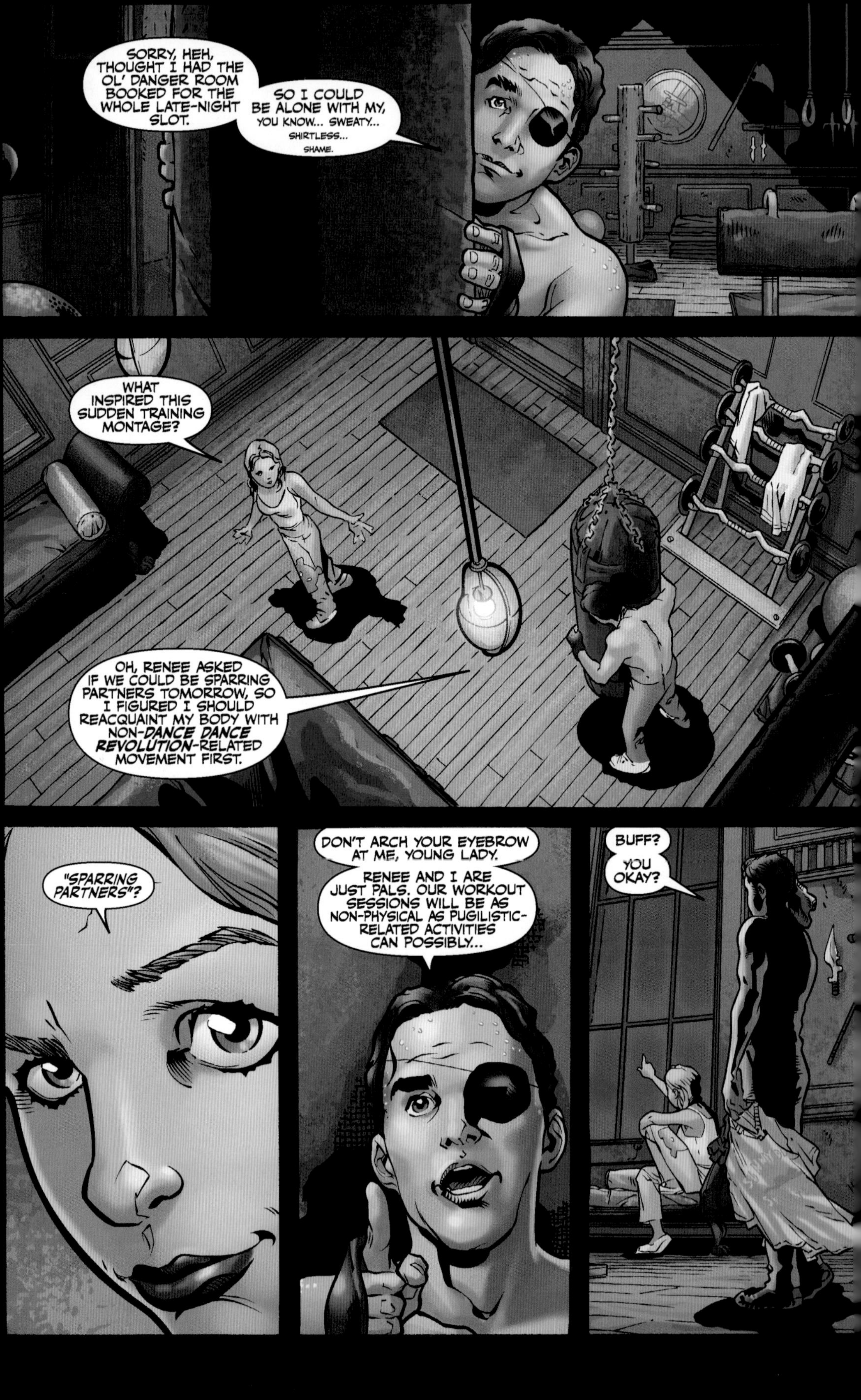
SORRY, HEH, THOUGHT I HAD THE OL' DANGER ROOM BOOKED FOR THE WHOLE LATE-NIGHT SLOT.
SO I COULD BE ALONE WITH MY, YOU KNOW... SWEATY... SHIRTLESS... SHAME.
WHAT INSPIRED THIS SUDDEN TRAINING MONTAGE?
OH, RENEE ASKED IF WE COULD BE SPARRING PARTNERS TOMORROW, SO I FIGURED I SHOULD REACQUAINT MY BODY WITH NON-*DANCE DANCE REVOLUTION*-RELATED MOVEMENT FIRST.
"SPARRING PARTNERS"?
DON'T ARCH YOUR EYEBROW AT ME, YOUNG LADY.
RENEE AND I ARE JUST PALS. OUR WORKOUT SESSIONS WILL BE AS NON-PHYSICAL AS PUGILISTIC-RELATED ACTIVITIES CAN POSSIBLY...
BUFF?
YOU OKAY?

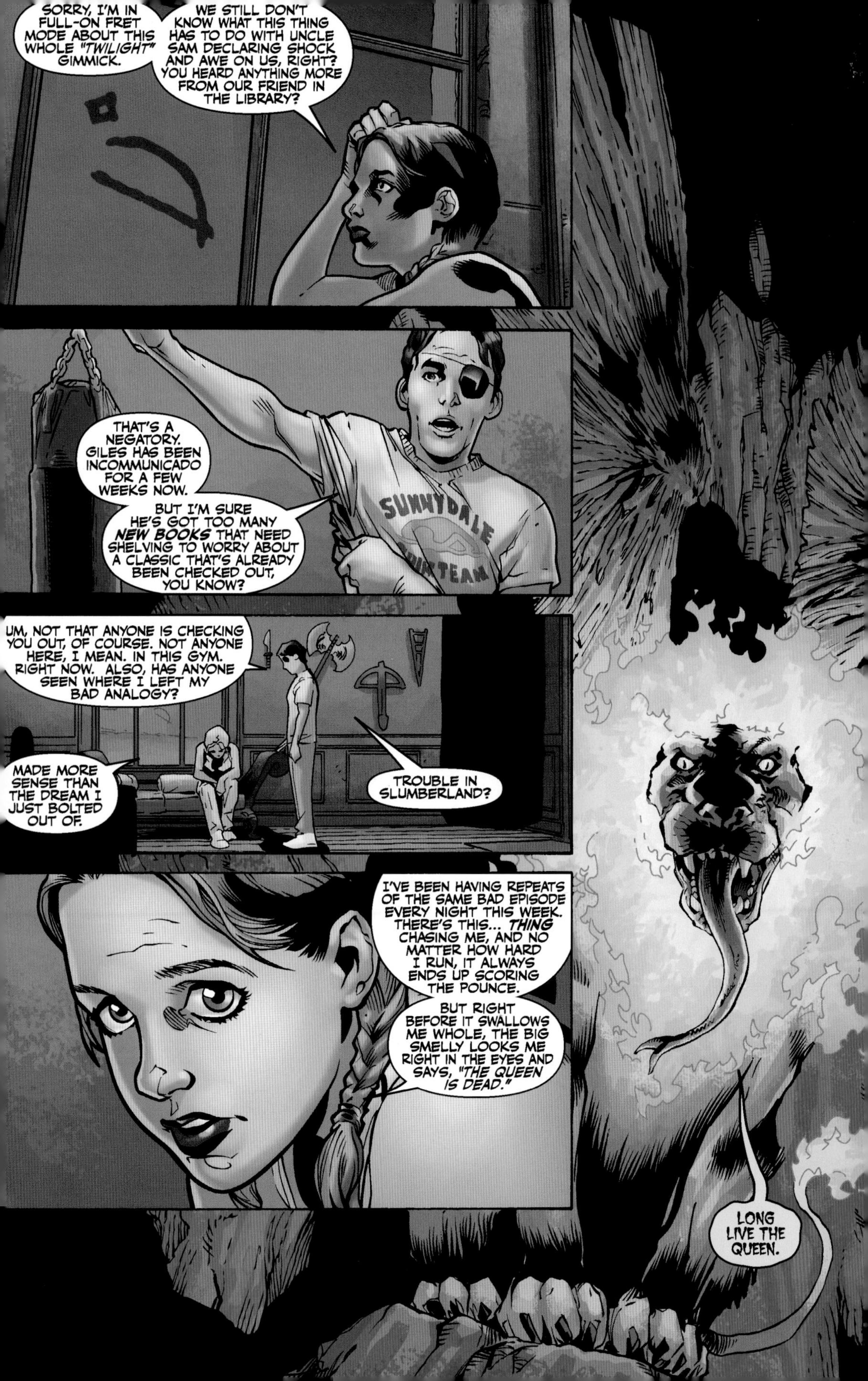
SORRY, I'M IN FULL-ON FRET MODE ABOUT THIS WHOLE "TWILIGHT" GIMMICK.
WE STILL DON'T KNOW WHAT THIS THING HAS TO DO WITH UNCLE SAM DECLARING SHOCK AND AWE ON US, RIGHT? YOU HEARD ANYTHING MORE FROM OUR FRIEND IN THE LIBRARY?
THAT'S A NEGATORY. GILES HAS BEEN INCOMMUNICADO FOR A FEW WEEKS NOW.
BUT I'M SURE HE'S GOT TOO MANY NEW BOOKS THAT NEED SHELVING TO WORRY ABOUT A CLASSIC THAT'S ALREADY BEEN CHECKED OUT, YOU KNOW?
SUNNYDALE SWIM TEAM
UM, NOT THAT ANYONE IS CHECKING YOU OUT, OF COURSE. NOT ANYONE HERE, I MEAN. IN THIS GYM. RIGHT NOW. ALSO, HAS ANYONE SEEN WHERE I LEFT MY BAD ANALOGY?
MADE MORE SENSE THAN THE DREAM I JUST BOLTED OUT OF.
TROUBLE IN SLUMBERLAND?
I'VE BEEN HAVING REPEATS OF THE SAME BAD EPISODE EVERY NIGHT THIS WEEK. THERE'S THIS... THING CHASING ME, AND NO MATTER HOW HARD I RUN, IT ALWAYS ENDS UP SCORING THE POUNCE.
BUT RIGHT BEFORE IT SWALLOWS ME WHOLE, THE BIG SMELLY LOOKS ME RIGHT IN THE EYES AND SAYS, "THE QUEEN IS DEAD."
LONG LIVE THE QUEEN.

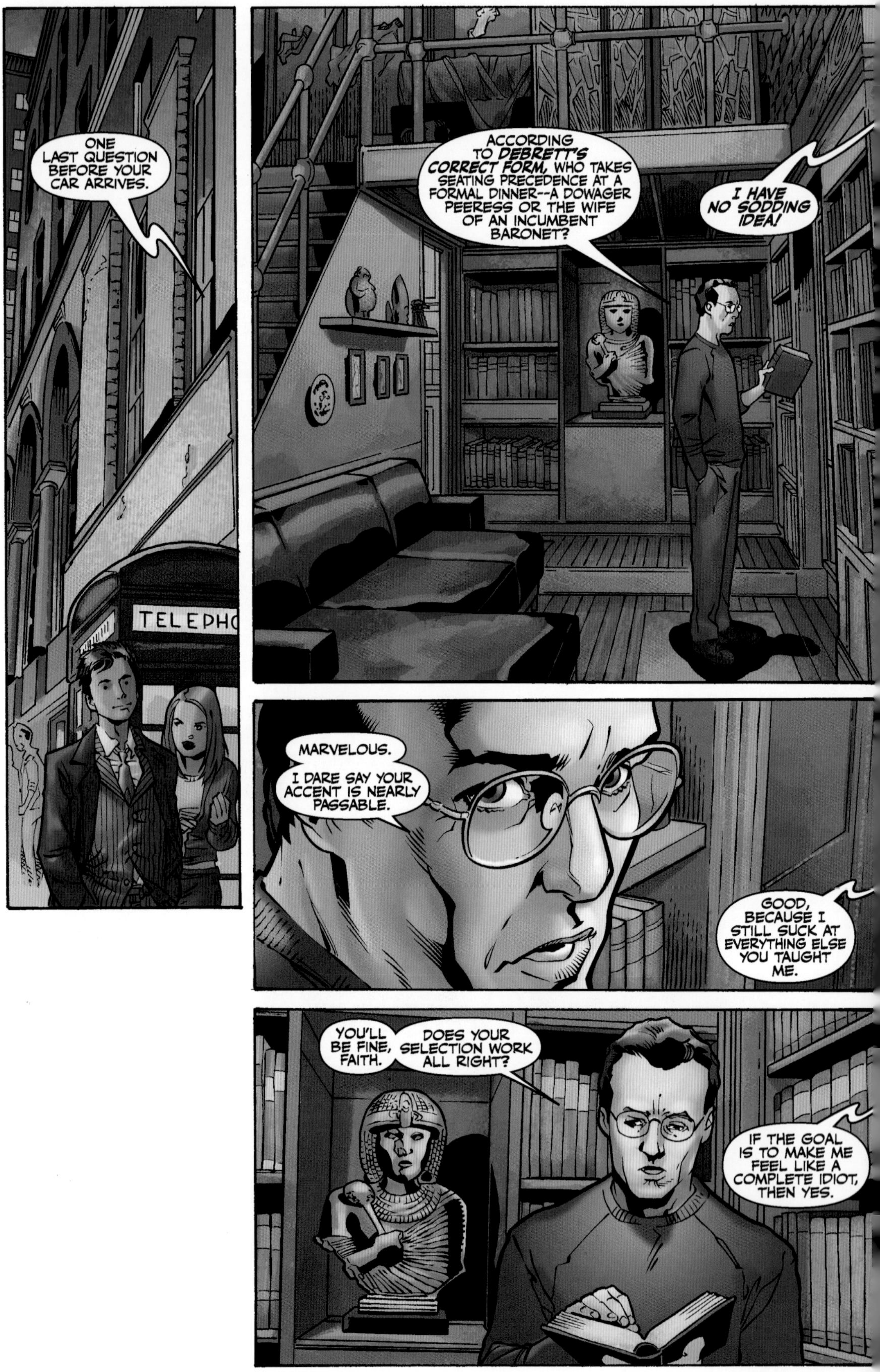

ONE LAST QUESTION BEFORE YOUR CAR ARRIVES.
TELEPHO
ACCORDING TO DEBRETT'S CORRECT FORM, WHO TAKES SEATING PRECEDENCE AT A FORMAL DINNER--A DOWAGER PEERESS OR THE WIFE OF AN INCUMBENT BARONET?
I HAVE NO SODDING IDEA!
MARVELOUS.
I DARE SAY YOUR ACCENT IS NEARLY PASSABLE.
GOOD, BECAUSE I STILL SUCK AT EVERYTHING ELSE YOU TAUGHT ME.
YOU'LL BE FINE, FAITH.
DOES YOUR SELECTION WORK ALL RIGHT?
IF THE GOAL IS TO MAKE ME FEEL LIKE A COMPLETE IDIOT, THEN YES.

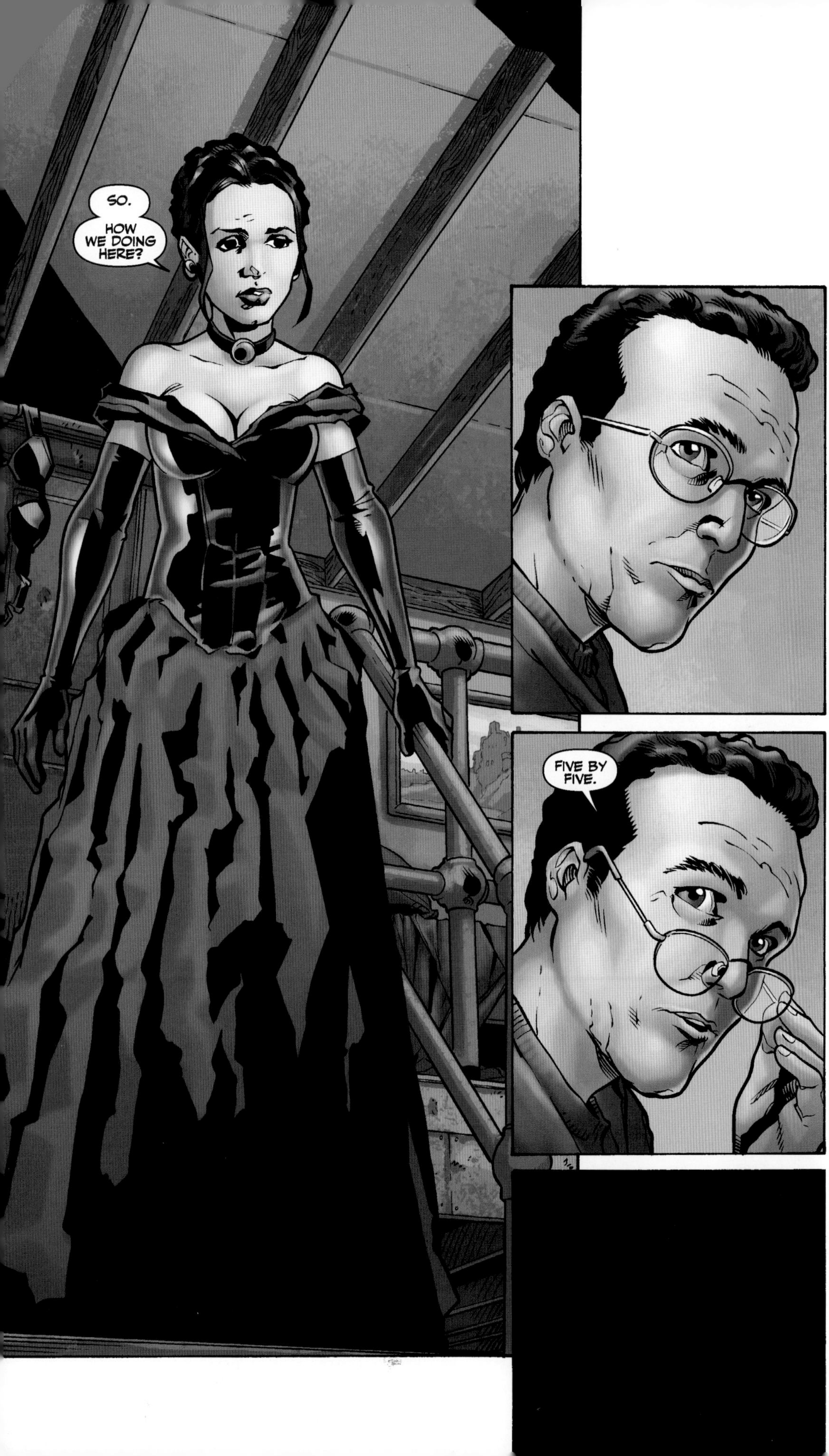
SO.
HOW WE DOING HERE?
FIVE BY FIVE.

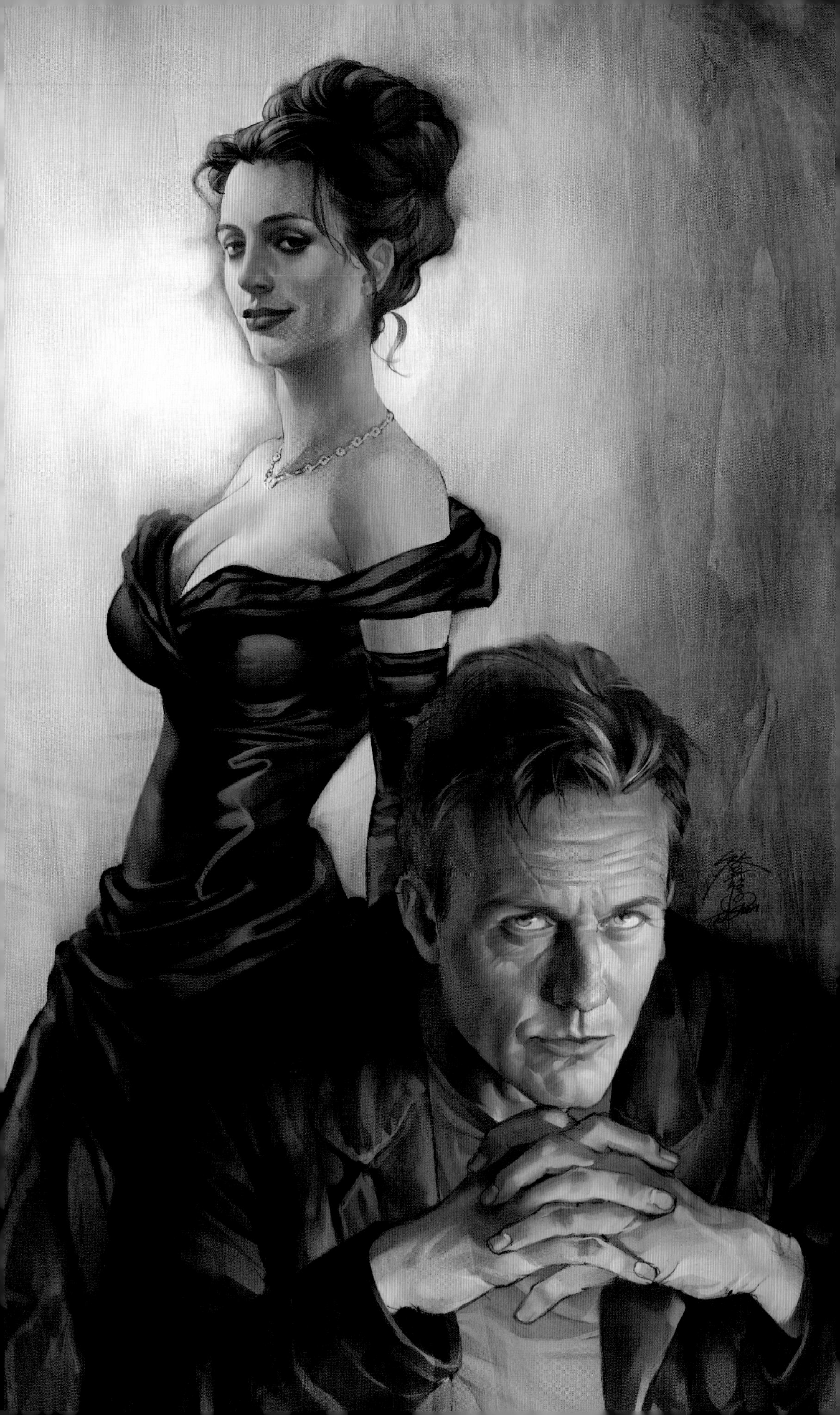

NO FUTURE FOR YOU

PART TWO

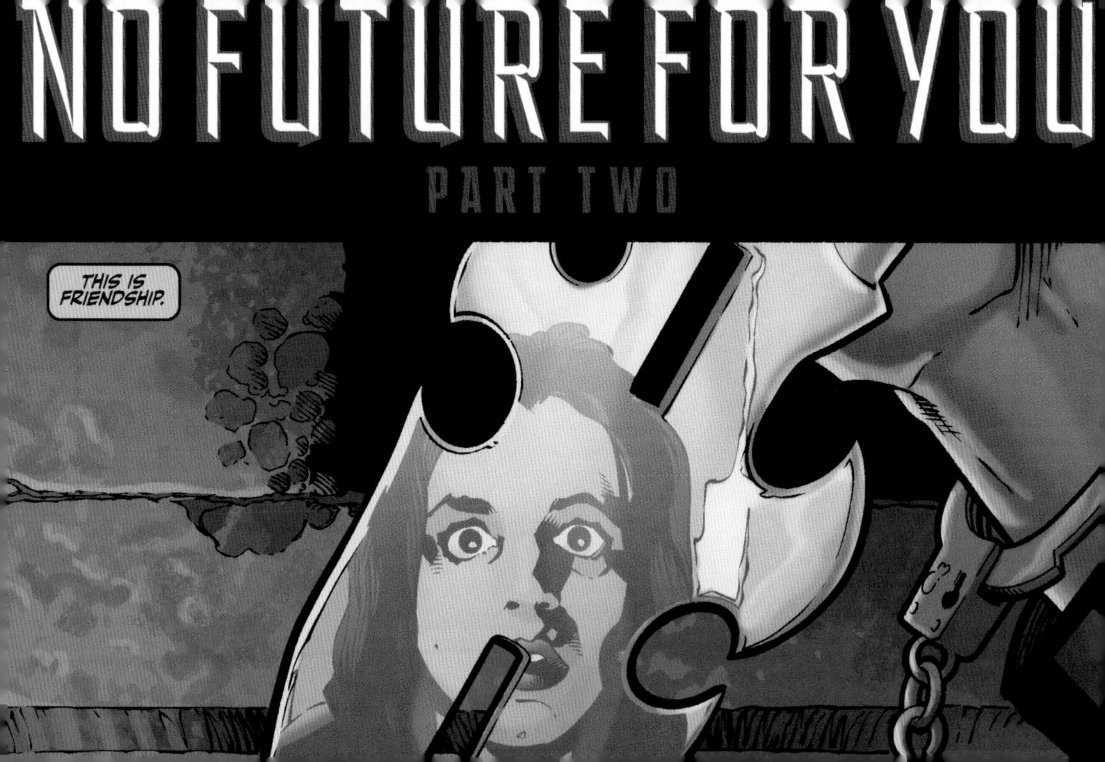
THIS IS FRIENDSHIP.

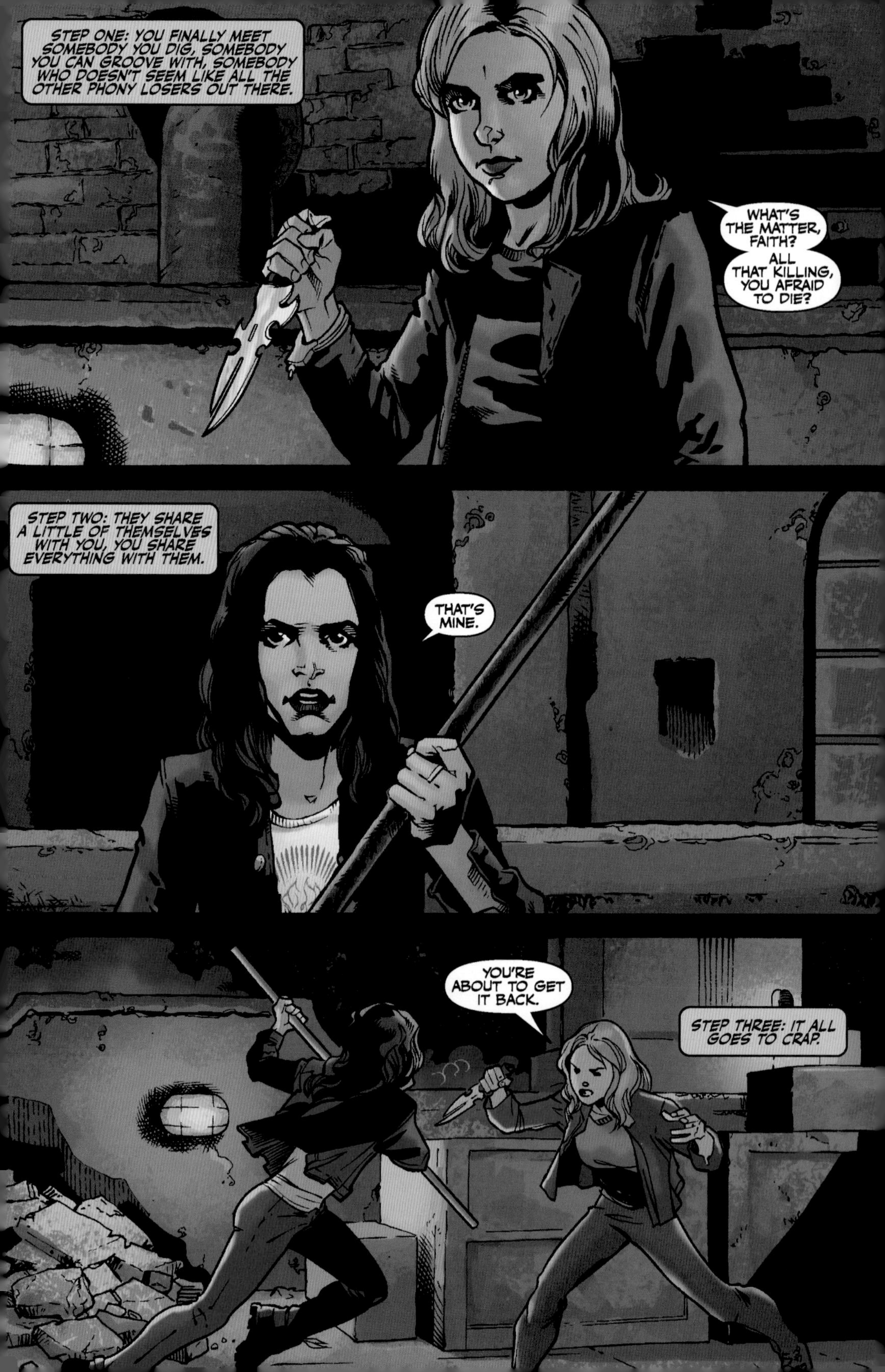
STEP ONE: YOU FINALLY MEET SOMEBODY YOU DIG, SOMEBODY YOU CAN GROOVE WITH, SOMEBODY WHO DOESN'T SEEM LIKE ALL THE OTHER PHONY LOSERS OUT THERE.
WHAT'S THE MATTER, FAITH?
ALL THAT KILLING, YOU AFRAID TO DIE?
STEP TWO: THEY SHARE A LITTLE OF THEMSELVES WITH YOU, YOU SHARE EVERYTHING WITH THEM.
THAT'S MINE.
YOU'RE ABOUT TO GET IT BACK.
STEP THREE: IT ALL GOES TO CRAP.

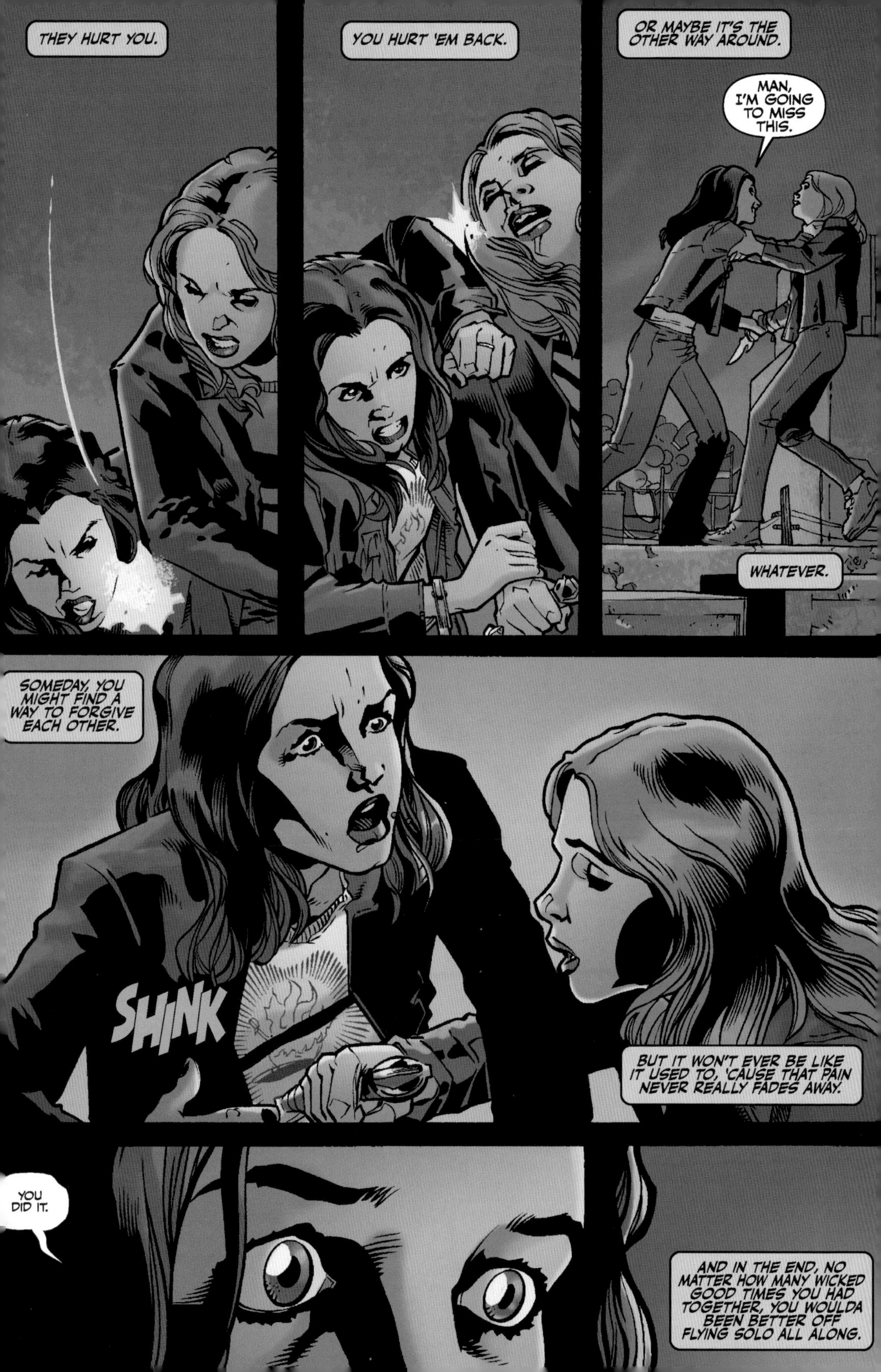

THEY HURT YOU.
YOU HURT 'EM BACK.
OR MAYBE IT'S THE OTHER WAY AROUND.
MAN, I'M GOING TO MISS THIS.
WHATEVER.
SOMEDAY, YOU MIGHT FIND A WAY TO FORGIVE EACH OTHER.
SHINK
BUT IT WON'T EVER BE LIKE IT USED TO, 'CAUSE THAT PAIN NEVER REALLY FADES AWAY.
YOU DID IT.
AND IN THE END, NO MATTER HOW MANY WICKED GOOD TIMES YOU HAD TOGETHER, YOU WOULDA BEEN BETTER OFF FLYING SOLO ALL ALONG.

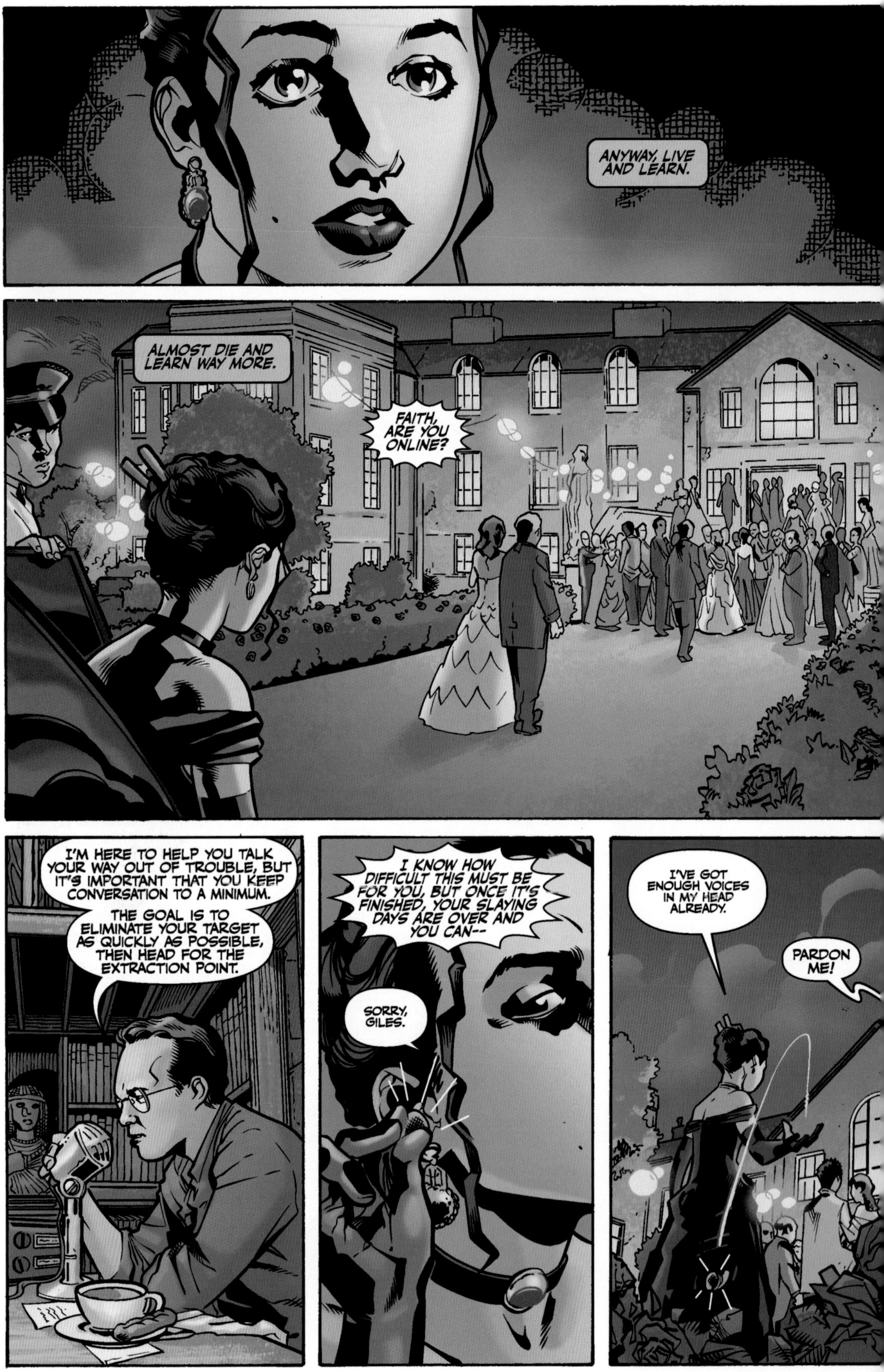
ANYWAY, LIVE AND LEARN.
ALMOST DIE AND LEARN WAY MORE.
FAITH, ARE YOU ONLINE?
I'M HERE TO HELP YOU TALK YOUR WAY OUT OF TROUBLE, BUT IT'S IMPORTANT THAT YOU KEEP CONVERSATION TO A MINIMUM.
THE GOAL IS TO ELIMINATE YOUR TARGET AS QUICKLY AS POSSIBLE, THEN HEAD FOR THE EXTRACTION POINT.
I KNOW HOW DIFFICULT THIS MUST BE FOR YOU, BUT ONCE IT'S FINISHED, YOUR SLAYING DAYS ARE OVER AND YOU CAN--
SORRY, GILES.
I'VE GOT ENOUGH VOICES IN MY HEAD ALREADY.
PARDON ME!

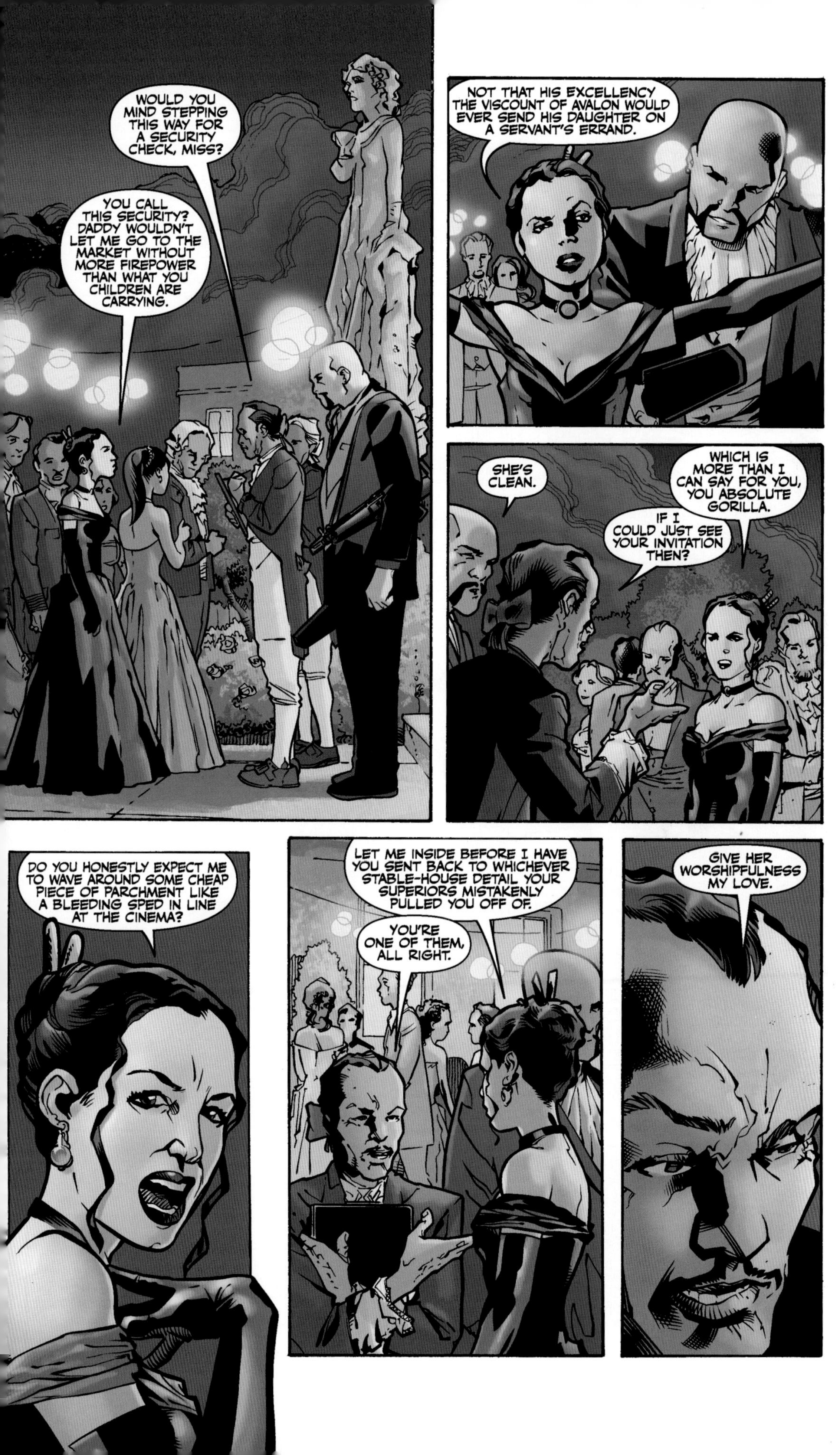
WOULD YOU MIND STEPPING THIS WAY FOR A SECURITY CHECK, MISS?
YOU CALL THIS SECURITY? DADDY WOULDN'T LET ME GO TO THE MARKET WITHOUT MORE FIREPOWER THAN WHAT YOU CHILDREN ARE CARRYING.
NOT THAT HIS EXCELLENCY THE VISCOUNT OF AVALON WOULD EVER SEND HIS DAUGHTER ON A SERVANT'S ERRAND.
SHE'S CLEAN.
WHICH IS MORE THAN I CAN SAY FOR YOU, YOU ABSOLUTE GORILLA.
IF I COULD JUST SEE YOUR INVITATION THEN?
DO YOU HONESTLY EXPECT ME TO WAVE AROUND SOME CHEAP PIECE OF PARCHMENT LIKE A BLEEDING SPED IN LINE AT THE CINEMA?
LET ME INSIDE BEFORE I HAVE YOU SENT BACK TO WHICHEVER STABLE-HOUSE DETAIL YOUR SUPERIORS MISTAKENLY PULLED YOU OFF OF.
YOU'RE ONE OF THEM, ALL RIGHT.
GIVE HER WORSHIPFULNESS MY LOVE.

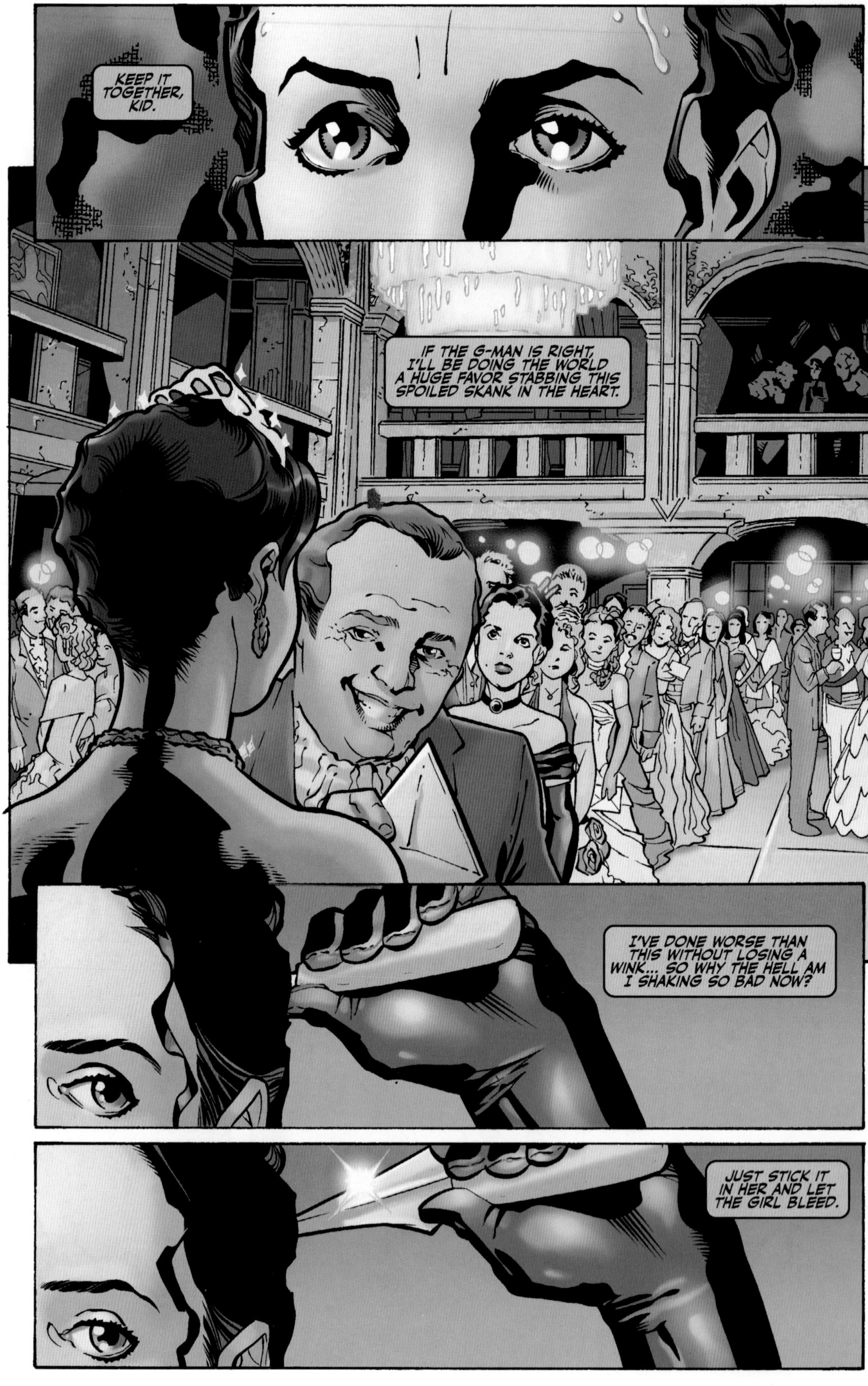
KEEP IT TOGETHER, KID.
IF THE G-MAN IS RIGHT, I'LL BE DOING THE WORLD A HUGE FAVOR STABBING THIS SPOILED SKANK IN THE HEART.
I'VE DONE WORSE THAN THIS WITHOUT LOSING A WINK... SO WHY THE HELL AM I SHAKING SO BAD NOW?
JUST STICK IT IN HER AND LET THE GIRL BLEED.

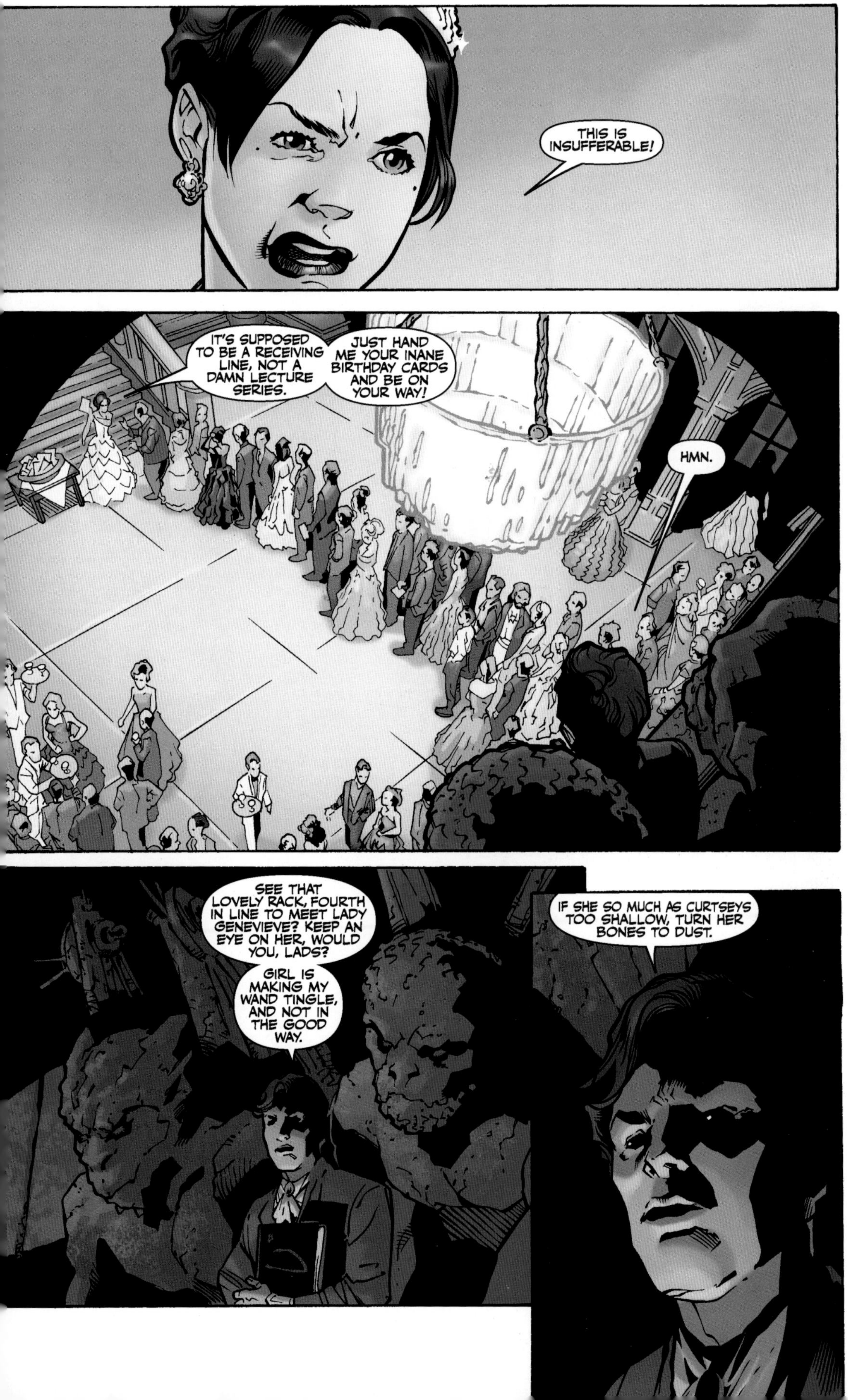

THIS IS INSUFFERABLE!
IT'S SUPPOSED TO BE A RECEIVING LINE, NOT A DAMN LECTURE SERIES.
JUST HAND ME YOUR INANE BIRTHDAY CARDS AND BE ON YOUR WAY!
HMN.
SEE THAT LOVELY RACK, FOURTH IN LINE TO MEET LADY GENEVIEVE? KEEP AN EYE ON HER, WOULD YOU, LADS?
GIRL IS MAKING MY WAND TINGLE, AND NOT IN THE GOOD WAY.
IF SHE SO MUCH AS CURTSEYS TOO SHALLOW, TURN HER BONES TO DUST.

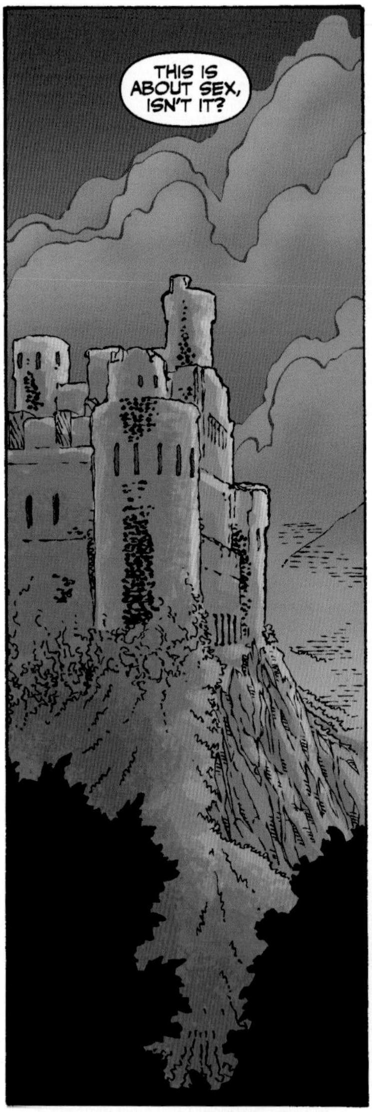
THIS IS ABOUT SEX, ISN'T IT?

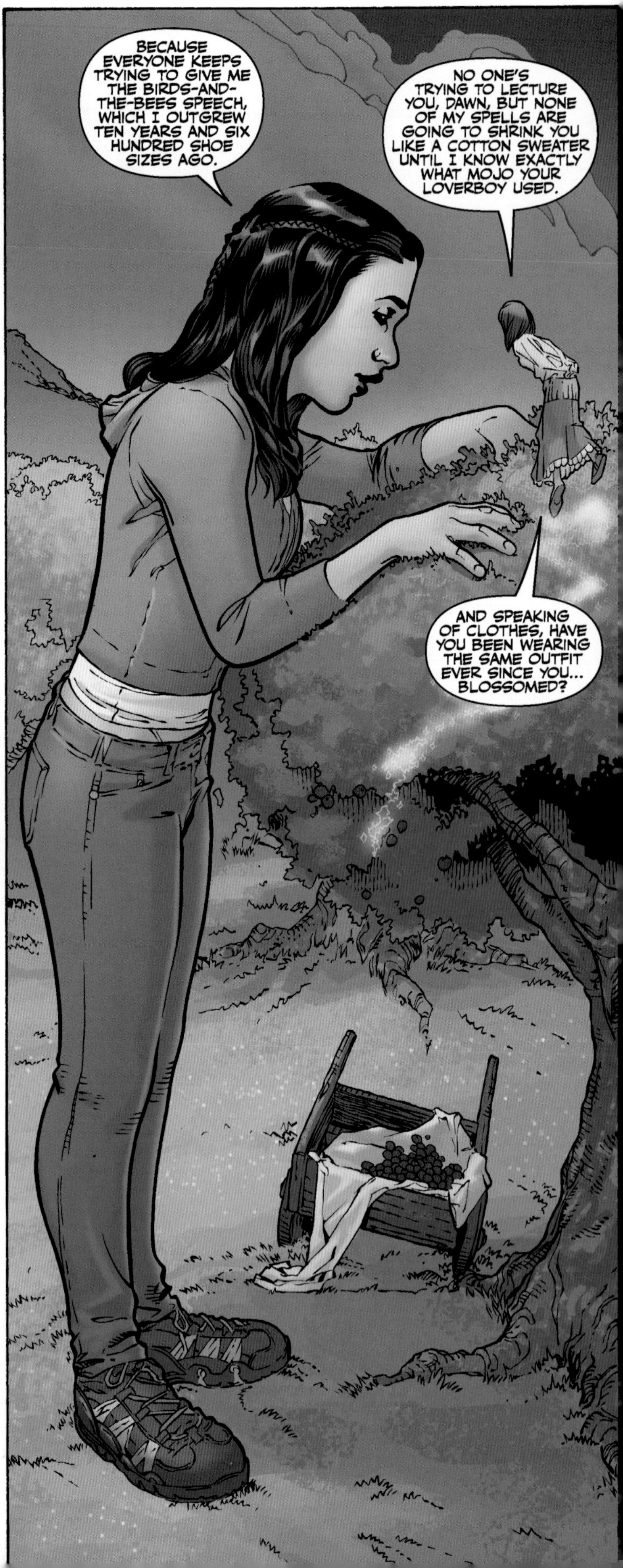
BECAUSE EVERYONE KEEPS TRYING TO GIVE ME THE BIRDS-AND-THE-BEES SPEECH, WHICH I OUTGREW TEN YEARS AND SIX HUNDRED SHOE SIZES AGO.
NO ONE'S TRYING TO LECTURE YOU, DAWN, BUT NONE OF MY SPELLS ARE GOING TO SHRINK YOU LIKE A COTTON SWEATER UNTIL I KNOW EXACTLY WHAT MOJO YOUR LOVERBOY USED.
AND SPEAKING OF CLOTHES, HAVE YOU BEEN WEARING THE SAME OUTFIT EVER SINCE YOU... BLOSSOMED?

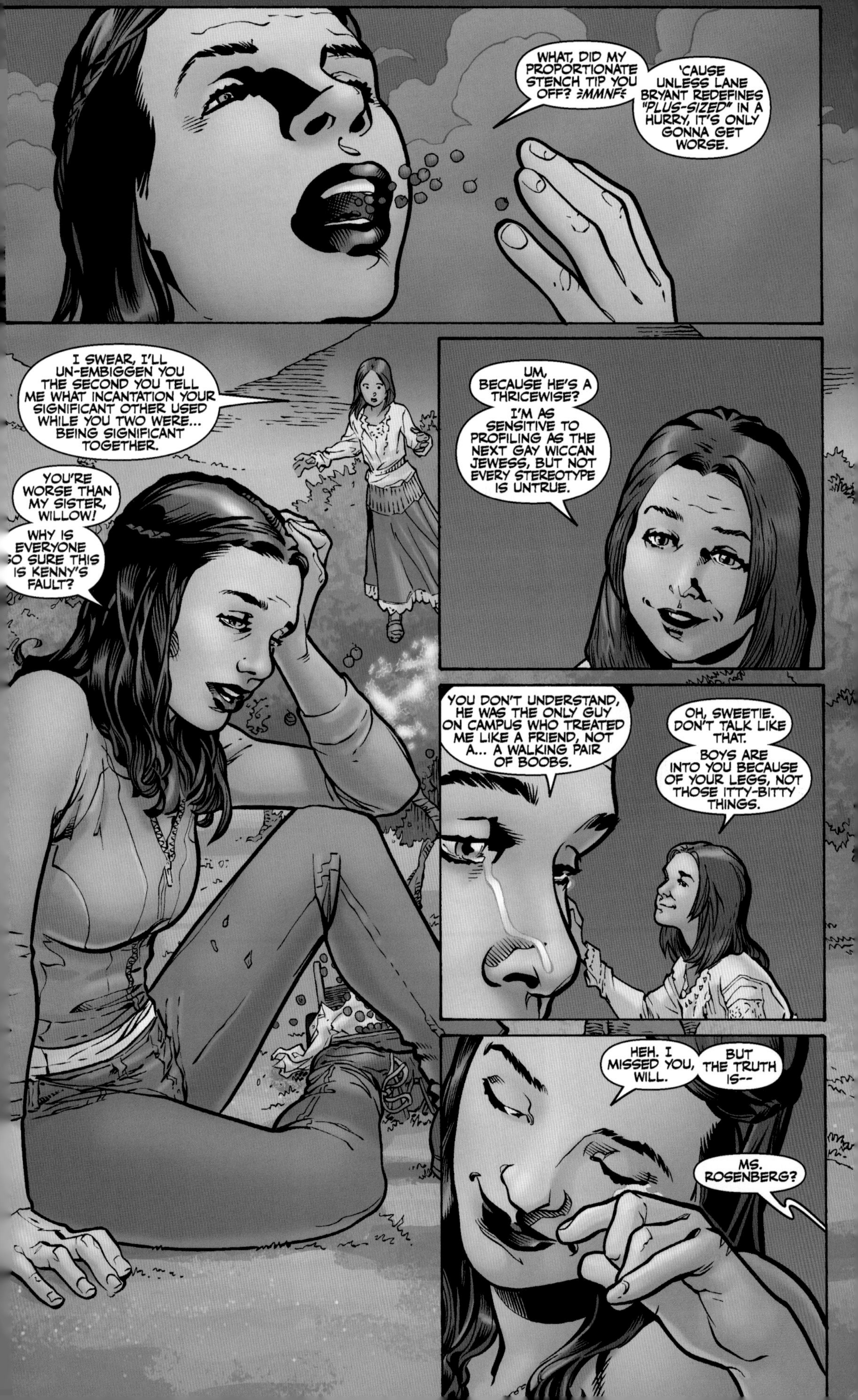
WHAT, DID MY PROPORTIONATE STENCH TIP YOU OFF? *MMNF*
'CAUSE UNLESS LANE BRYANT REDEFINES "PLUS-SIZED" IN A HURRY, IT'S ONLY GONNA GET WORSE.
I SWEAR, I'LL UN-EMBIGGEN YOU THE SECOND YOU TELL ME WHAT INCANTATION YOUR SIGNIFICANT OTHER USED WHILE YOU TWO WERE... BEING SIGNIFICANT TOGETHER.
YOU'RE WORSE THAN MY SISTER, WILLOW!
WHY IS EVERYONE SO SURE THIS IS KENNY'S FAULT?
UM, BECAUSE HE'S A THRICEWISE?
I'M AS SENSITIVE TO PROFILING AS THE NEXT GAY WICCAN JEWESS, BUT NOT EVERY STEREOTYPE IS UNTRUE.
YOU DON'T UNDERSTAND, HE WAS THE ONLY GUY ON CAMPUS WHO TREATED ME LIKE A FRIEND, NOT A... A WALKING PAIR OF BOOBS.
OH, SWEETIE. DON'T TALK LIKE THAT.
BOYS ARE INTO YOU BECAUSE OF YOUR LEGS, NOT THOSE ITTY-BITTY THINGS.
HEH. I MISSED YOU, WILL.
BUT THE TRUTH IS--
MS. ROSENBERG?

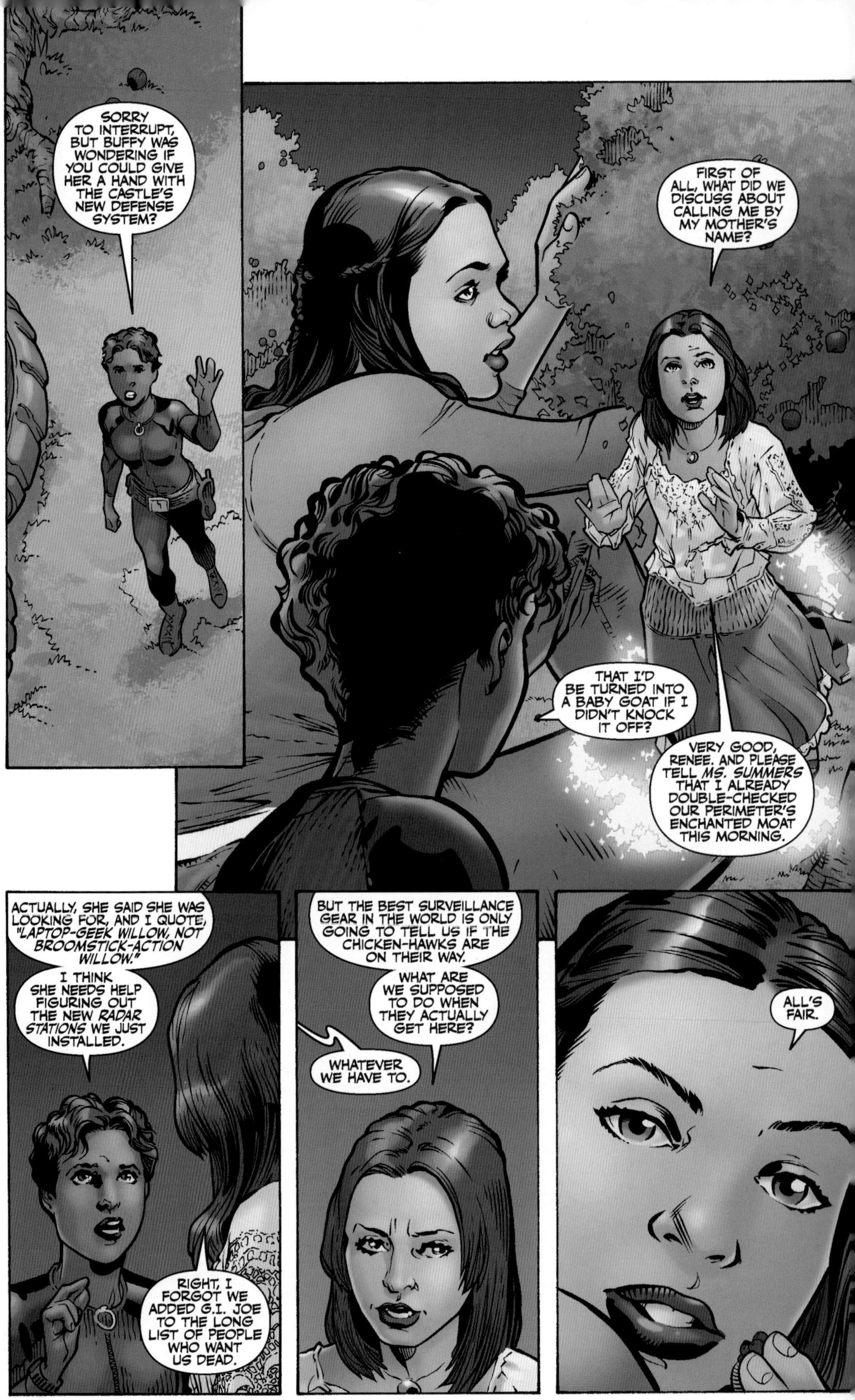
SORRY TO INTERRUPT, BUT BUFFY WAS WONDERING IF YOU COULD GIVE HER A HAND WITH THE CASTLE'S NEW DEFENSE SYSTEM?
FIRST OF ALL, WHAT DID WE DISCUSS ABOUT CALLING ME BY MY MOTHER'S NAME?
THAT I'D BE TURNED INTO A BABY GOAT IF I DIDN'T KNOCK IT OFF?
VERY GOOD, RENEE. AND PLEASE TELL *MS. SUMMERS* THAT I ALREADY DOUBLE-CHECKED OUR PERIMETER'S ENCHANTED MOAT THIS MORNING.
ACTUALLY, SHE SAID SHE WAS LOOKING FOR, AND I QUOTE, *"LAPTOP-GEEK WILLOW, NOT BROOMSTICK-ACTION WILLOW."*
I THINK SHE NEEDS HELP FIGURING OUT THE NEW *RADAR STATIONS* WE JUST INSTALLED.
RIGHT, I FORGOT WE ADDED G.I. JOE TO THE LONG LIST OF PEOPLE WHO WANT US DEAD.
BUT THE BEST SURVEILLANCE GEAR IN THE WORLD IS ONLY GOING TO TELL US IF THE CHICKEN-HAWKS ARE ON THEIR WAY.
WHAT ARE WE SUPPOSED TO DO WHEN THEY ACTUALLY GET HERE?
WHATEVER WE HAVE TO.
ALL'S FAIR.

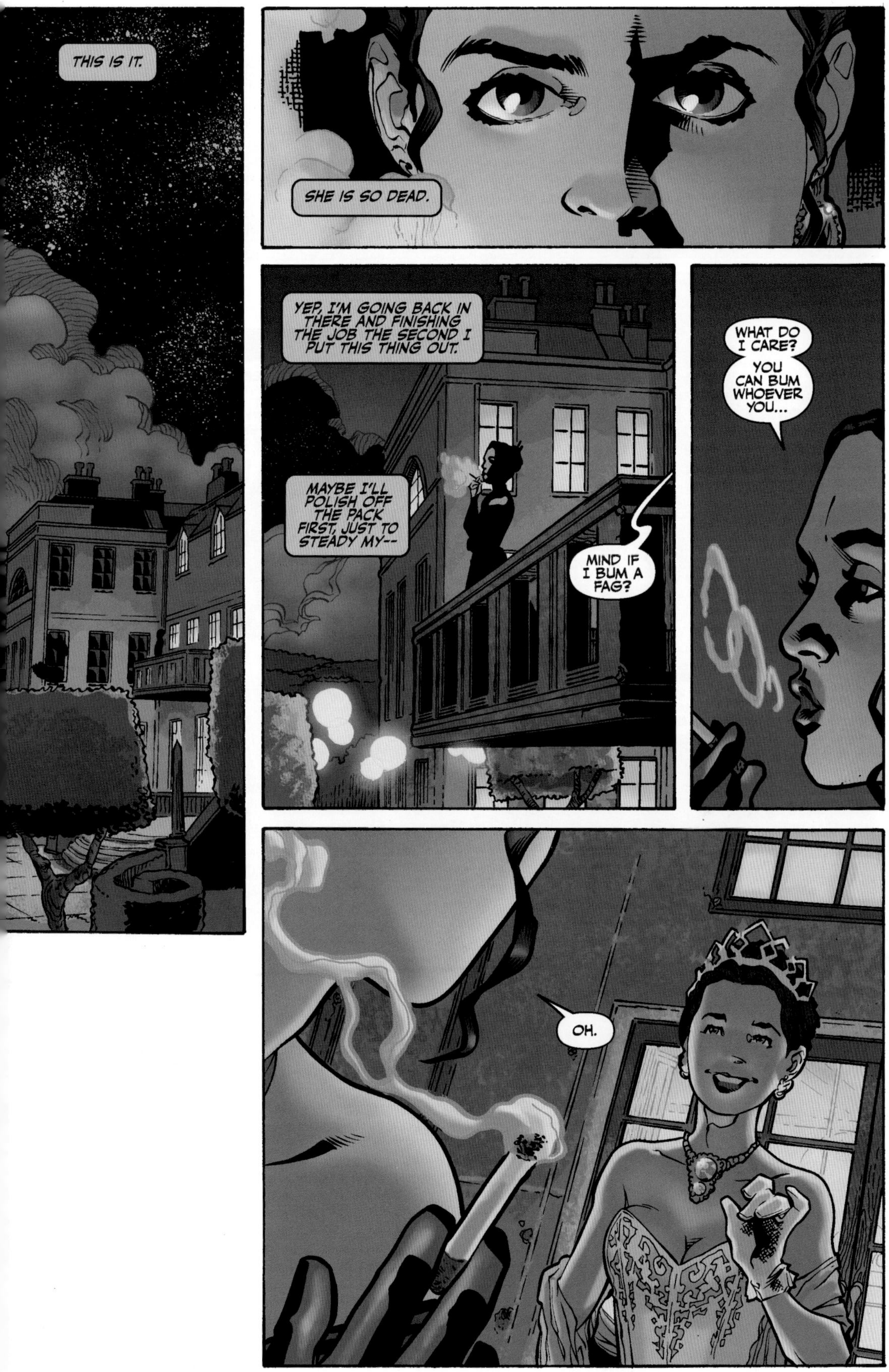
THIS IS IT.
SHE IS SO DEAD.
YEP, I'M GOING BACK IN THERE AND FINISHING THE JOB THE SECOND I PUT THIS THING OUT.
MAYBE I'LL POLISH OFF THE PACK FIRST, JUST TO STEADY MY--
MIND IF I BUM A FAG?
WHAT DO I CARE?
YOU CAN BUM WHOEVER YOU...
OH.

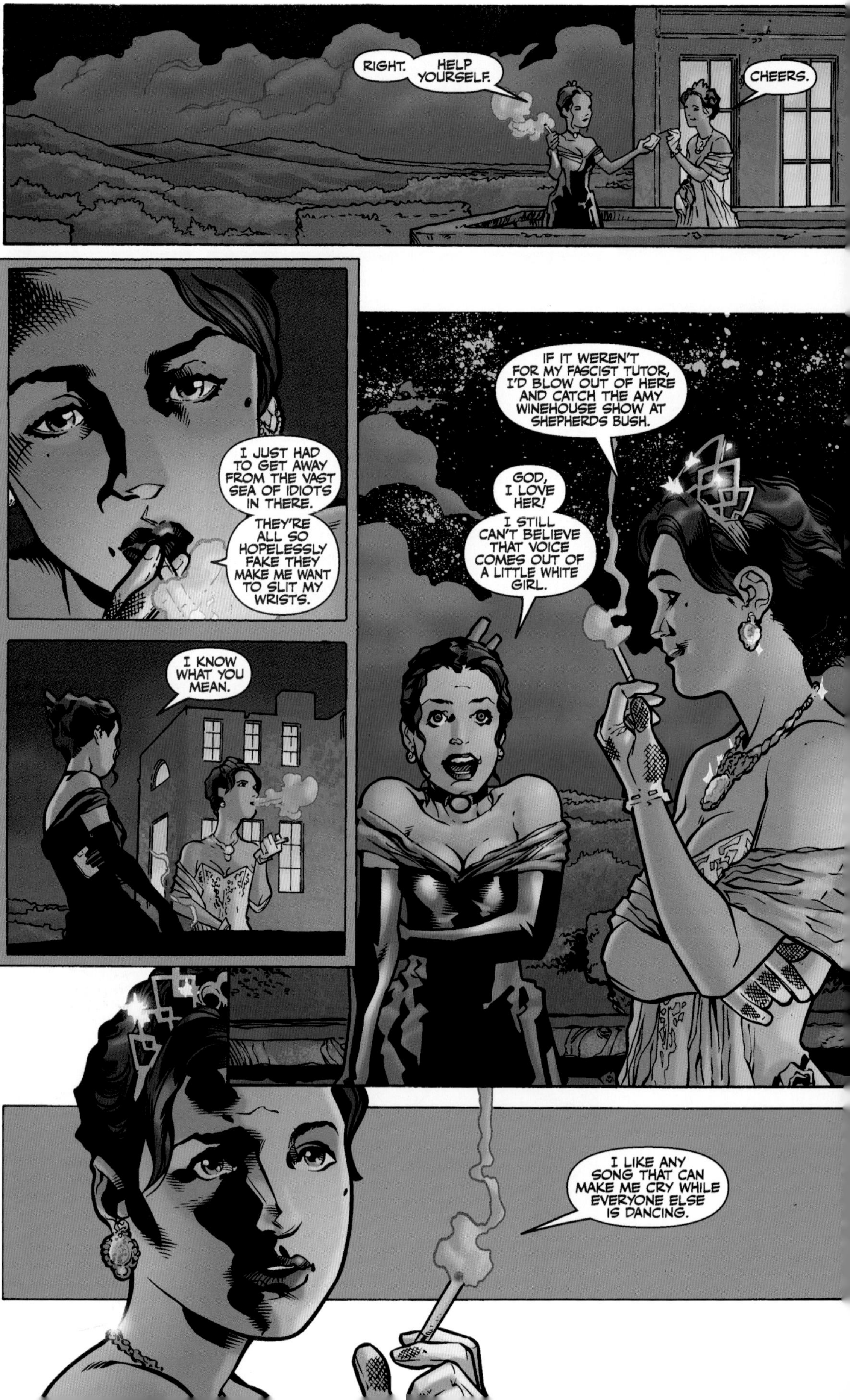
RIGHT.
HELP YOURSELF.
CHEERS.
I JUST HAD TO GET AWAY FROM THE VAST SEA OF IDIOTS IN THERE.
THEY'RE ALL SO HOPELESSLY FAKE THEY MAKE ME WANT TO SLIT MY WRISTS.
I KNOW WHAT YOU MEAN.
IF IT WEREN'T FOR MY FASCIST TUTOR, I'D BLOW OUT OF HERE AND CATCH THE AMY WINEHOUSE SHOW AT SHEPHERDS BUSH.
GOD, I LOVE HER!
I STILL CAN'T BELIEVE THAT VOICE COMES OUT OF A LITTLE WHITE GIRL.
I LIKE ANY SONG THAT CAN MAKE ME CRY WHILE EVERYONE ELSE IS DANCING.

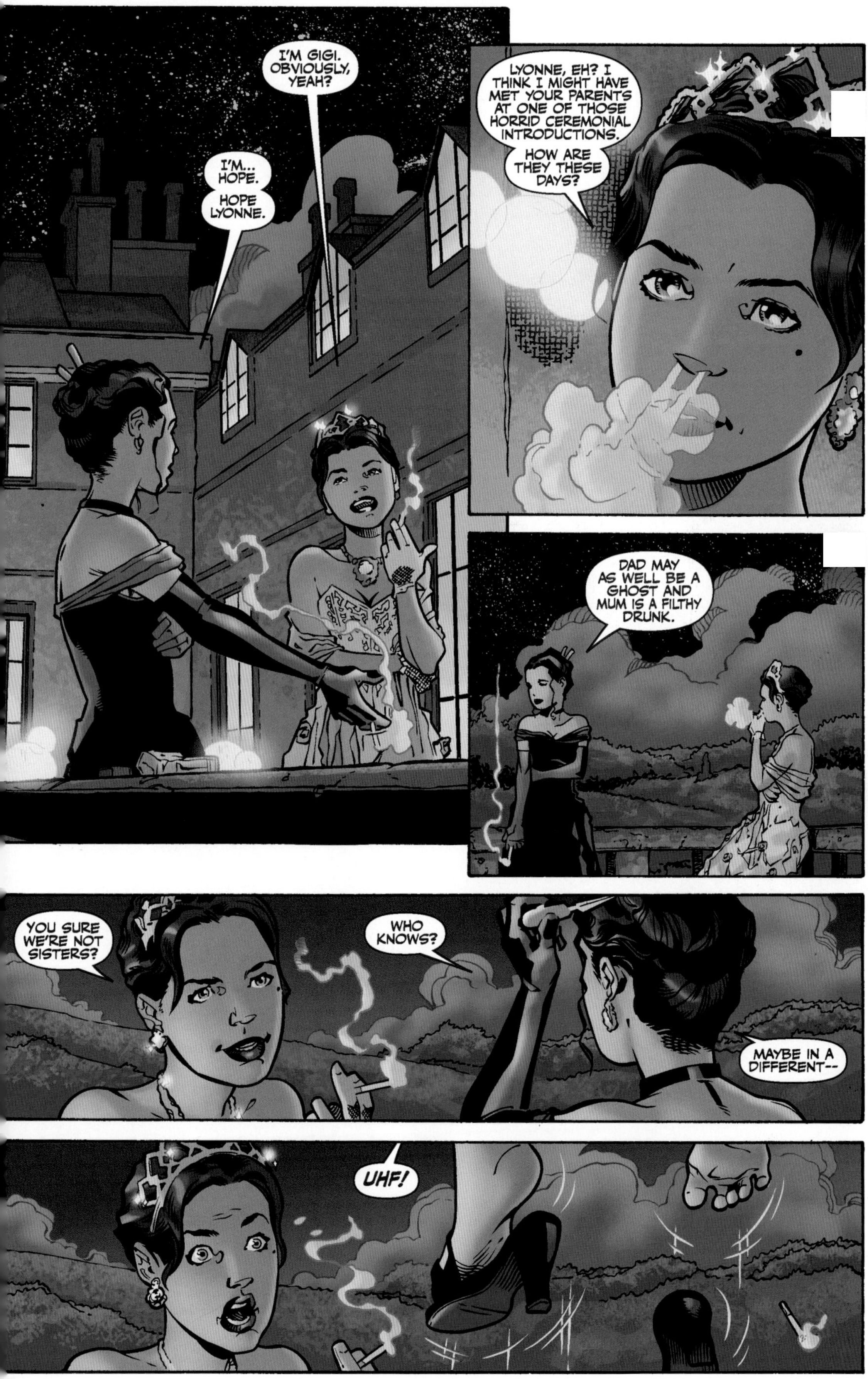
I'M GIGI. OBVIOUSLY, YEAH?
I'M... HOPE.
HOPE LYONNE.
LYONNE, EH? I THINK I MIGHT HAVE MET YOUR PARENTS AT ONE OF THOSE HORRID CEREMONIAL INTRODUCTIONS.
HOW ARE THEY THESE DAYS?
DAD MAY AS WELL BE A GHOST AND MUM IS A FILTHY DRUNK.
YOU SURE WE'RE NOT SISTERS?
WHO KNOWS?
MAYBE IN A DIFFERENT--
UHF!

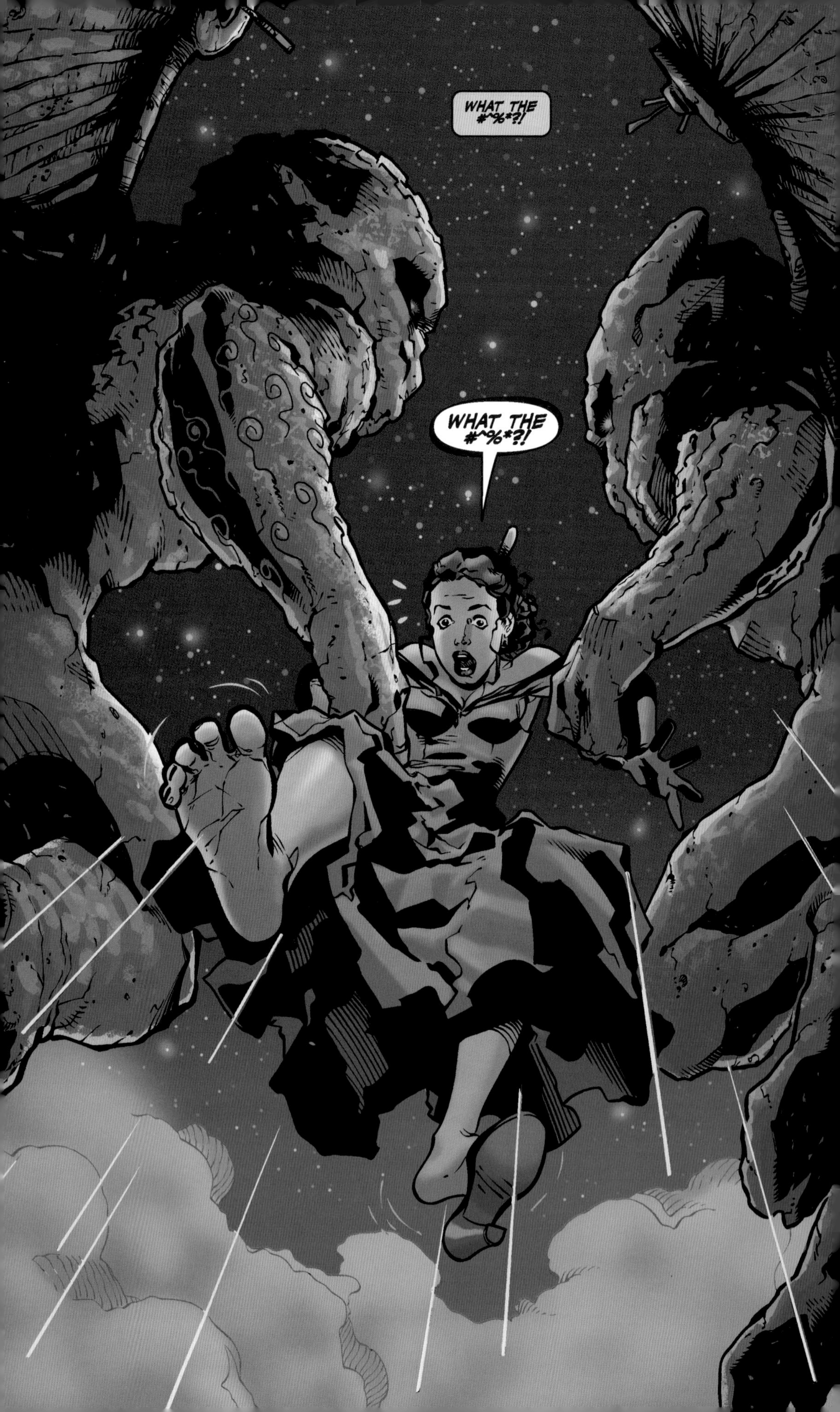
WHAT THE #^%*?!
WHAT THE #^%*?!

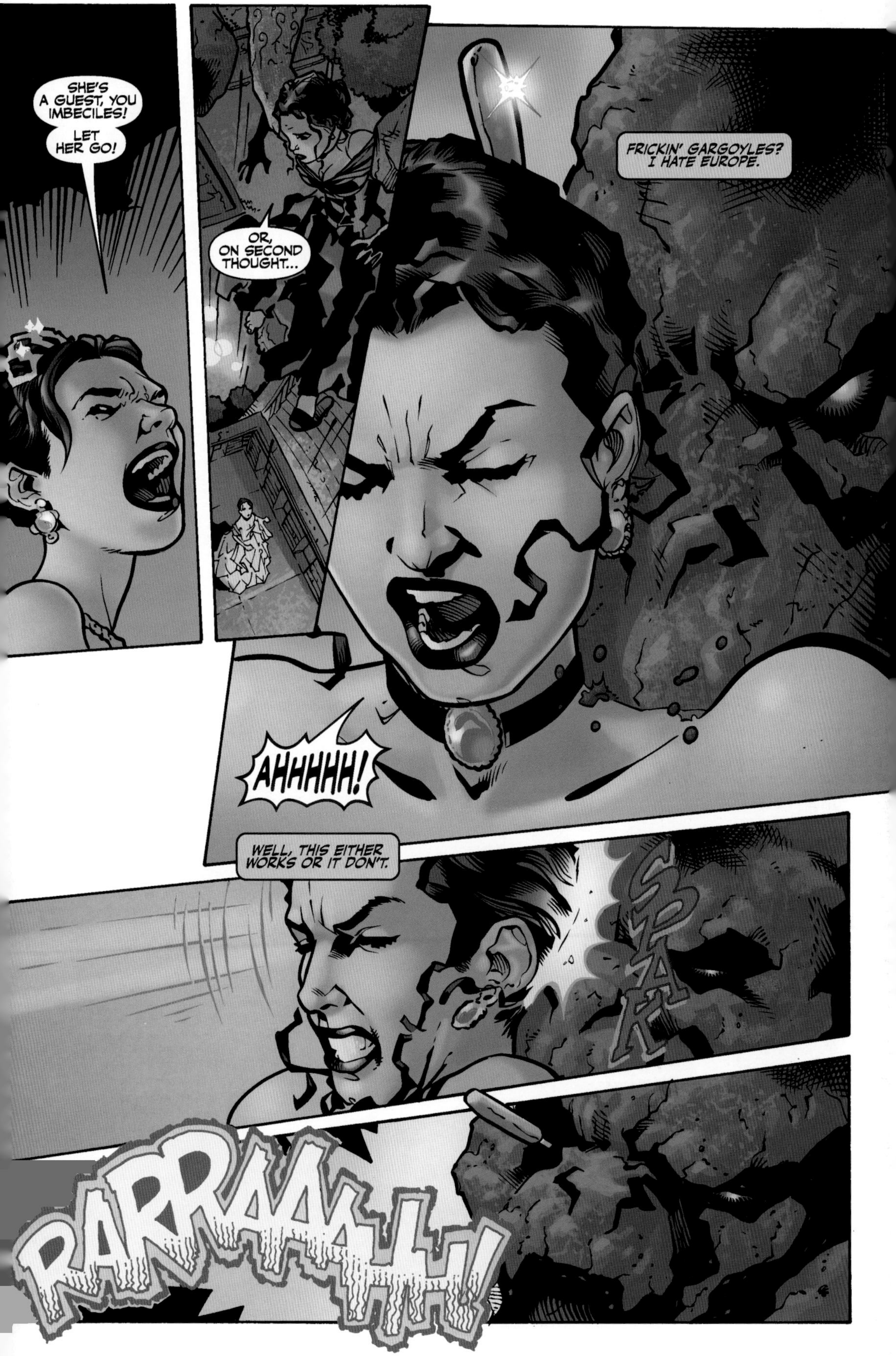
SHE'S A GUEST, YOU IMBECILES!
LET HER GO!
OR, ON SECOND THOUGHT...
FRICKIN' GARGOYLES? I HATE EUROPE.
AHHHHH!
WELL, THIS EITHER WORKS OR IT DON'T.
SHAK
RARRAAAHH!

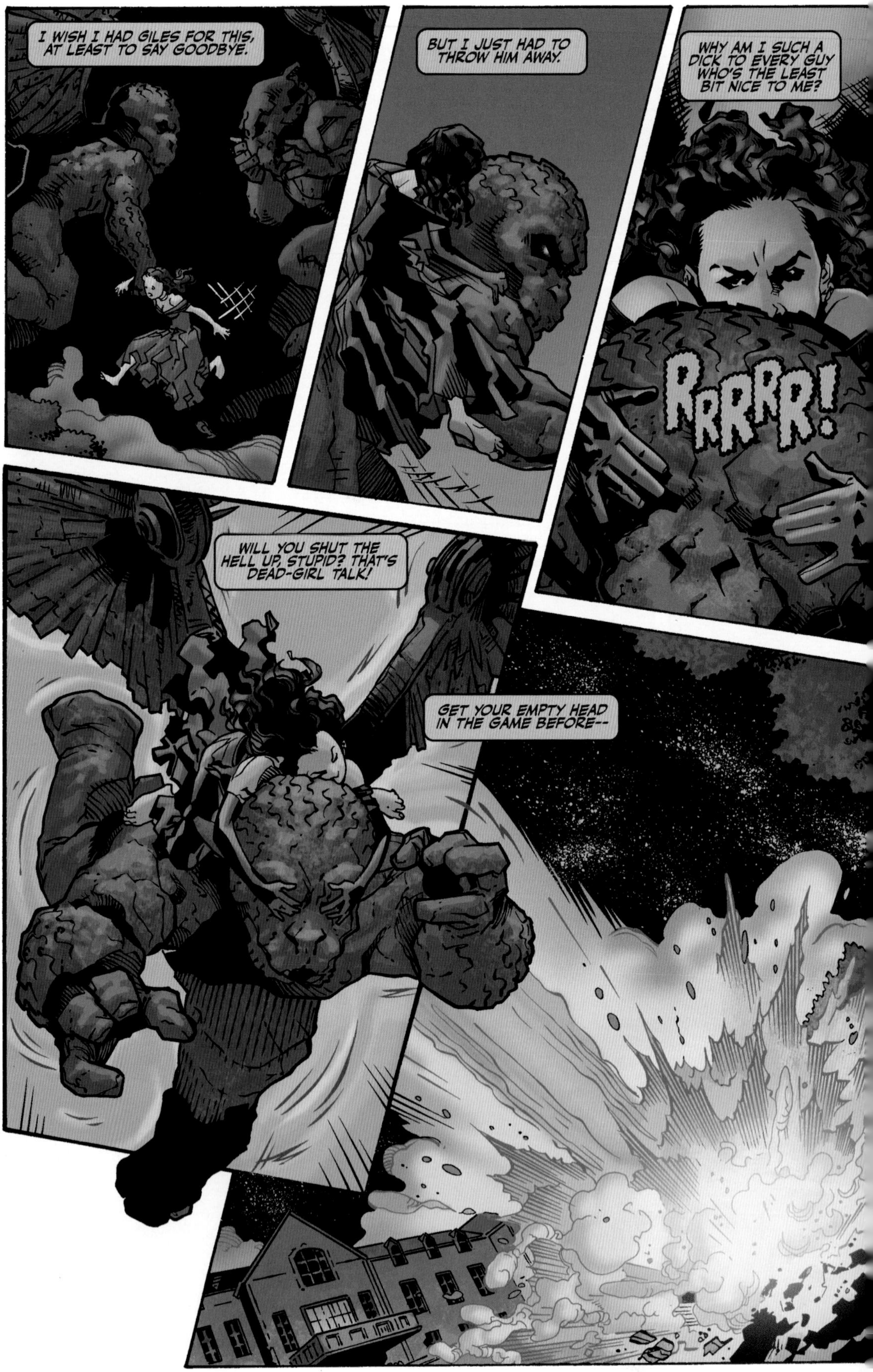
I WISH I HAD GILES FOR THIS, AT LEAST TO SAY GOODBYE.
BUT I JUST HAD TO THROW HIM AWAY.
WHY AM I SUCH A DICK TO EVERY GUY WHO'S THE LEAST BIT NICE TO ME?
RRRRR!
WILL YOU SHUT THE HELL UP, STUPID? THAT'S DEAD-GIRL TALK!
GET YOUR EMPTY HEAD IN THE GAME BEFORE--

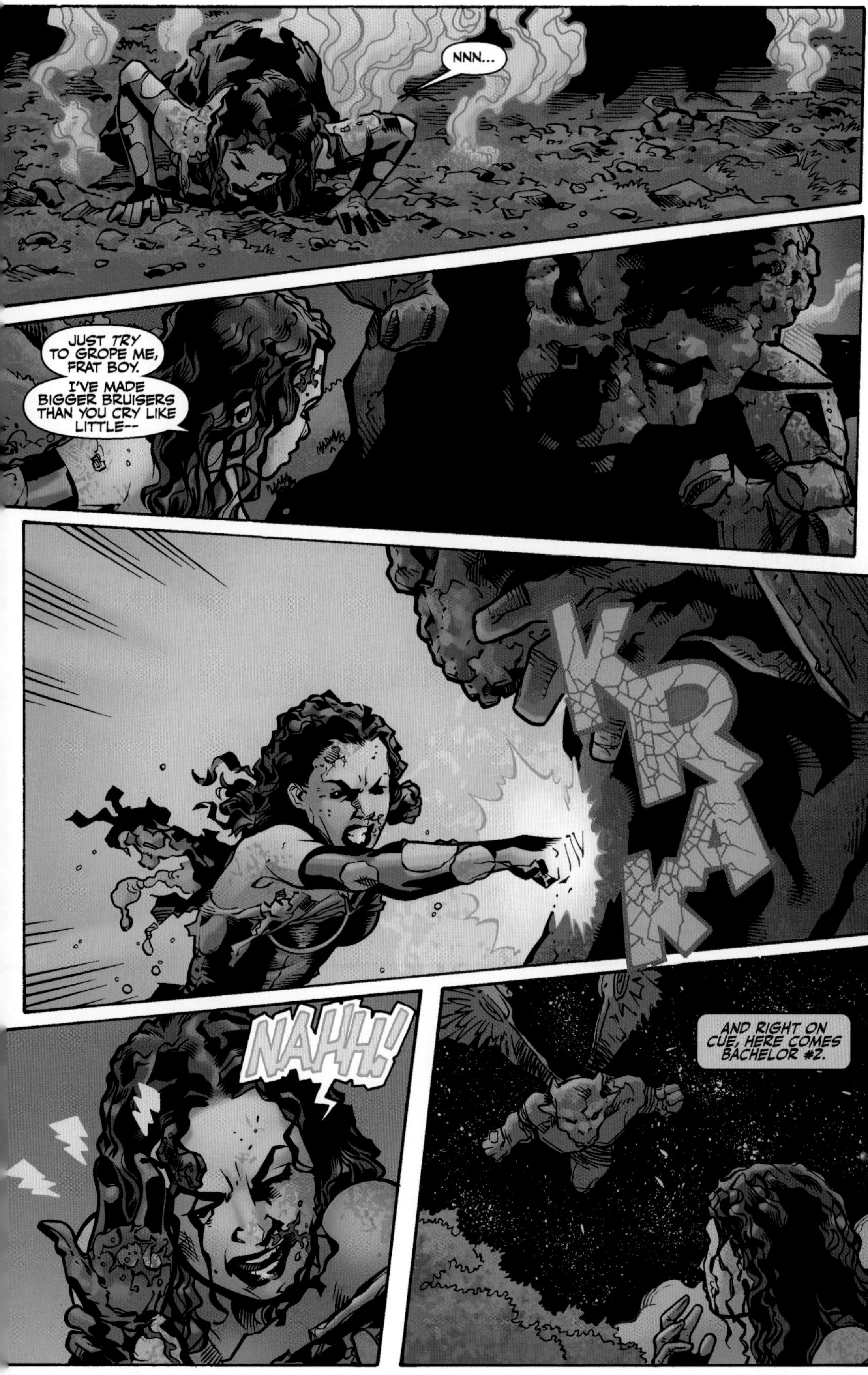
NNN...
JUST TRY TO GROPE ME, FRAT BOY.
I'VE MADE BIGGER BRUISERS THAN YOU CRY LIKE LITTLE--
KRAKA
NAHH!
AND RIGHT ON CUE, HERE COMES BACHELOR #2.

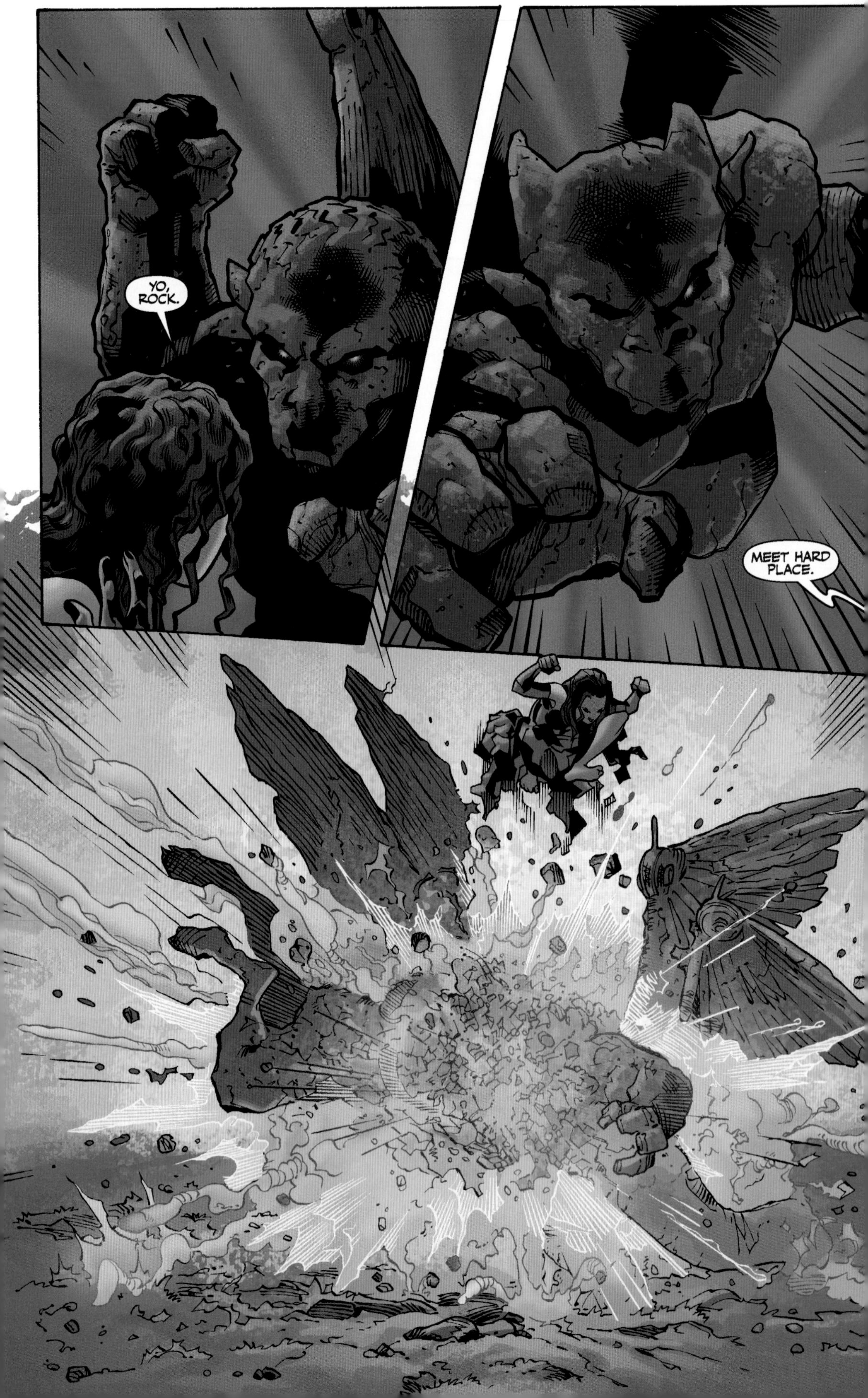
YO, ROCK.
MEET HARD PLACE.

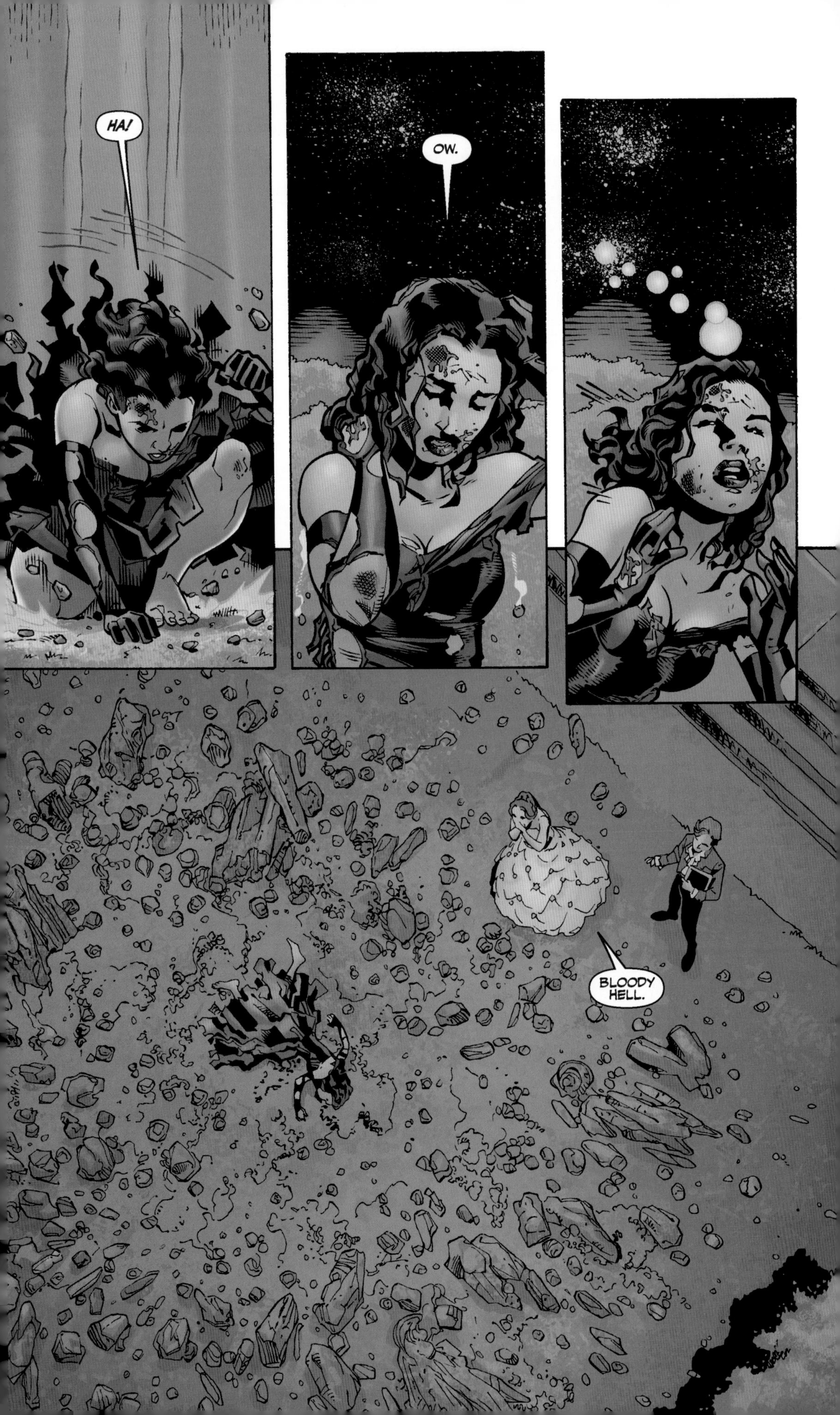
HA!
OW.
BLOODY HELL.

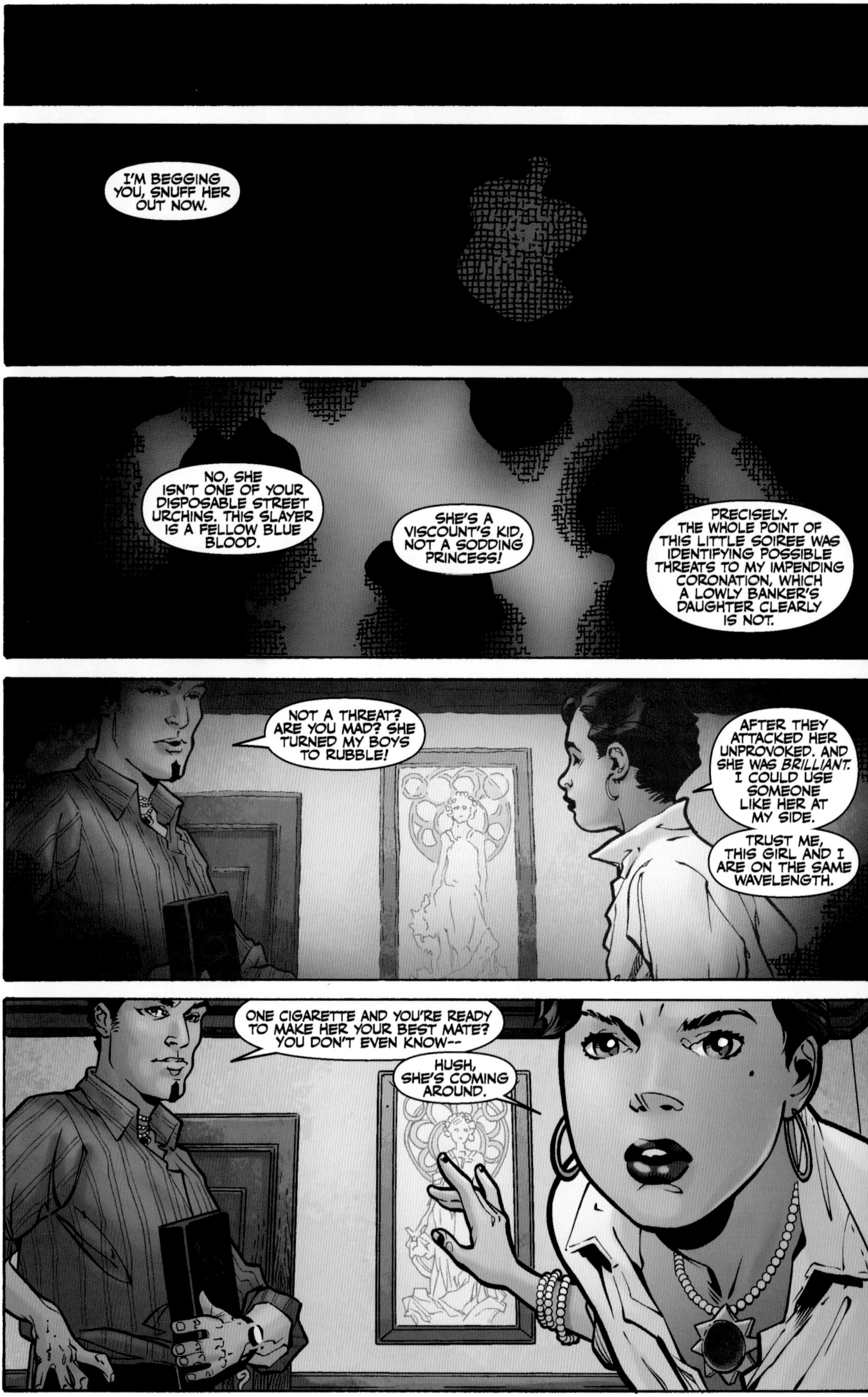
I'M BEGGING YOU, SNUFF HER OUT NOW.
NO, SHE ISN'T ONE OF YOUR DISPOSABLE STREET URCHINS. THIS SLAYER IS A FELLOW BLUE BLOOD.
SHE'S A VISCOUNT'S KID, NOT A SODDING PRINCESS!
PRECISELY. THE WHOLE POINT OF THIS LITTLE SOIREE WAS IDENTIFYING POSSIBLE THREATS TO MY IMPENDING CORONATION, WHICH A LOWLY BANKER'S DAUGHTER CLEARLY IS NOT.
NOT A THREAT? ARE YOU MAD? SHE TURNED MY BOYS TO RUBBLE!
AFTER THEY ATTACKED HER UNPROVOKED. AND SHE WAS *BRILLIANT.* I COULD USE SOMEONE LIKE HER AT MY SIDE.
TRUST ME, THIS GIRL AND I ARE ON THE SAME WAVELENGTH.
ONE CIGARETTE AND YOU'RE READY TO MAKE HER YOUR BEST MATE? YOU DON'T EVEN KNOW--
HUSH, SHE'S COMING AROUND.

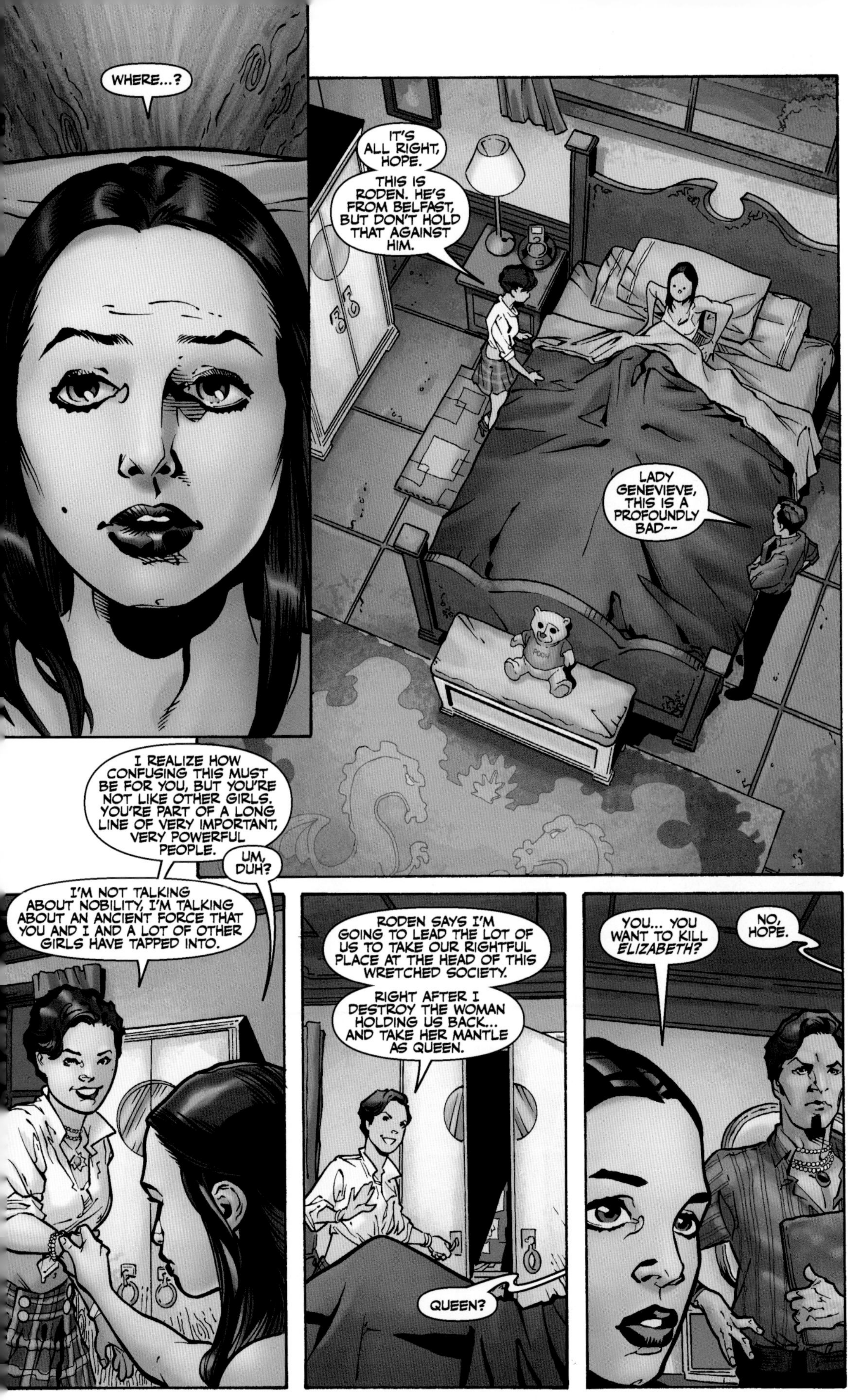

WHERE...?
IT'S ALL RIGHT, HOPE.
THIS IS RODEN. HE'S FROM BELFAST, BUT DON'T HOLD THAT AGAINST HIM.
LADY GENEVIEVE, THIS IS A PROFOUNDLY BAD--
I REALIZE HOW CONFUSING THIS MUST BE FOR YOU, BUT YOU'RE NOT LIKE OTHER GIRLS. YOU'RE PART OF A LONG LINE OF VERY IMPORTANT, VERY POWERFUL PEOPLE.
UM, DUH?
I'M NOT TALKING ABOUT NOBILITY, I'M TALKING ABOUT AN ANCIENT FORCE THAT YOU AND I AND A LOT OF OTHER GIRLS HAVE TAPPED INTO.
RODEN SAYS I'M GOING TO LEAD THE LOT OF US TO TAKE OUR RIGHTFUL PLACE AT THE HEAD OF THIS WRETCHED SOCIETY.
RIGHT AFTER I DESTROY THE WOMAN HOLDING US BACK... AND TAKE HER MANTLE AS QUEEN.
QUEEN?
YOU... YOU WANT TO KILL *ELIZABETH*?
NO, HOPE.

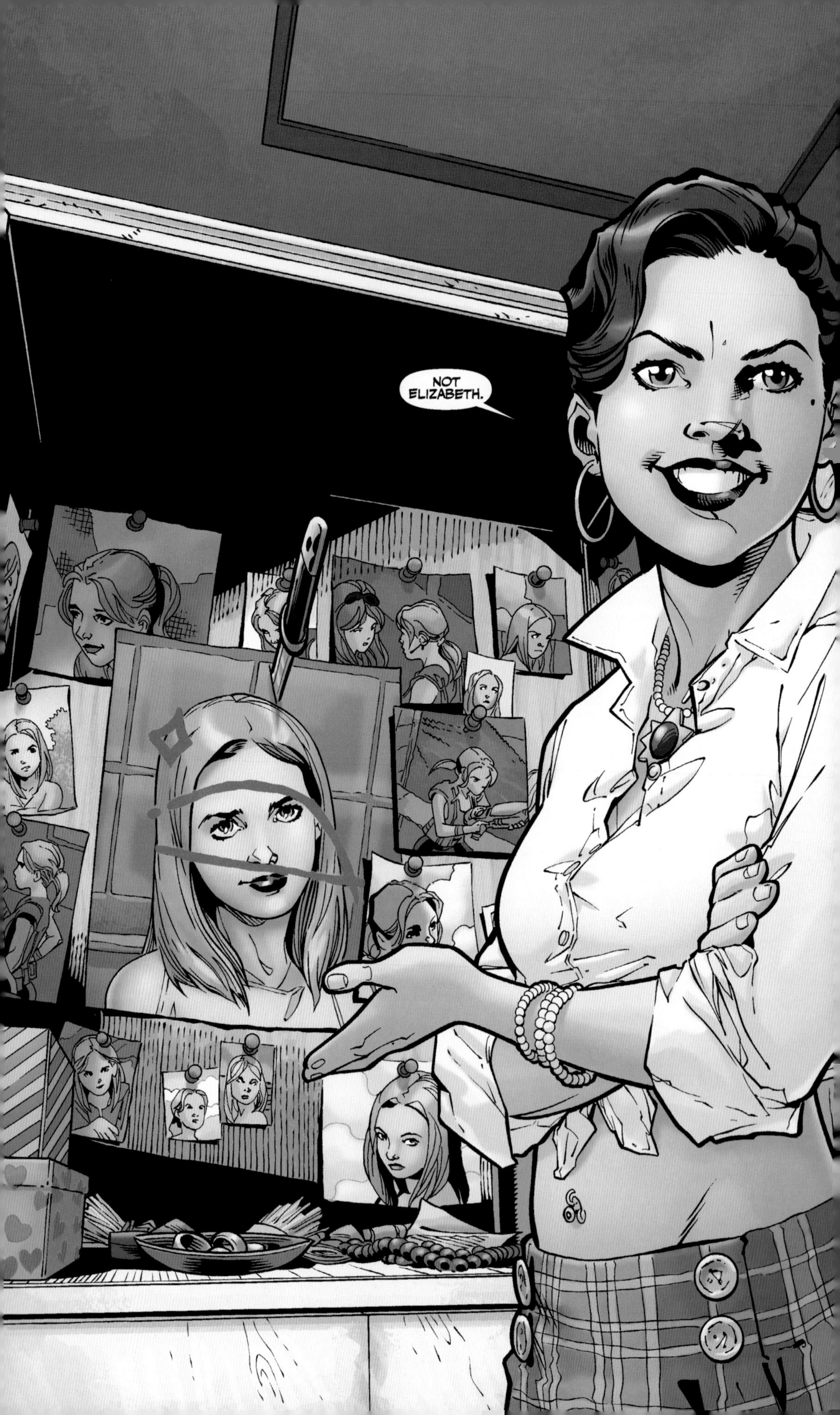
NOT ELIZABETH.

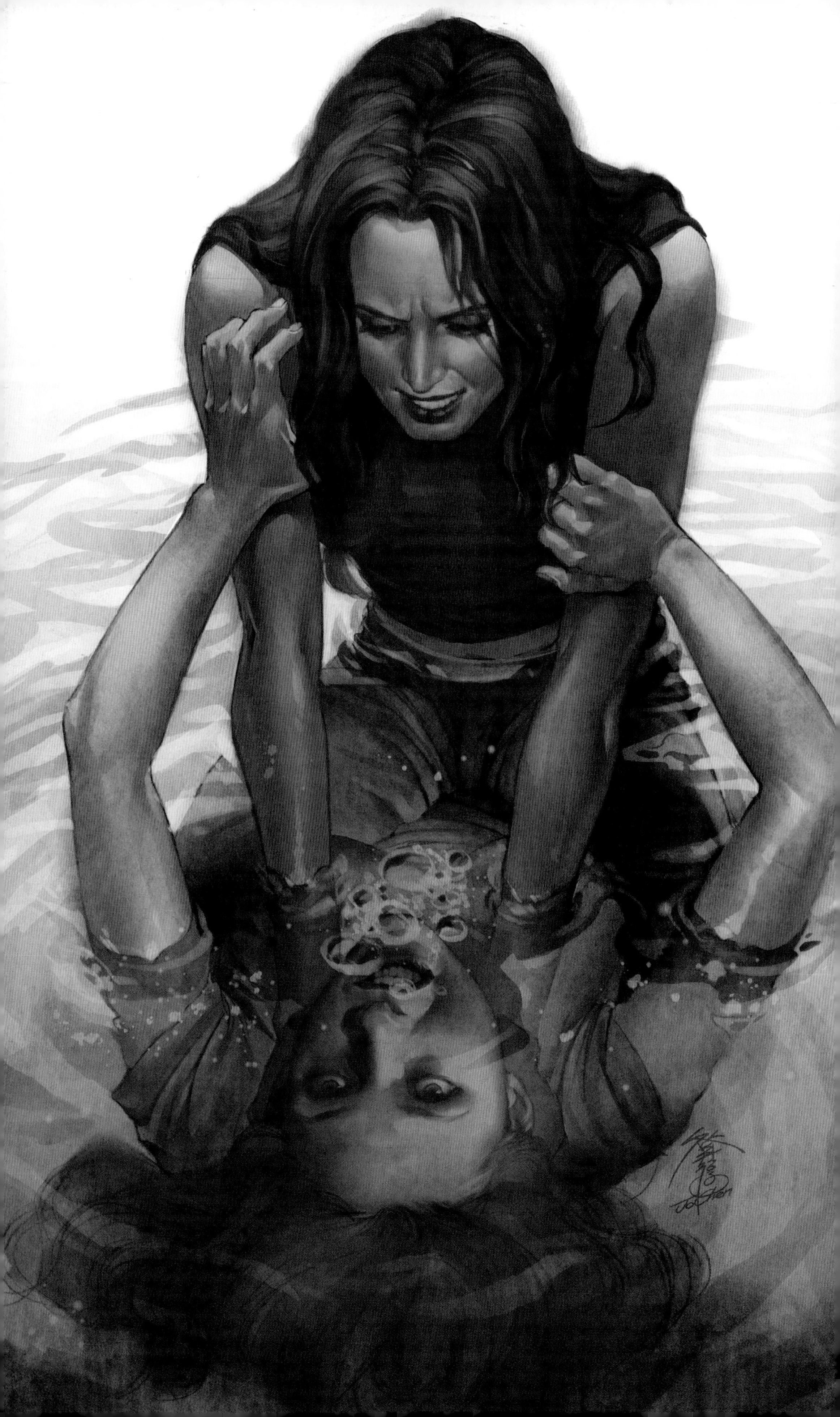

NO FUTURE FOR YOU

PART THREE

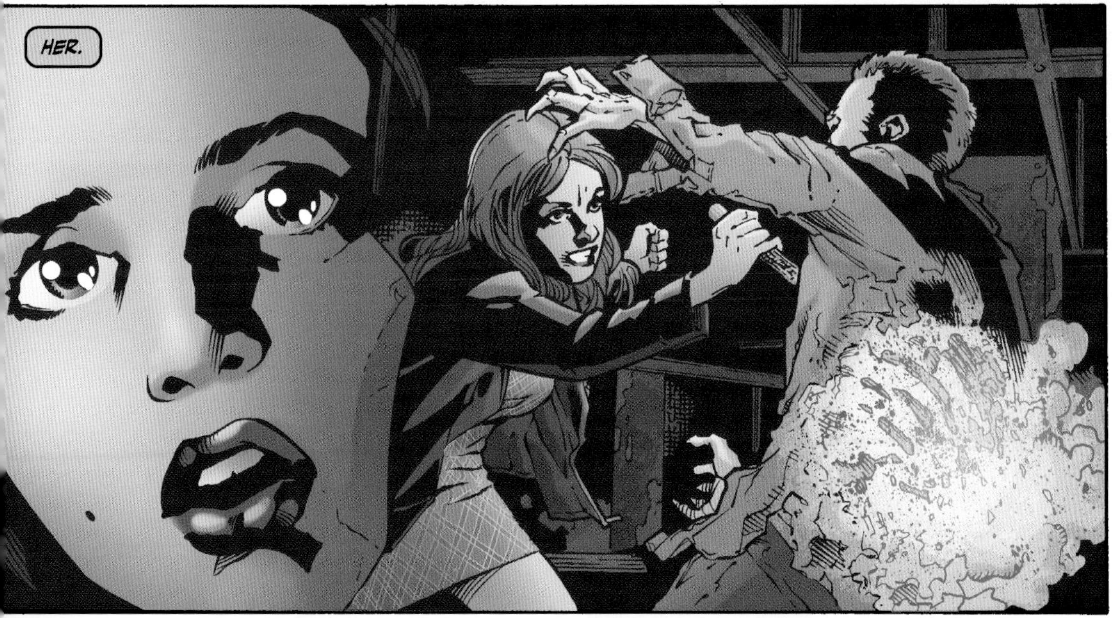
HER.

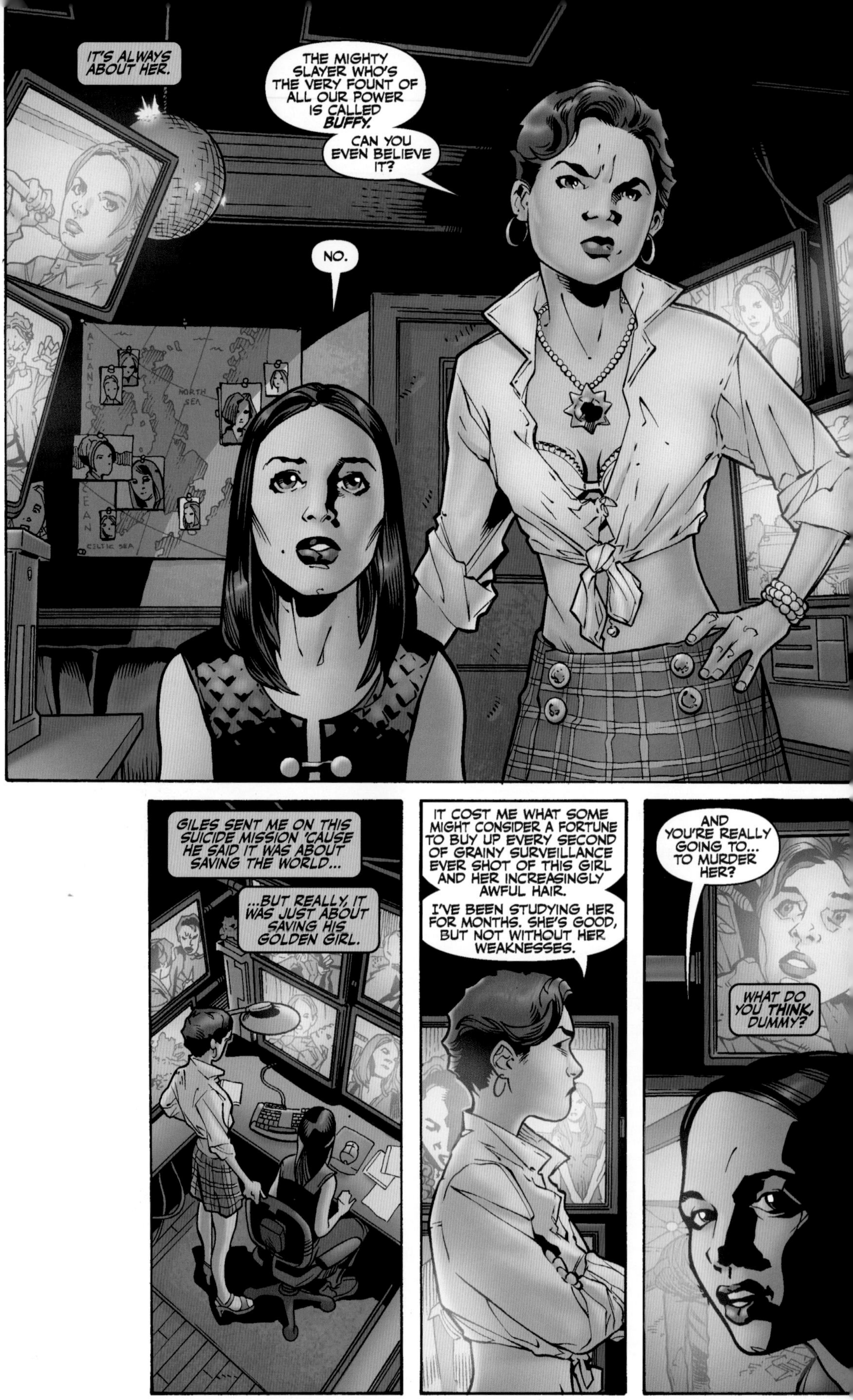

IT'S ALWAYS ABOUT HER.
THE MIGHTY SLAYER WHO'S THE VERY FOUNT OF ALL OUR POWER IS CALLED BUFFY.
CAN YOU EVEN BELIEVE IT?
NO.
ATLANTIC OCEAN
NORTH SEA
CELTIC SEA
GILES SENT ME ON THIS SUICIDE MISSION 'CAUSE HE SAID IT WAS ABOUT SAVING THE WORLD...
...BUT REALLY, IT WAS JUST ABOUT SAVING HIS GOLDEN GIRL.
IT COST ME WHAT SOME MIGHT CONSIDER A FORTUNE TO BUY UP EVERY SECOND OF GRAINY SURVEILLANCE EVER SHOT OF THIS GIRL AND HER INCREASINGLY AWFUL HAIR.
I'VE BEEN STUDYING HER FOR MONTHS. SHE'S GOOD, BUT NOT WITHOUT HER WEAKNESSES.
AND YOU'RE REALLY GOING TO... TO MURDER HER?
WHAT DO YOU THINK, DUMMY?

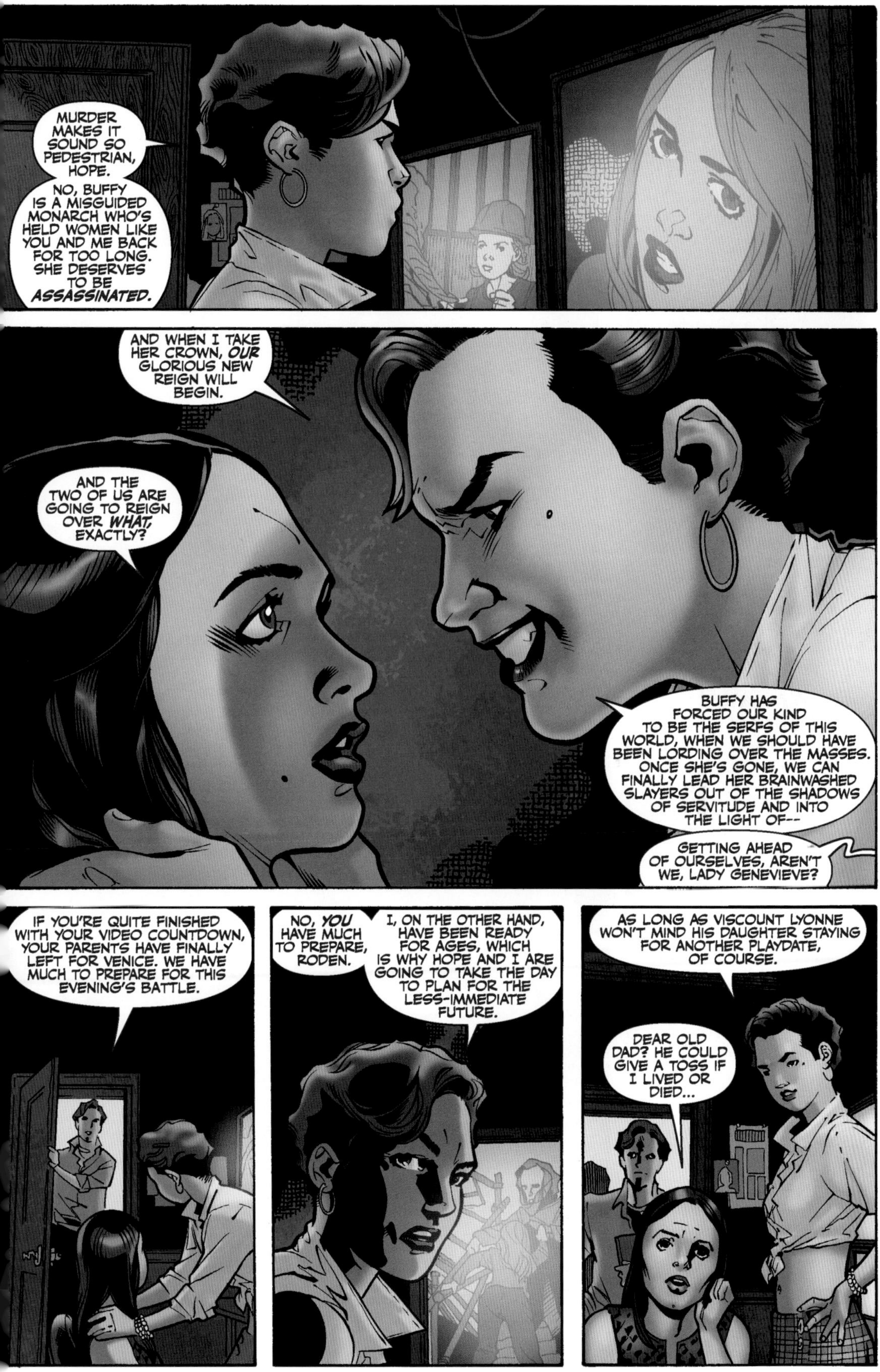
MURDER MAKES IT SOUND SO PEDESTRIAN, HOPE.
NO, BUFFY IS A MISGUIDED MONARCH WHO'S HELD WOMEN LIKE YOU AND ME BACK FOR TOO LONG. SHE DESERVES TO BE ASSASSINATED.
AND WHEN I TAKE HER CROWN, OUR GLORIOUS NEW REIGN WILL BEGIN.
AND THE TWO OF US ARE GOING TO REIGN OVER WHAT, EXACTLY?
BUFFY HAS FORCED OUR KIND TO BE THE SERFS OF THIS WORLD, WHEN WE SHOULD HAVE BEEN LORDING OVER THE MASSES. ONCE SHE'S GONE, WE CAN FINALLY LEAD HER BRAINWASHED SLAYERS OUT OF THE SHADOWS OF SERVITUDE AND INTO THE LIGHT OF--
GETTING AHEAD OF OURSELVES, AREN'T WE, LADY GENEVIEVE?
IF YOU'RE QUITE FINISHED WITH YOUR VIDEO COUNTDOWN, YOUR PARENTS HAVE FINALLY LEFT FOR VENICE. WE HAVE MUCH TO PREPARE FOR THIS EVENING'S BATTLE.
NO, YOU HAVE MUCH TO PREPARE, RODEN.
I, ON THE OTHER HAND, HAVE BEEN READY FOR AGES, WHICH IS WHY HOPE AND I ARE GOING TO TAKE THE DAY TO PLAN FOR THE LESS-IMMEDIATE FUTURE.
AS LONG AS VISCOUNT LYONNE WON'T MIND HIS DAUGHTER STAYING FOR ANOTHER PLAYDATE, OF COURSE.
DEAR OLD DAD? HE COULD GIVE A TOSS IF I LIVED OR DIED...

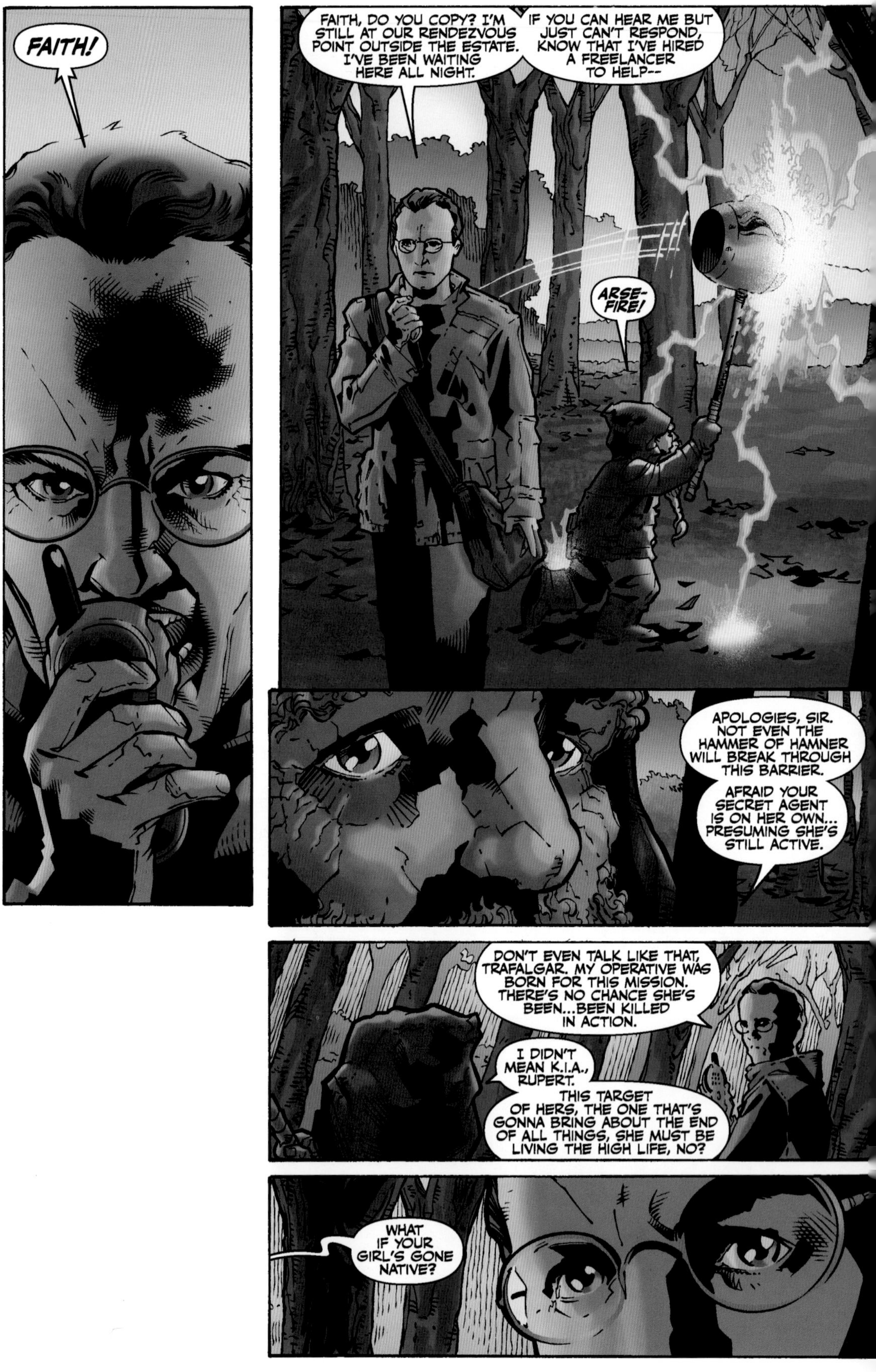
FAITH!
FAITH, DO YOU COPY? I'M STILL AT OUR RENDEZVOUS POINT OUTSIDE THE ESTATE. I'VE BEEN WAITING HERE ALL NIGHT.
IF YOU CAN HEAR ME BUT JUST CAN'T RESPOND, KNOW THAT I'VE HIRED A FREELANCER TO HELP--
ARSE-FIRE!
APOLOGIES, SIR. NOT EVEN THE HAMMER OF HAMNER WILL BREAK THROUGH THIS BARRIER.
AFRAID YOUR SECRET AGENT IS ON HER OWN... PRESUMING SHE'S STILL ACTIVE.
DON'T EVEN TALK LIKE THAT, TRAFALGAR. MY OPERATIVE WAS BORN FOR THIS MISSION. THERE'S NO CHANCE SHE'S BEEN...BEEN KILLED IN ACTION.
I DIDN'T MEAN K.I.A., RUPERT.
THIS TARGET OF HERS, THE ONE THAT'S GONNA BRING ABOUT THE END OF ALL THINGS, SHE MUST BE LIVING THE HIGH LIFE, NO?
WHAT IF YOUR GIRL'S GONE NATIVE?

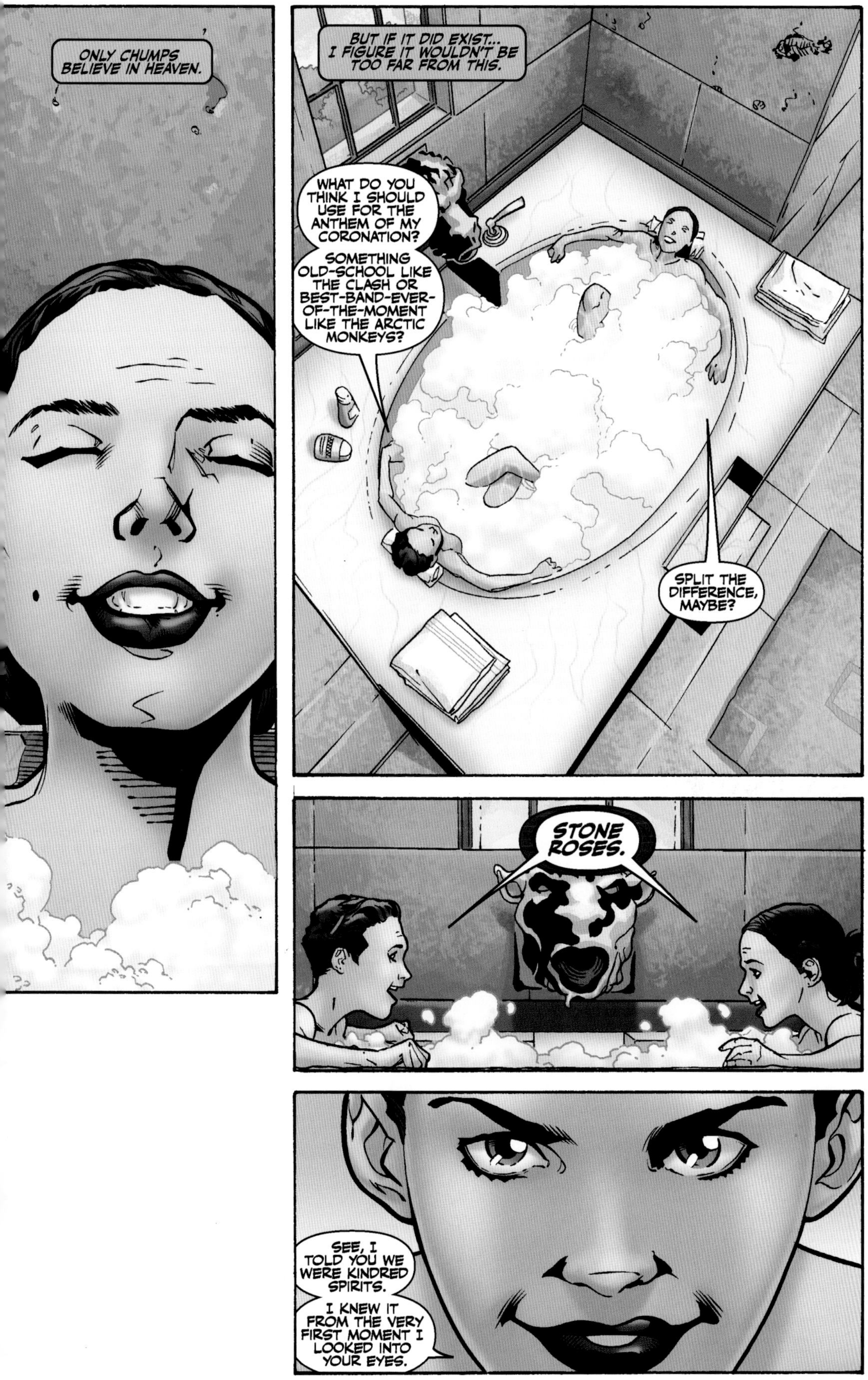
ONLY CHUMPS BELIEVE IN HEAVEN.
BUT IF IT DID EXIST... I FIGURE IT WOULDN'T BE TOO FAR FROM THIS.
WHAT DO YOU THINK I SHOULD USE FOR THE ANTHEM OF MY CORONATION?
SOMETHING OLD-SCHOOL LIKE THE CLASH OR BEST-BAND-EVER-OF-THE-MOMENT LIKE THE ARCTIC MONKEYS?
SPLIT THE DIFFERENCE, MAYBE?
STONE ROSES.
SEE, I TOLD YOU WE WERE KINDRED SPIRITS.
I KNEW IT FROM THE VERY FIRST MOMENT I LOOKED INTO YOUR EYES.

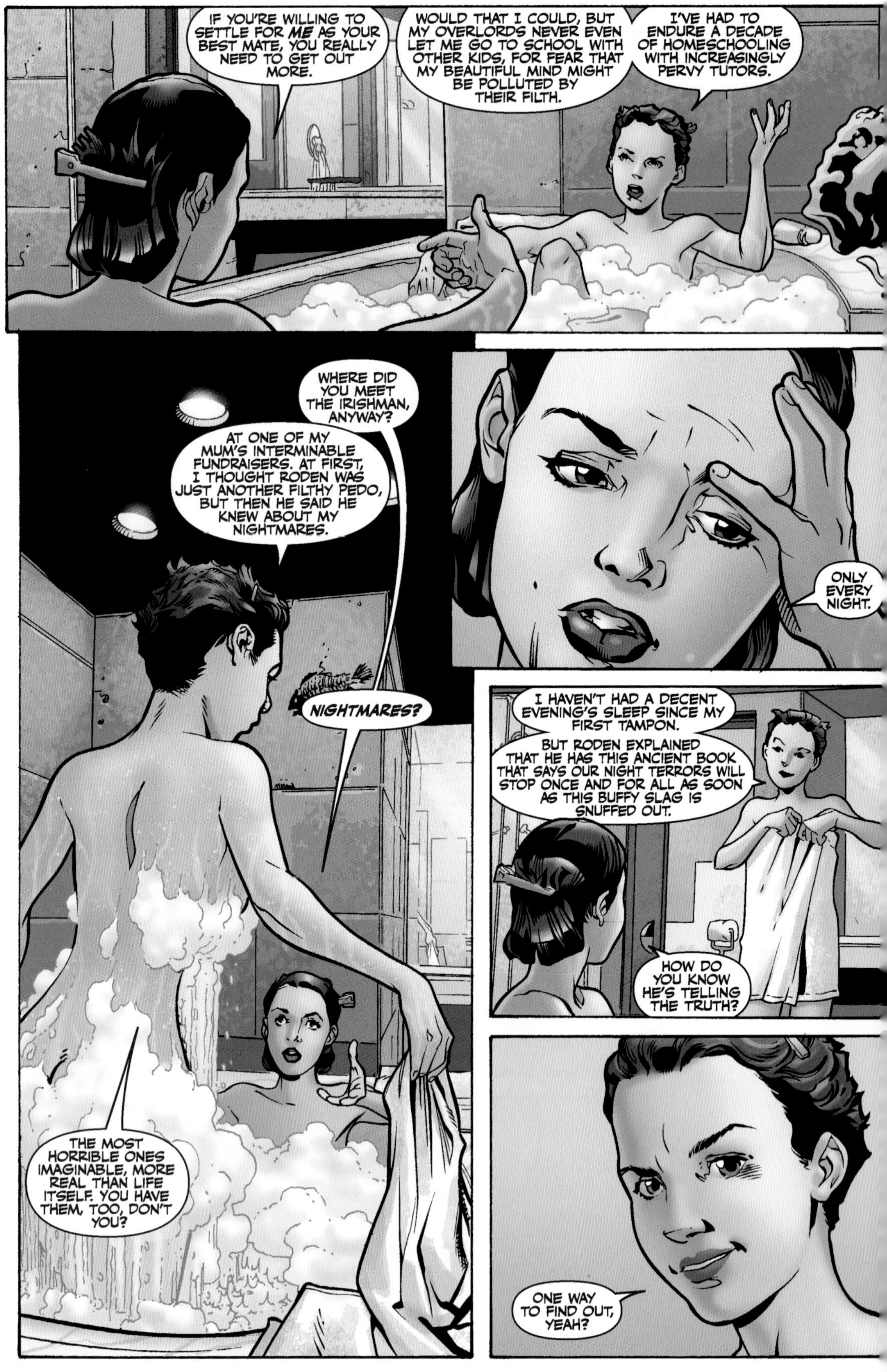
IF YOU'RE WILLING TO SETTLE FOR *ME* AS YOUR BEST MATE, YOU REALLY NEED TO GET OUT MORE.
WOULD THAT I COULD, BUT MY OVERLORDS NEVER EVEN LET ME GO TO SCHOOL WITH OTHER KIDS, FOR FEAR THAT MY BEAUTIFUL MIND MIGHT BE POLLUTED BY THEIR FILTH.
I'VE HAD TO ENDURE A DECADE OF HOMESCHOOLING WITH INCREASINGLY PERVY TUTORS.
WHERE DID YOU MEET THE IRISHMAN, ANYWAY?
AT ONE OF MY MUM'S INTERMINABLE FUNDRAISERS. AT FIRST, I THOUGHT RODEN WAS JUST ANOTHER FILTHY PEDO, BUT THEN HE SAID HE KNEW ABOUT MY NIGHTMARES.
NIGHTMARES?
THE MOST HORRIBLE ONES IMAGINABLE, MORE REAL THAN LIFE ITSELF. YOU HAVE THEM, TOO, DON'T YOU?
ONLY EVERY NIGHT.
I HAVEN'T HAD A DECENT EVENING'S SLEEP SINCE MY FIRST TAMPON.
BUT RODEN EXPLAINED THAT HE HAS THIS ANCIENT BOOK THAT SAYS OUR NIGHT TERRORS WILL STOP ONCE AND FOR ALL AS SOON AS THIS BUFFY SLAG IS SNUFFED OUT.
HOW DO YOU KNOW HE'S TELLING THE TRUTH?
ONE WAY TO FIND OUT, YEAH?

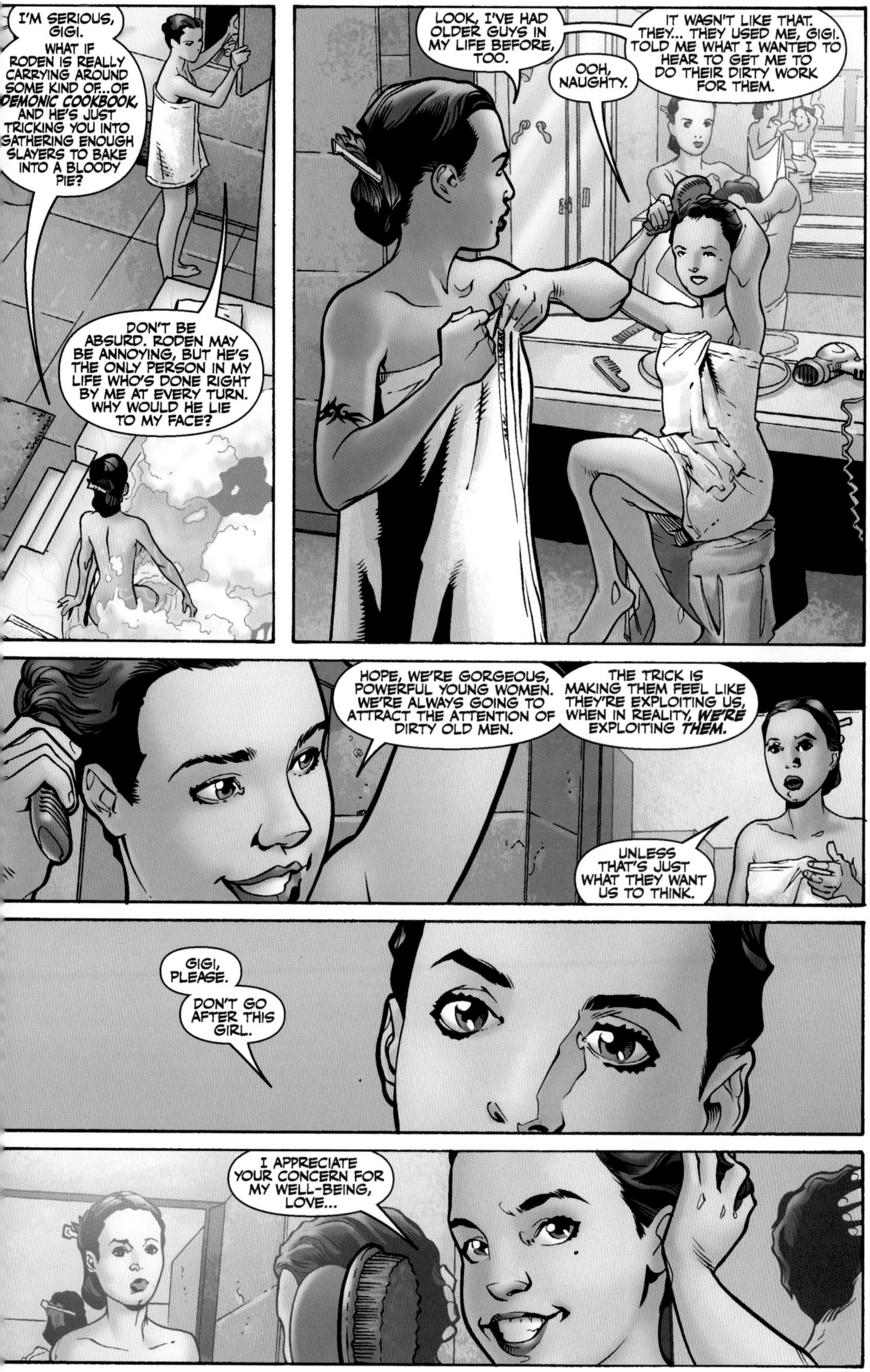
I'M SERIOUS, GIGI.
WHAT IF RODEN IS REALLY CARRYING AROUND SOME KIND OF...OF *DEMONIC COOKBOOK,* AND HE'S JUST TRICKING YOU INTO GATHERING ENOUGH SLAYERS TO BAKE INTO A BLOODY PIE?
DON'T BE ABSURD. RODEN MAY BE ANNOYING, BUT HE'S THE ONLY PERSON IN MY LIFE WHO'S DONE RIGHT BY ME AT EVERY TURN. WHY WOULD HE LIE TO MY FACE?
LOOK, I'VE HAD OLDER GUYS IN MY LIFE BEFORE, TOO.
OOH, NAUGHTY.
IT WASN'T LIKE THAT. THEY... THEY USED ME, GIGI. TOLD ME WHAT I WANTED TO HEAR TO GET ME TO DO THEIR DIRTY WORK FOR THEM.
HOPE, WE'RE GORGEOUS, POWERFUL YOUNG WOMEN. WE'RE ALWAYS GOING TO ATTRACT THE ATTENTION OF DIRTY OLD MEN.
THE TRICK IS MAKING THEM FEEL LIKE THEY'RE EXPLOITING US, WHEN IN REALITY, *WE'RE* EXPLOITING *THEM.*
UNLESS THAT'S JUST WHAT THEY WANT US TO THINK.
GIGI, PLEASE.
DON'T GO AFTER THIS GIRL.
I APPRECIATE YOUR CONCERN FOR MY WELL-BEING, LOVE...

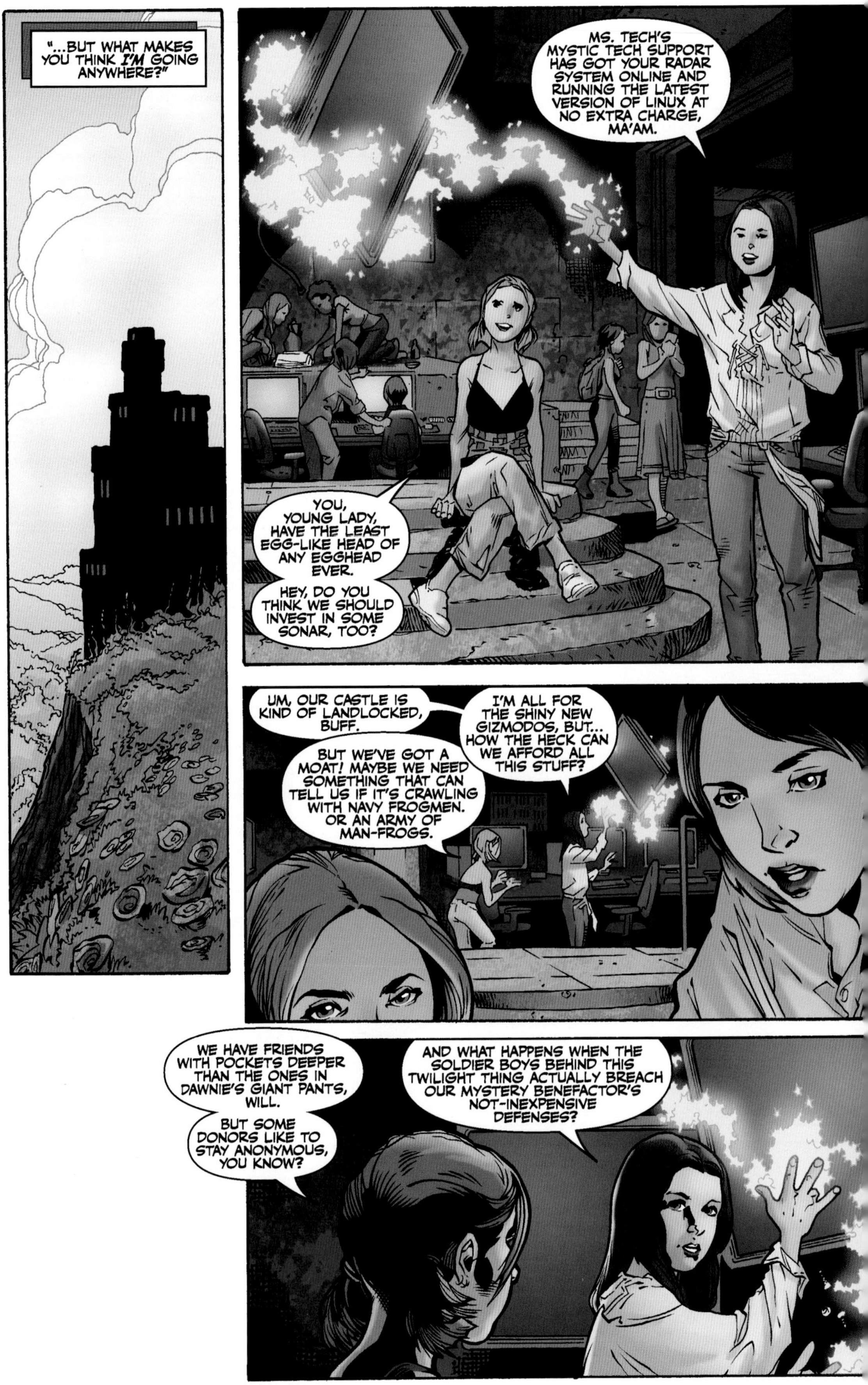
"...BUT WHAT MAKES YOU THINK *I'M* GOING ANYWHERE?"
MS. TECH'S MYSTIC TECH SUPPORT HAS GOT YOUR RADAR SYSTEM ONLINE AND RUNNING THE LATEST VERSION OF LINUX AT NO EXTRA CHARGE, MA'AM.
YOU, YOUNG LADY, HAVE THE LEAST EGG-LIKE HEAD OF ANY EGGHEAD EVER.
HEY, DO YOU THINK WE SHOULD INVEST IN SOME SONAR, TOO?
UM, OUR CASTLE IS KIND OF LANDLOCKED, BUFF.
BUT WE'VE GOT A MOAT! MAYBE WE NEED SOMETHING THAT CAN TELL US IF IT'S CRAWLING WITH NAVY FROGMEN. OR AN ARMY OF MAN-FROGS.
I'M ALL FOR THE SHINY NEW GIZMODOS, BUT... HOW THE HECK CAN WE AFFORD ALL THIS STUFF?
WE HAVE FRIENDS WITH POCKETS DEEPER THAN THE ONES IN DAWNIE'S GIANT PANTS, WILL.
BUT SOME DONORS LIKE TO STAY ANONYMOUS, YOU KNOW?
AND WHAT HAPPENS WHEN THE SOLDIER BOYS BEHIND THIS TWILIGHT THING ACTUALLY BREACH OUR MYSTERY BENEFACTOR'S NOT-INEXPENSIVE DEFENSES?

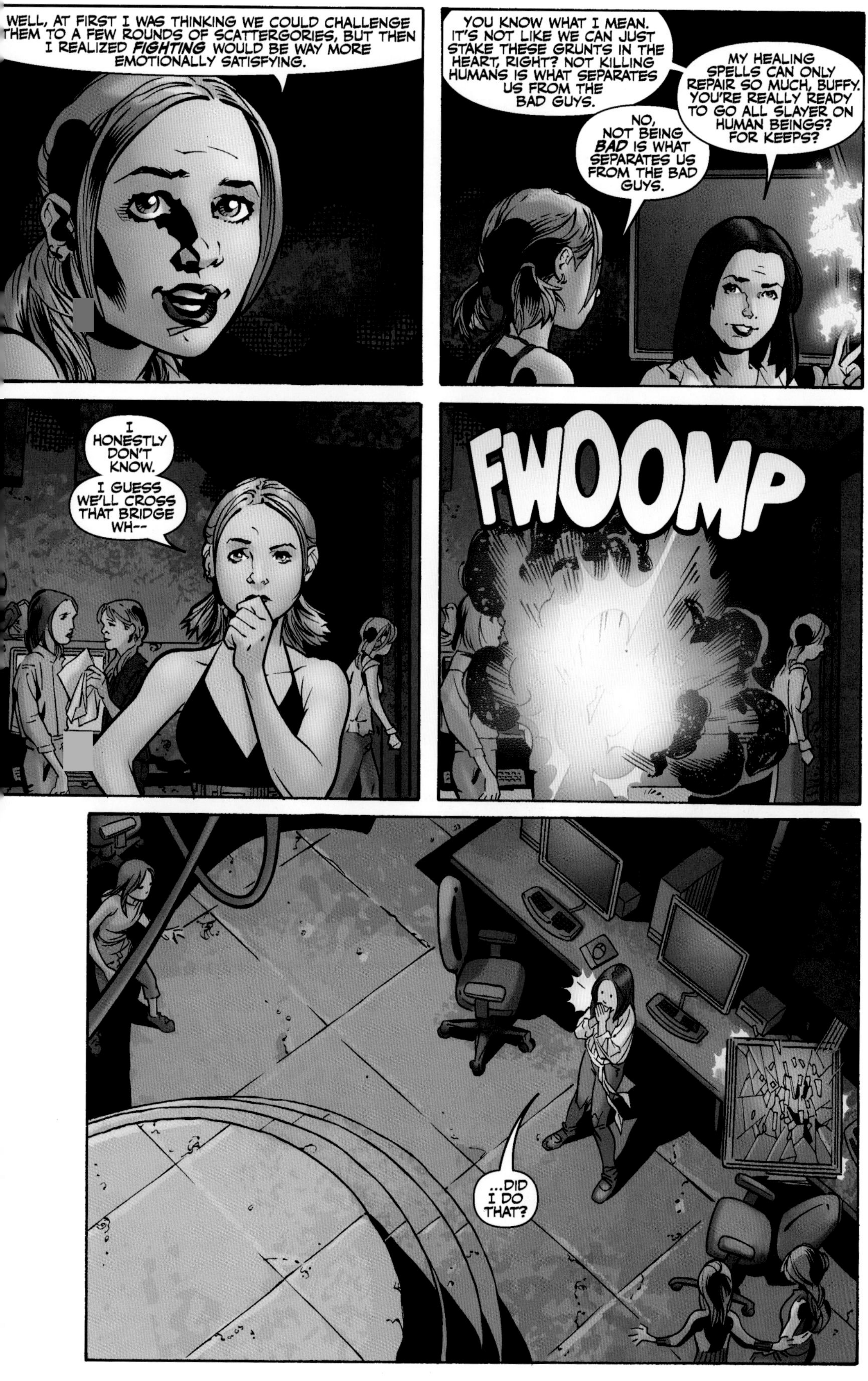

WELL, AT FIRST I WAS THINKING WE COULD CHALLENGE THEM TO A FEW ROUNDS OF SCATTERGORIES, BUT THEN I REALIZED *FIGHTING* WOULD BE WAY MORE EMOTIONALLY SATISFYING.
YOU KNOW WHAT I MEAN. IT'S NOT LIKE WE CAN JUST STAKE THESE GRUNTS IN THE HEART, RIGHT? NOT KILLING HUMANS IS WHAT SEPARATES US FROM THE BAD GUYS.
MY HEALING SPELLS CAN ONLY REPAIR SO MUCH, BUFFY. YOU'RE REALLY READY TO GO ALL SLAYER ON HUMAN BEINGS? FOR KEEPS?
NO, NOT BEING *BAD* IS WHAT SEPARATES US FROM THE BAD GUYS.
I HONESTLY DON'T KNOW.
I GUESS WE'LL CROSS THAT BRIDGE WH--
FWOOMP
...DID I DO THAT?

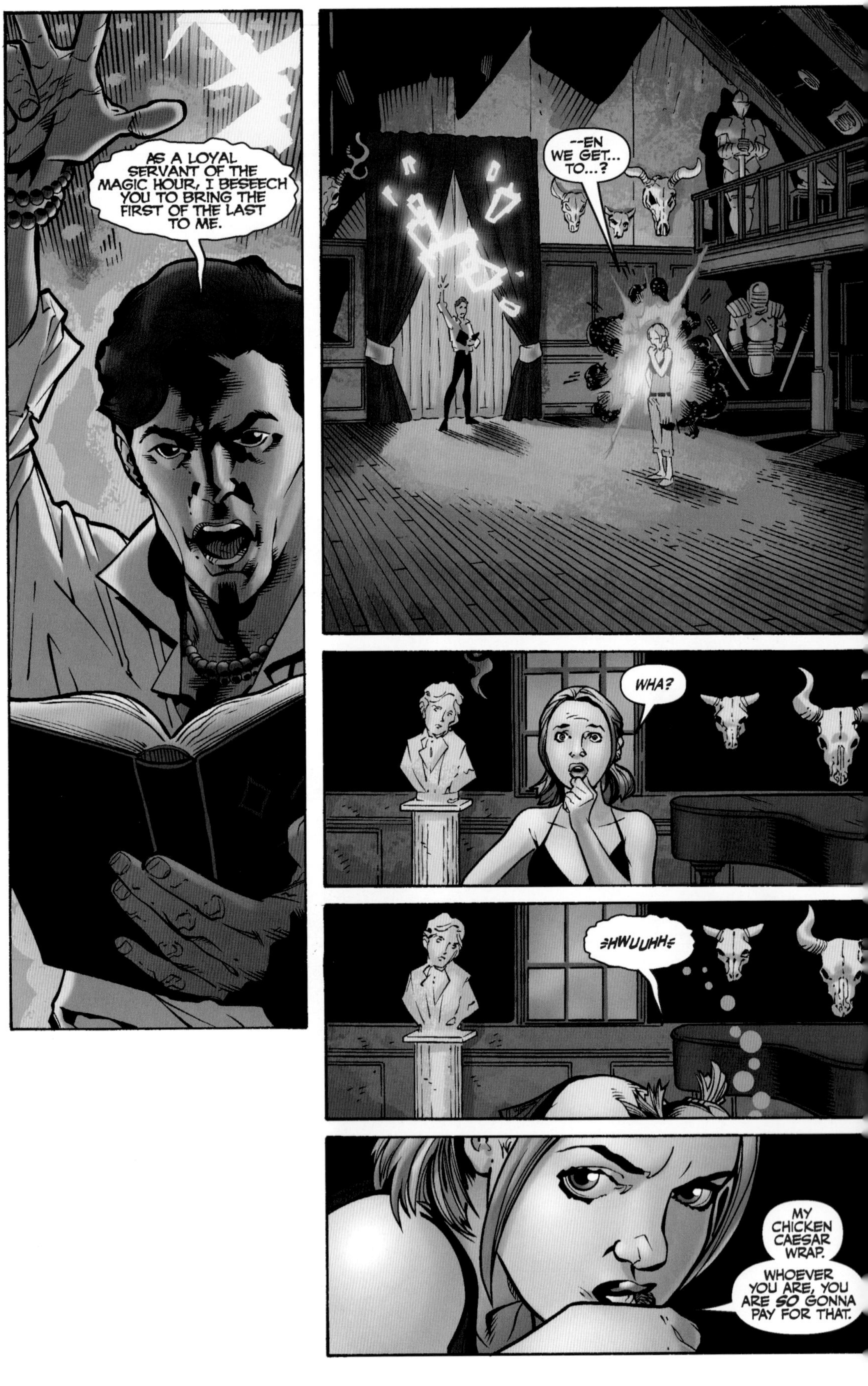
AS A LOYAL SERVANT OF THE MAGIC HOUR, I BESEECH YOU TO BRING THE FIRST OF THE LAST TO ME.
--EN WE GET... TO...?
WHA?
HWUUHH
MY CHICKEN CAESAR WRAP.
WHOEVER YOU ARE, YOU ARE SO GONNA PAY FOR THAT.

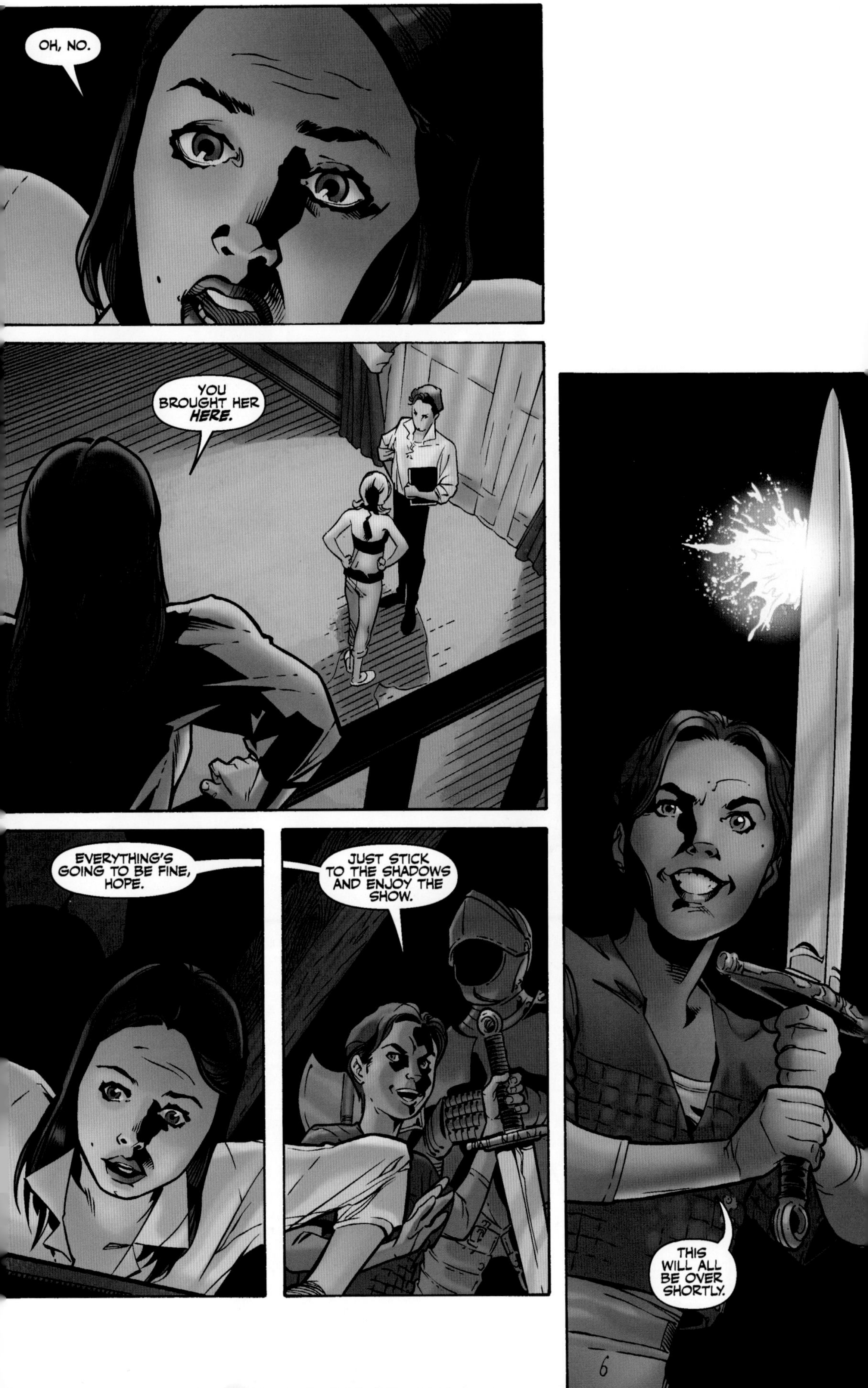
OH, NO.
YOU BROUGHT HER *HERE.*
EVERYTHING'S GOING TO BE FINE, HOPE.
JUST STICK TO THE SHADOWS AND ENJOY THE SHOW.
THIS WILL ALL BE OVER SHORTLY.

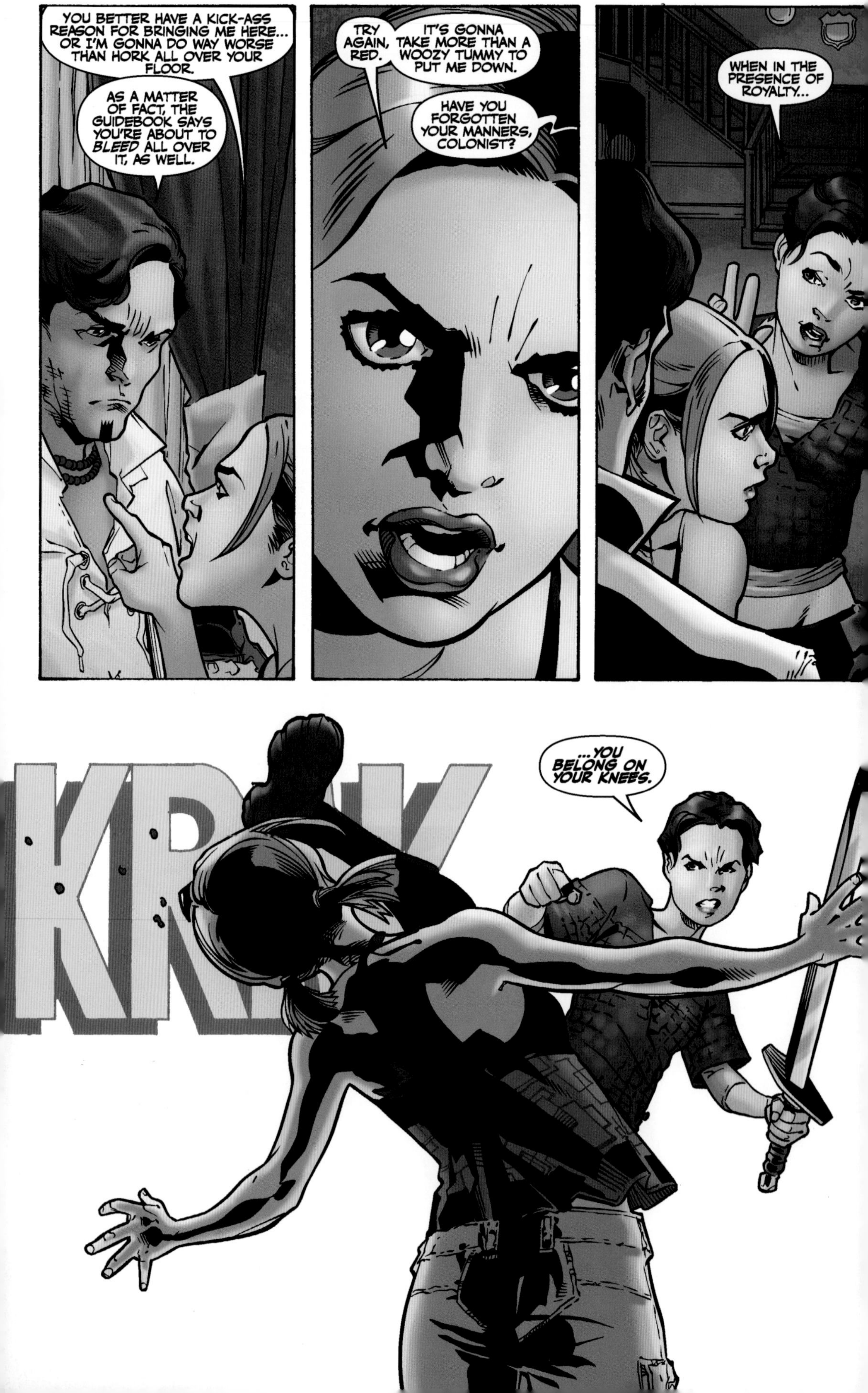
YOU BETTER HAVE A KICK-ASS REASON FOR BRINGING ME HERE... OR I'M GONNA DO WAY WORSE THAN HORK ALL OVER YOUR FLOOR.
AS A MATTER OF FACT, THE GUIDEBOOK SAYS YOU'RE ABOUT TO *BLEED* ALL OVER IT, AS WELL.
TRY AGAIN, RED.
IT'S GONNA TAKE MORE THAN A WOOZY TUMMY TO PUT ME DOWN.
HAVE YOU FORGOTTEN YOUR MANNERS, COLONIST?
WHEN IN THE PRESENCE OF ROYALTY...
...YOU BELONG ON YOUR KNEES.

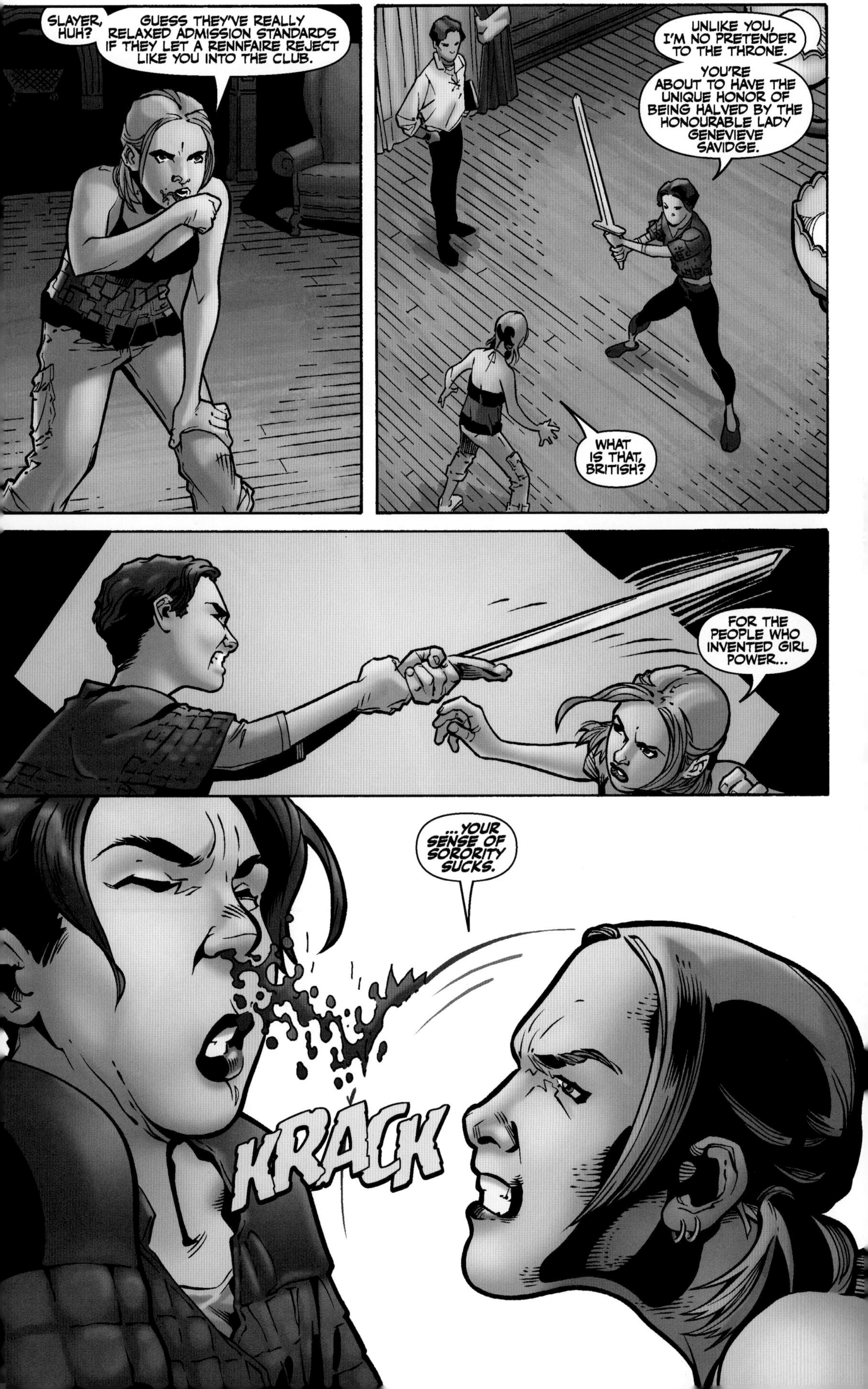
SLAYER, HUH?
GUESS THEY'VE REALLY RELAXED ADMISSION STANDARDS IF THEY LET A RENNFAIRE REJECT LIKE YOU INTO THE CLUB.
UNLIKE YOU, I'M NO PRETENDER TO THE THRONE.
YOU'RE ABOUT TO HAVE THE UNIQUE HONOR OF BEING HALVED BY THE HONOURABLE LADY GENEVIEVE SAVIDGE.
WHAT IS THAT, BRITISH?
FOR THE PEOPLE WHO INVENTED GIRL POWER...
...YOUR SENSE OF SORORITY SUCKS.
KRACK

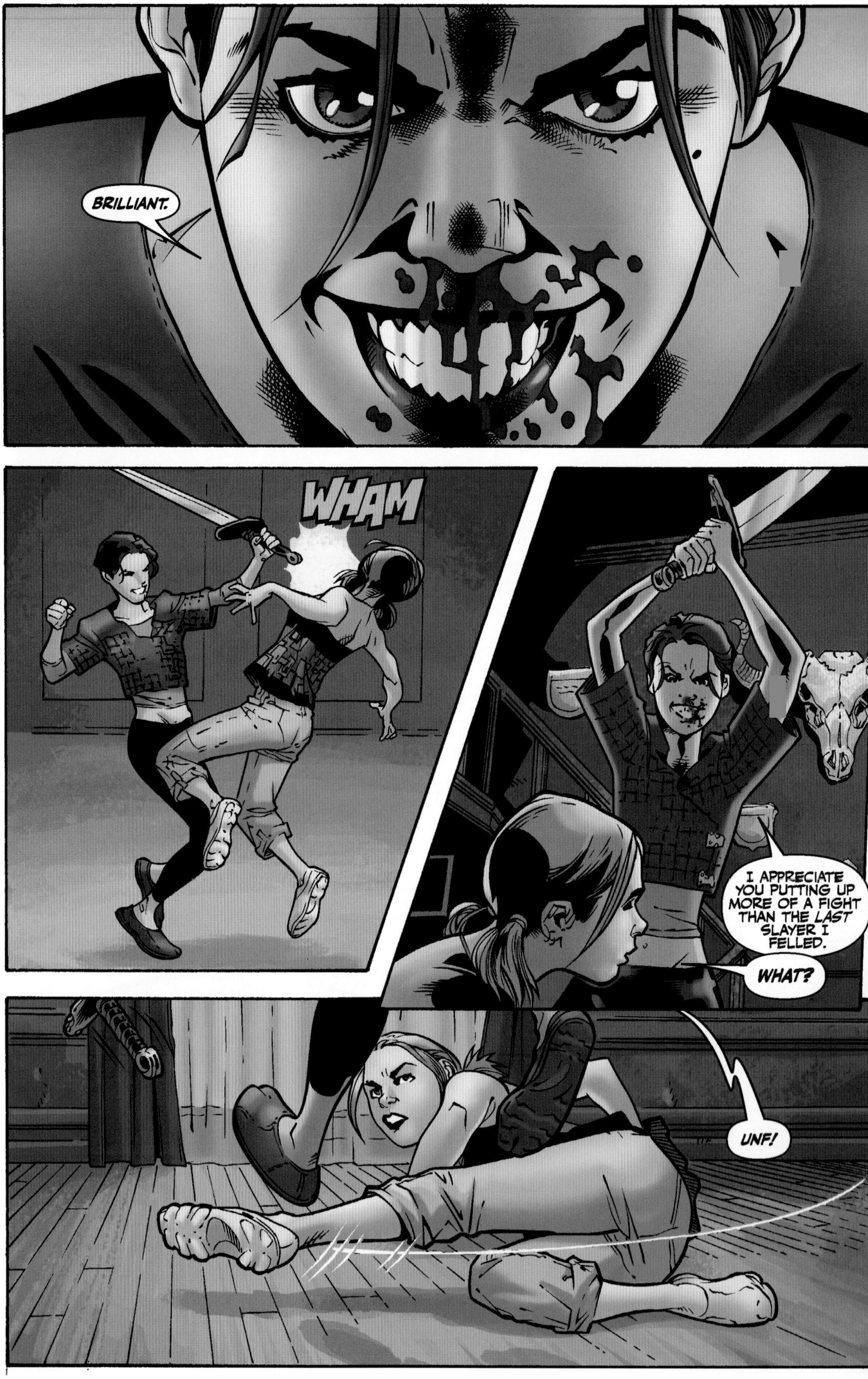
BRILLIANT.
WHAM
I APPRECIATE YOU PUTTING UP MORE OF A FIGHT THAN THE *LAST* SLAYER I FELLED.
WHAT?
UNF!

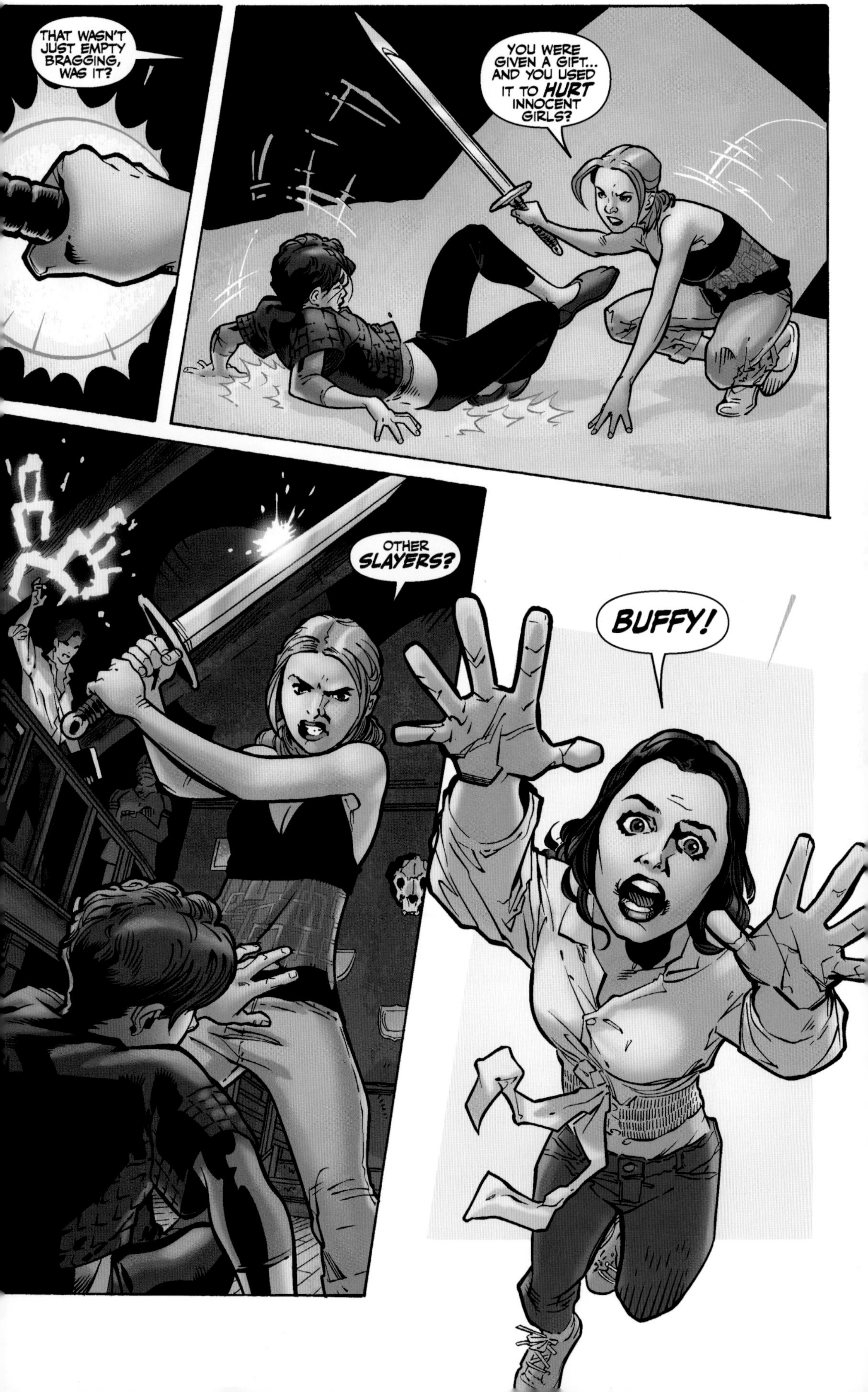
THAT WASN'T JUST EMPTY BRAGGING, WAS IT?
YOU WERE GIVEN A GIFT... AND YOU USED IT TO HURT INNOCENT GIRLS?
OTHER SLAYERS?
BUFFY!

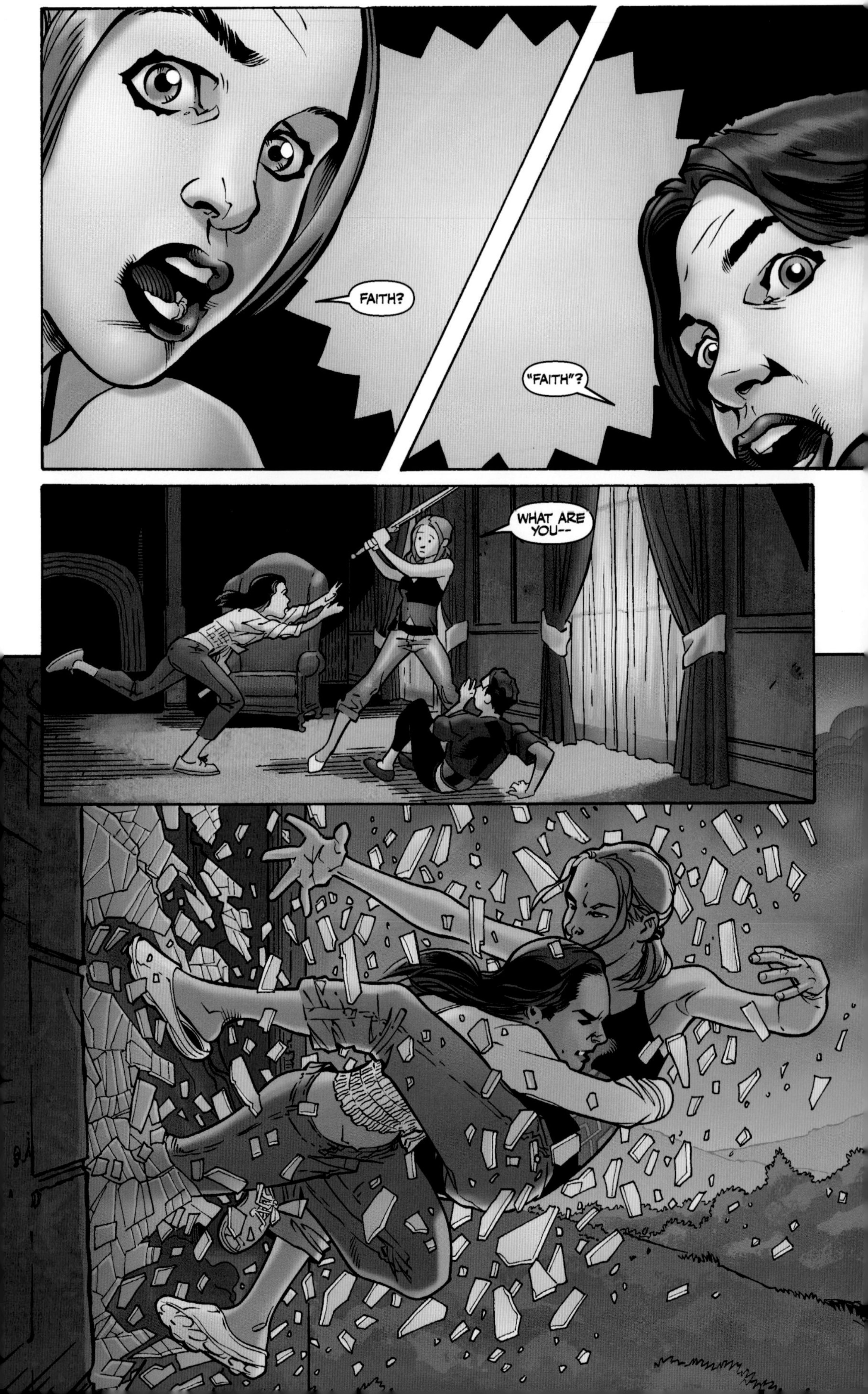
FAITH?
"FAITH"?
WHAT ARE YOU--

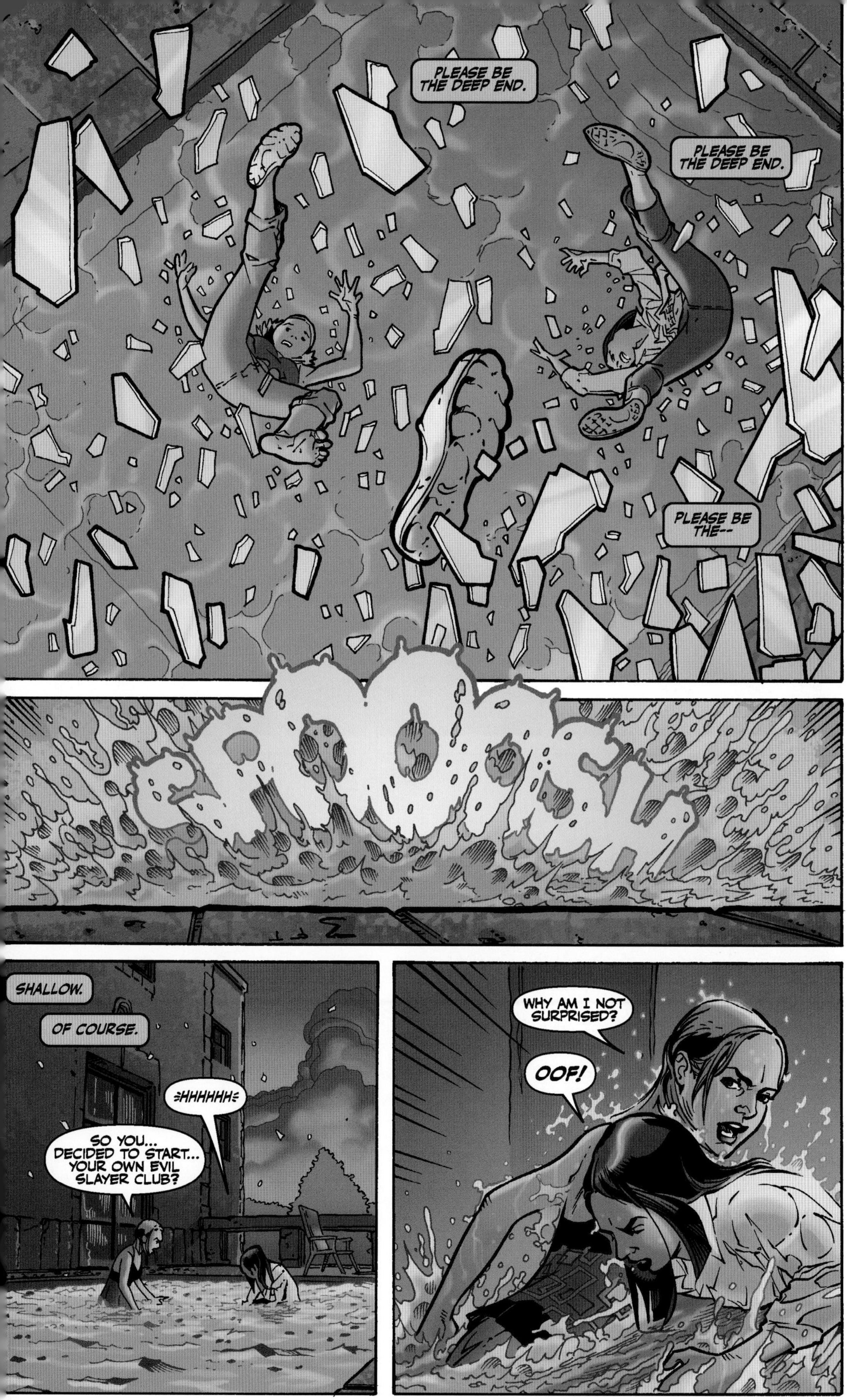
PLEASE BE THE DEEP END.
PLEASE BE THE DEEP END.
PLEASE BE THE--
SHALLOW.
OF COURSE.
=HHHHHH=
SO YOU... DECIDED TO START... YOUR OWN EVIL SLAYER CLUB?
WHY AM I NOT SURPRISED?
OOF!

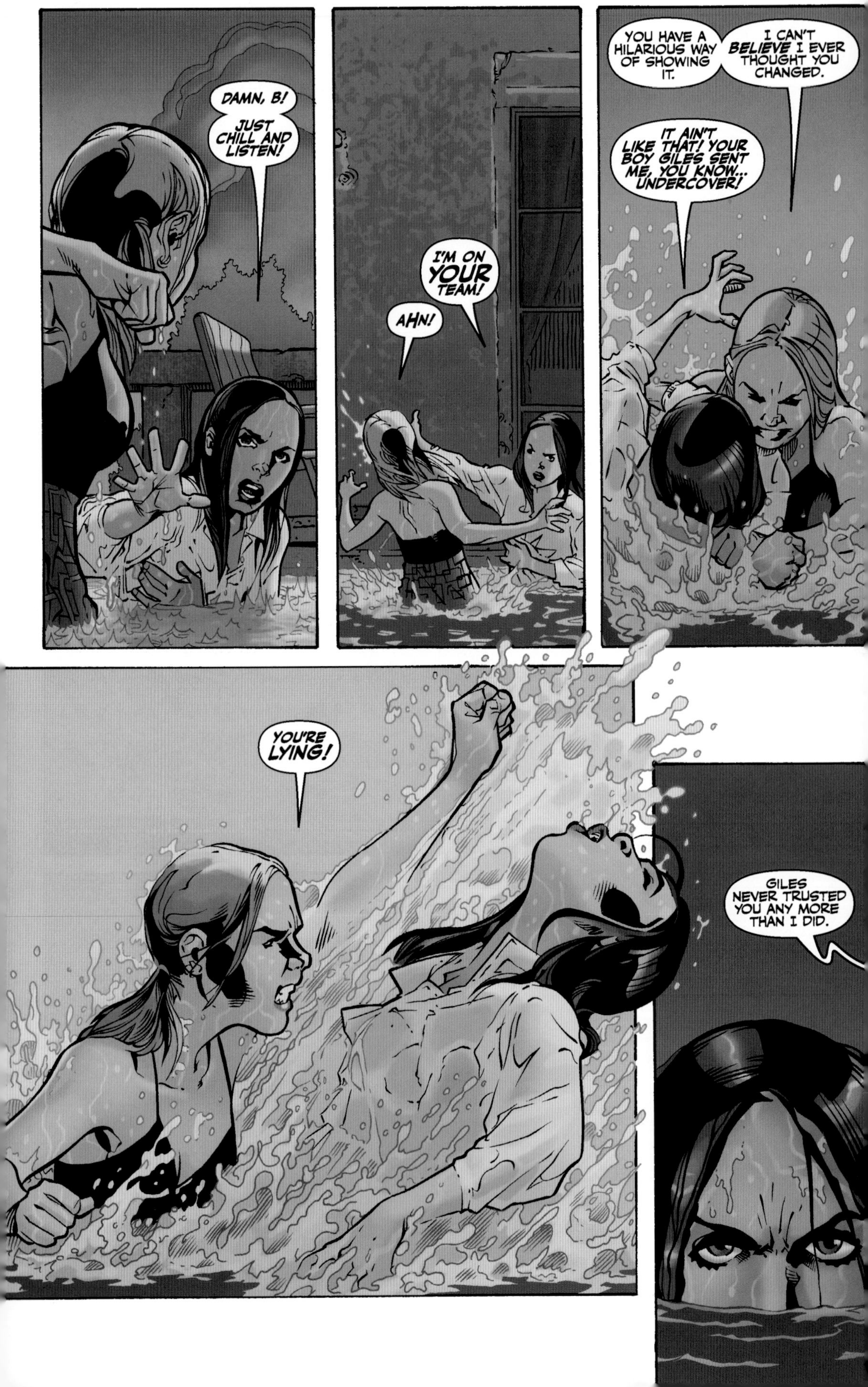
DAMN, B!
JUST CHILL AND LISTEN!
I'M ON YOUR TEAM!
AHN!
YOU HAVE A HILARIOUS WAY OF SHOWING IT.
I CAN'T BELIEVE I EVER THOUGHT YOU CHANGED.
IT AIN'T LIKE THAT! YOUR BOY GILES SENT ME, YOU KNOW... UNDERCOVER!
YOU'RE LYING!
GILES NEVER TRUSTED YOU ANY MORE THAN I DID.

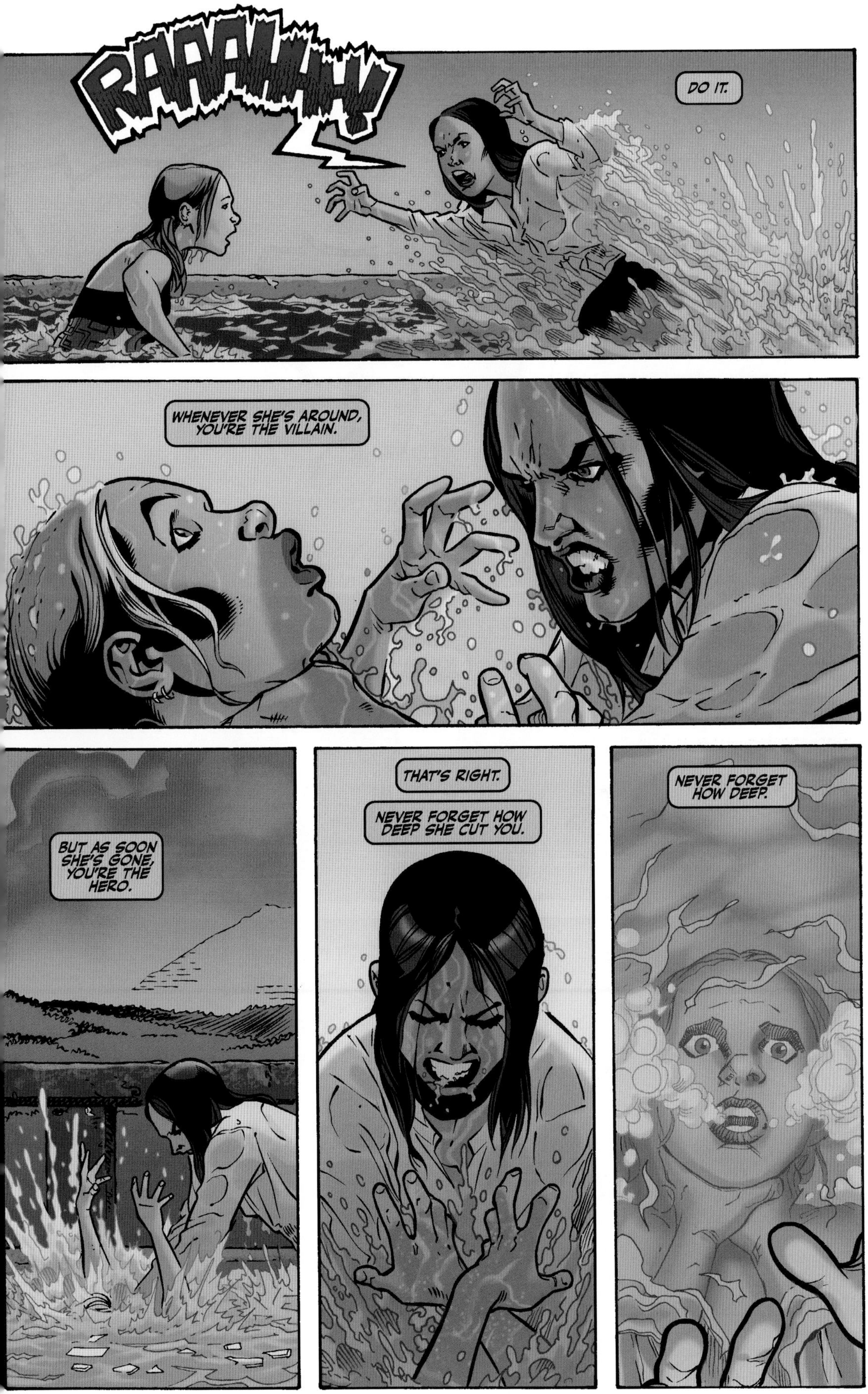
RAAAHHH!
DO IT.
WHENEVER SHE'S AROUND, YOU'RE THE VILLAIN.
BUT AS SOON SHE'S GONE, YOU'RE THE HERO.
THAT'S RIGHT.
NEVER FORGET HOW DEEP SHE CUT YOU.
NEVER FORGET HOW DEEP.

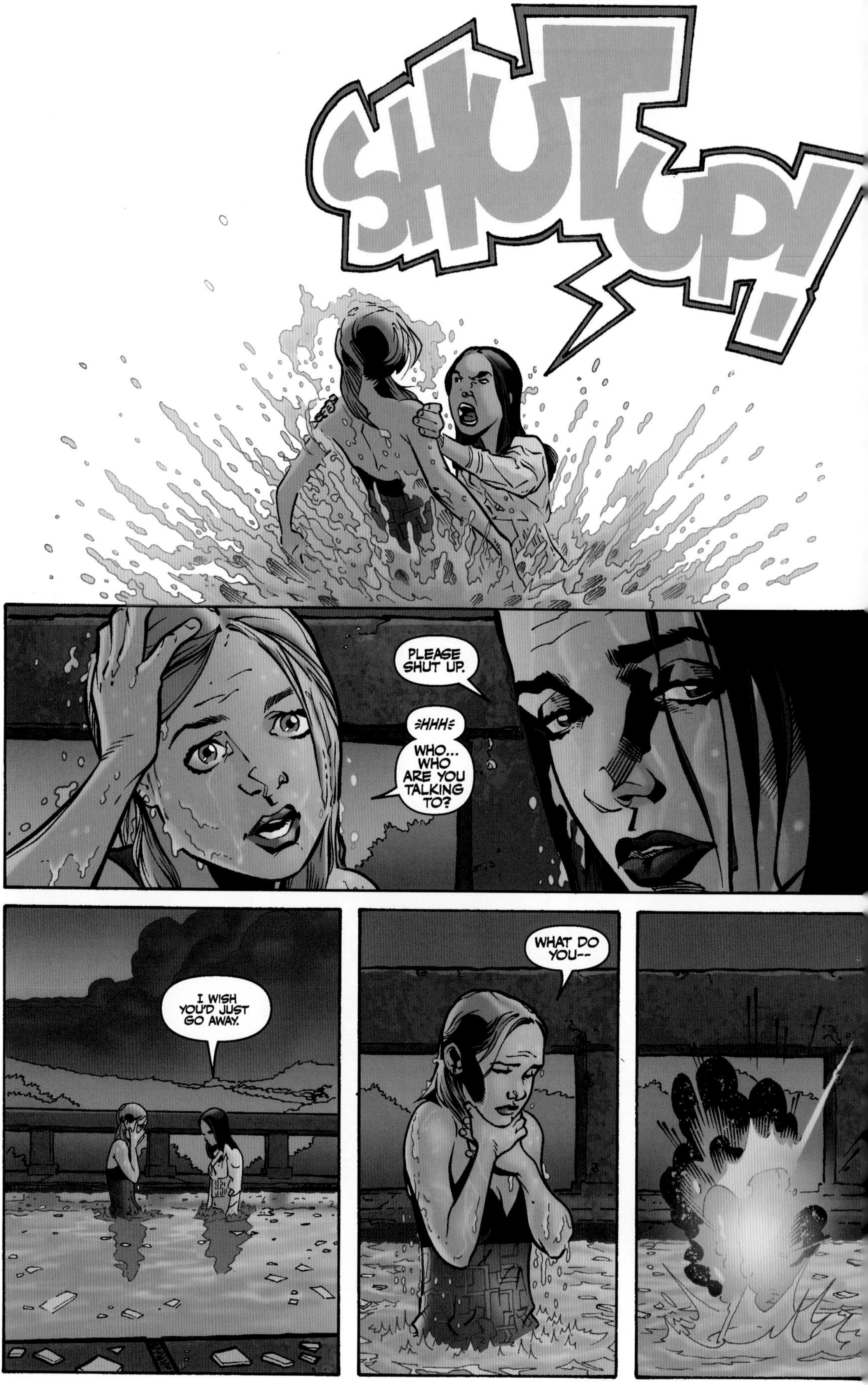
SHUT UP!
PLEASE SHUT UP.
HHH
WHO... WHO ARE YOU TALKING TO?
I WISH YOU'D JUST GO AWAY.
WHAT DO YOU--

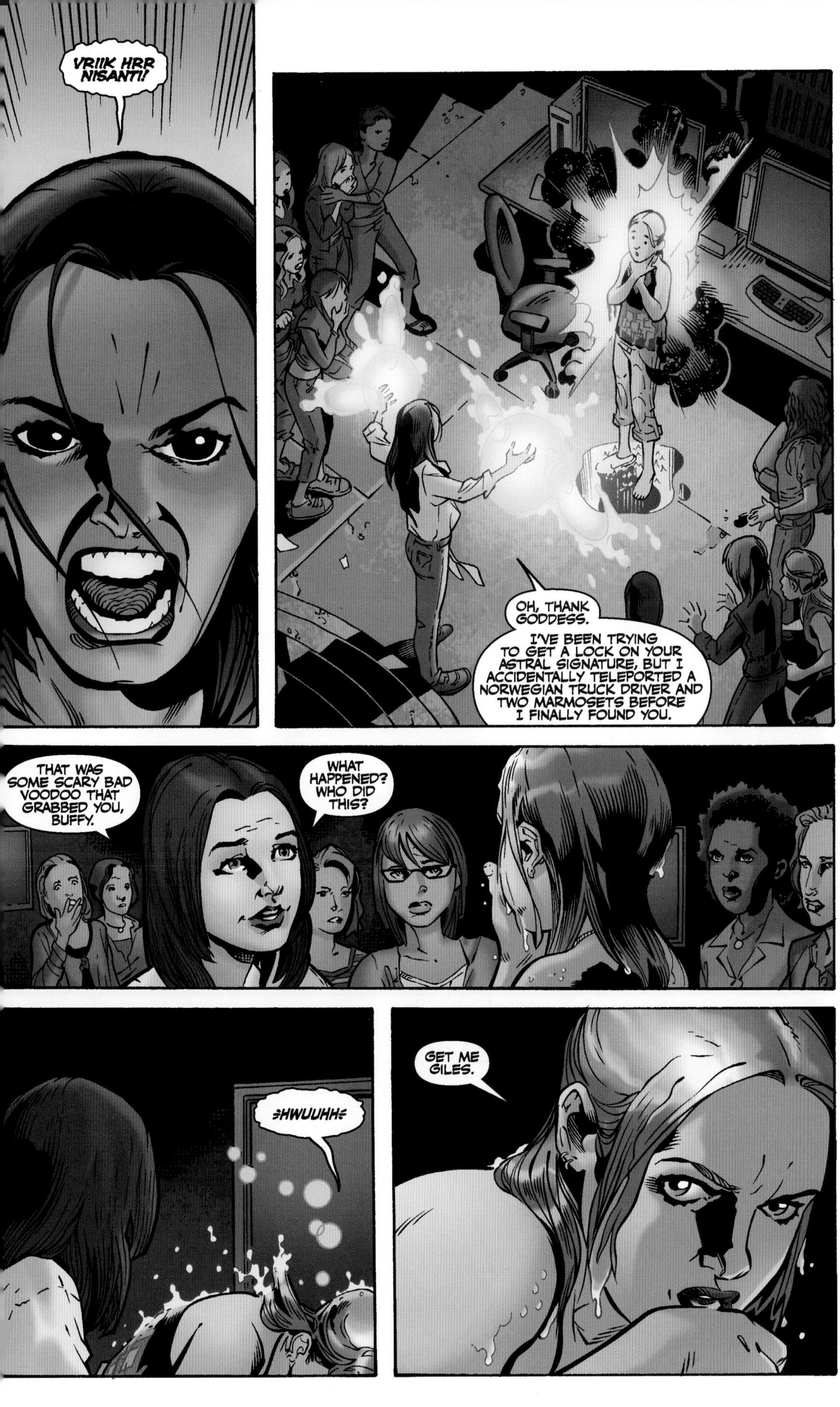
VRIIK HRR NISANTI!
OH, THANK GODDESS.
I'VE BEEN TRYING TO GET A LOCK ON YOUR ASTRAL SIGNATURE, BUT I ACCIDENTALLY TELEPORTED A NORWEGIAN TRUCK DRIVER AND TWO MARMOSETS BEFORE I FINALLY FOUND YOU.
THAT WAS SOME SCARY BAD VOODOO THAT GRABBED YOU, BUFFY.
WHAT HAPPENED? WHO DID THIS?
≠HWUUHH≠
GET ME GILES.

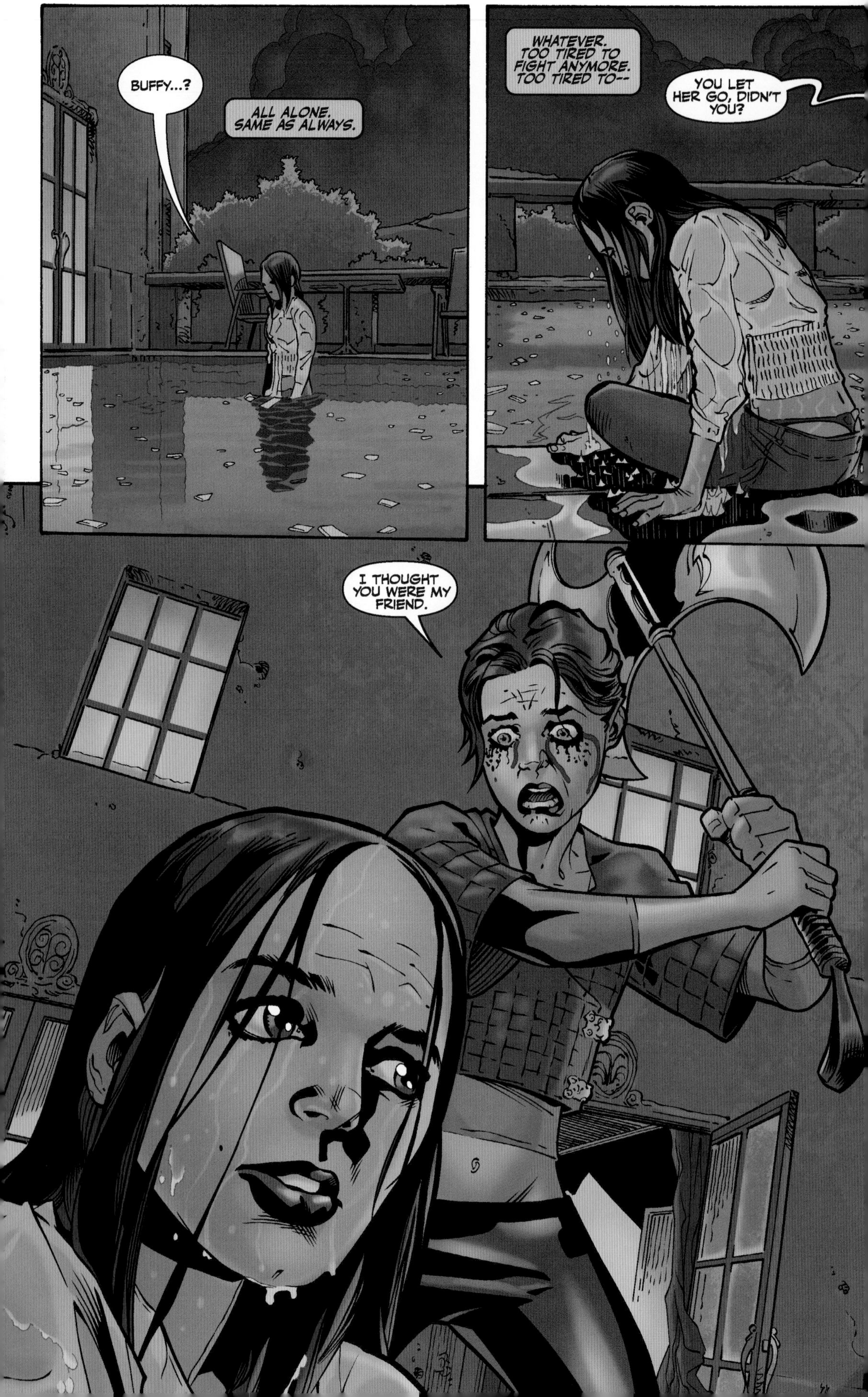
BUFFY...?
ALL ALONE. SAME AS ALWAYS.
WHATEVER. TOO TIRED TO FIGHT ANYMORE. TOO TIRED TO--
YOU LET HER GO, DIDN'T YOU?
I THOUGHT YOU WERE MY FRIEND.

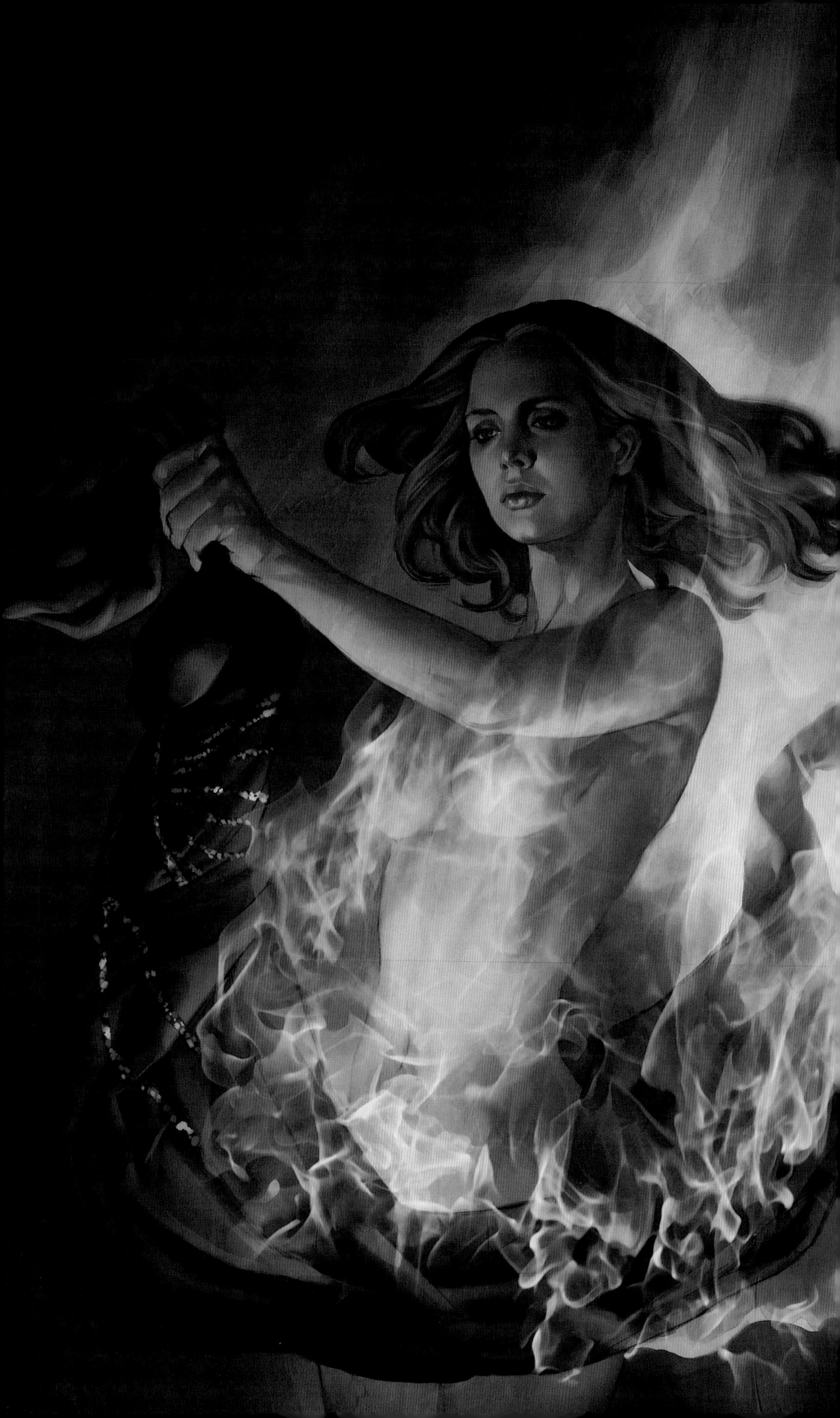

NO FUTURE FOR YOU
PART FOUR

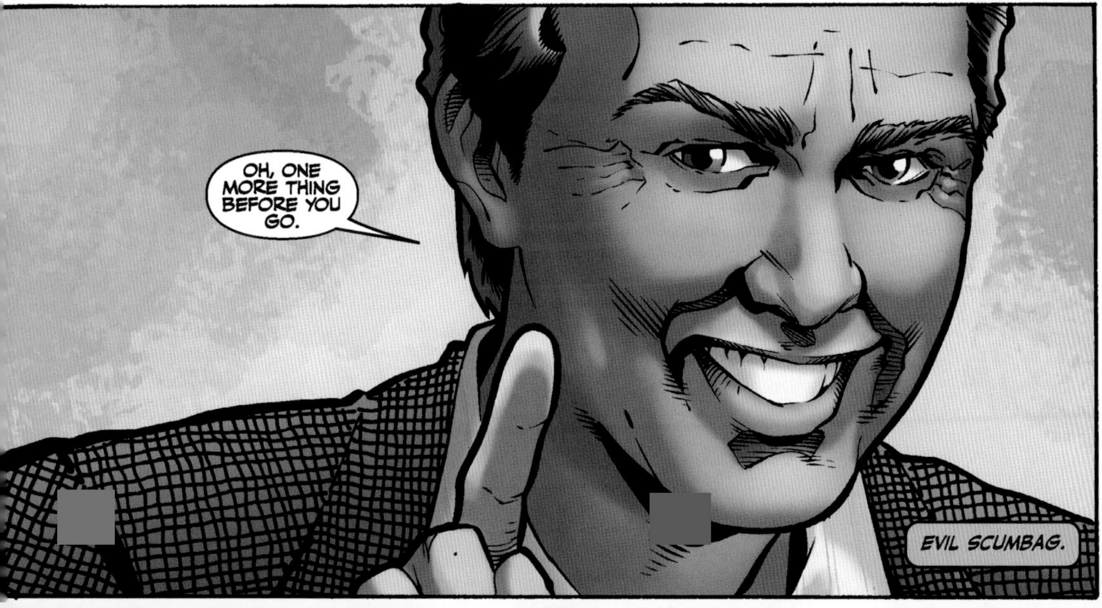
OH, ONE MORE THING BEFORE YOU GO.
EVIL SCUMBAG.

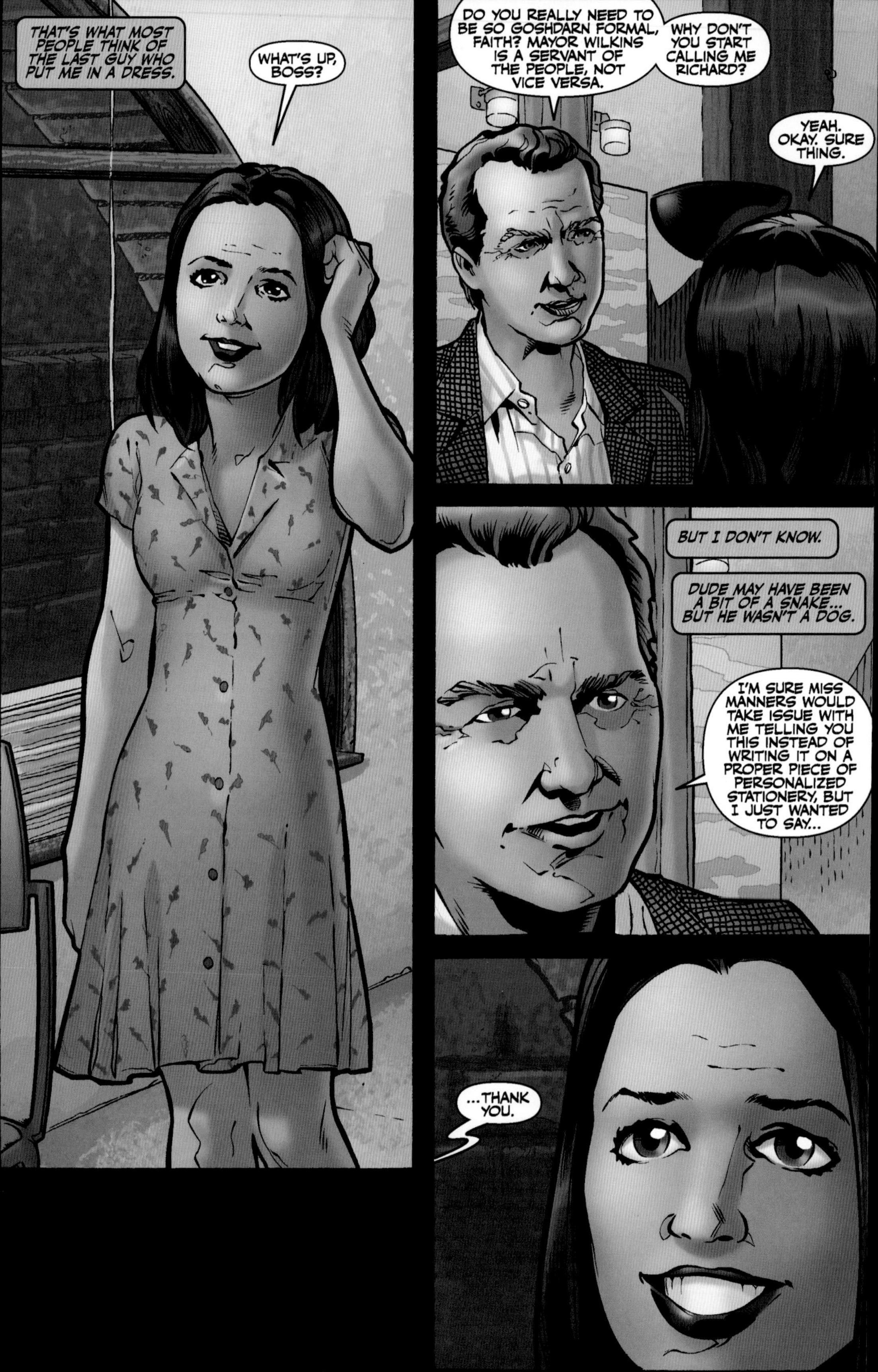
THAT'S WHAT MOST PEOPLE THINK OF THE LAST GUY WHO PUT ME IN A DRESS.
WHAT'S UP, BOSS?
DO YOU REALLY NEED TO BE SO GOSHDARN FORMAL, FAITH? MAYOR WILKINS IS A SERVANT OF THE PEOPLE, NOT VICE VERSA.
WHY DON'T YOU START CALLING ME RICHARD?
YEAH. OKAY. SURE THING.
BUT I DON'T KNOW.
DUDE MAY HAVE BEEN A BIT OF A SNAKE... BUT HE WASN'T A DOG.
I'M SURE MISS MANNERS WOULD TAKE ISSUE WITH ME TELLING YOU THIS INSTEAD OF WRITING IT ON A PROPER PIECE OF PERSONALIZED STATIONERY, BUT I JUST WANTED TO SAY...
...THANK YOU.

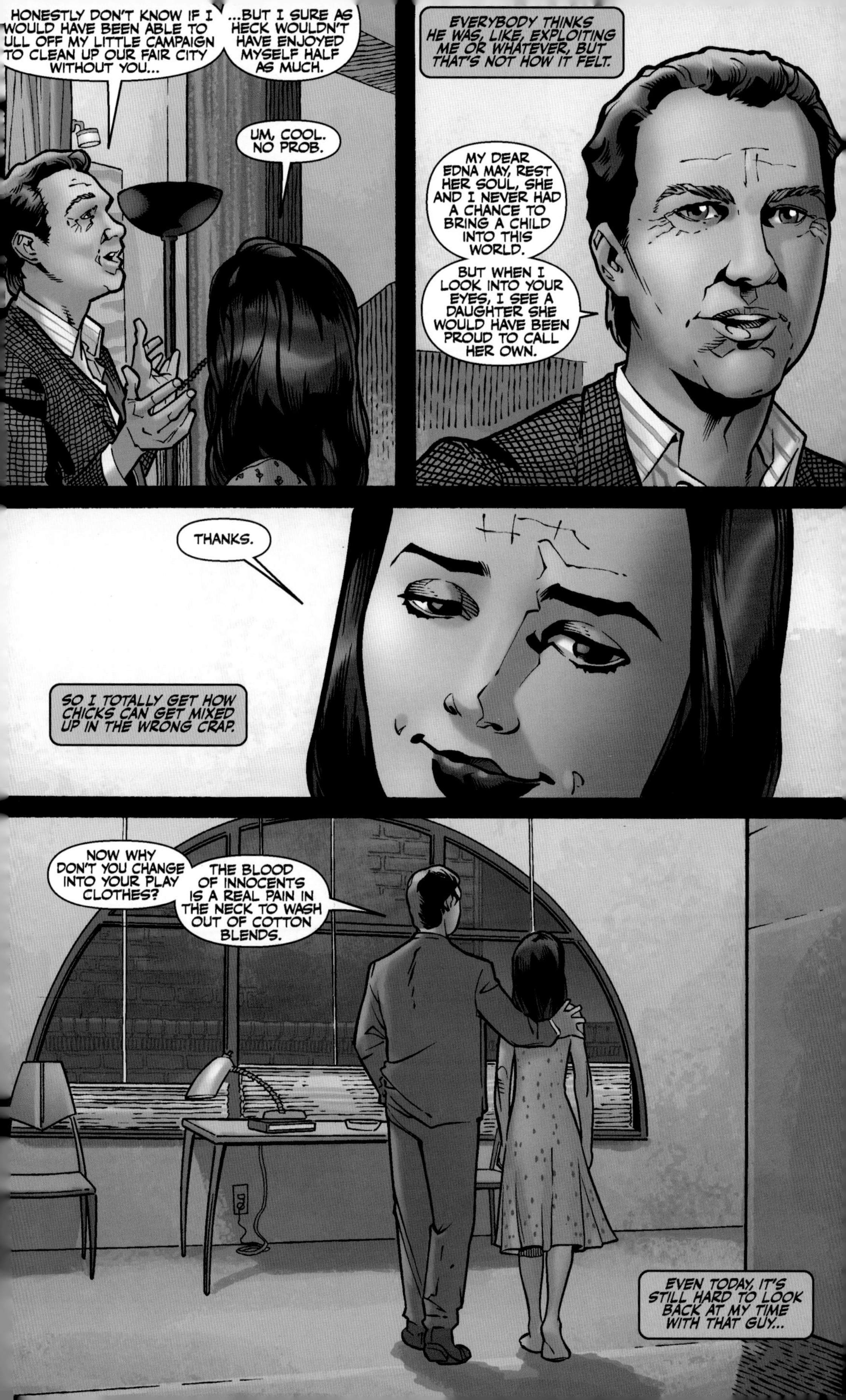
HONESTLY DON'T KNOW IF I WOULD HAVE BEEN ABLE TO ULL OFF MY LITTLE CAMPAIGN TO CLEAN UP OUR FAIR CITY WITHOUT YOU...
...BUT I SURE AS HECK WOULDN'T HAVE ENJOYED MYSELF HALF AS MUCH.
UM, COOL. NO PROB.
EVERYBODY THINKS HE WAS, LIKE, EXPLOITING ME OR WHATEVER, BUT THAT'S NOT HOW IT FELT.
MY DEAR EDNA MAY, REST HER SOUL, SHE AND I NEVER HAD A CHANCE TO BRING A CHILD INTO THIS WORLD.
BUT WHEN I LOOK INTO YOUR EYES, I SEE A DAUGHTER SHE WOULD HAVE BEEN PROUD TO CALL HER OWN.
THANKS.
SO I TOTALLY GET HOW CHICKS CAN GET MIXED UP IN THE WRONG CRAP.
NOW WHY DON'T YOU CHANGE INTO YOUR PLAY CLOTHES?
THE BLOOD OF INNOCENTS IS A REAL PAIN IN THE NECK TO WASH OUT OF COTTON BLENDS.
EVEN TODAY, IT'S STILL HARD TO LOOK BACK AT MY TIME WITH THAT GUY...

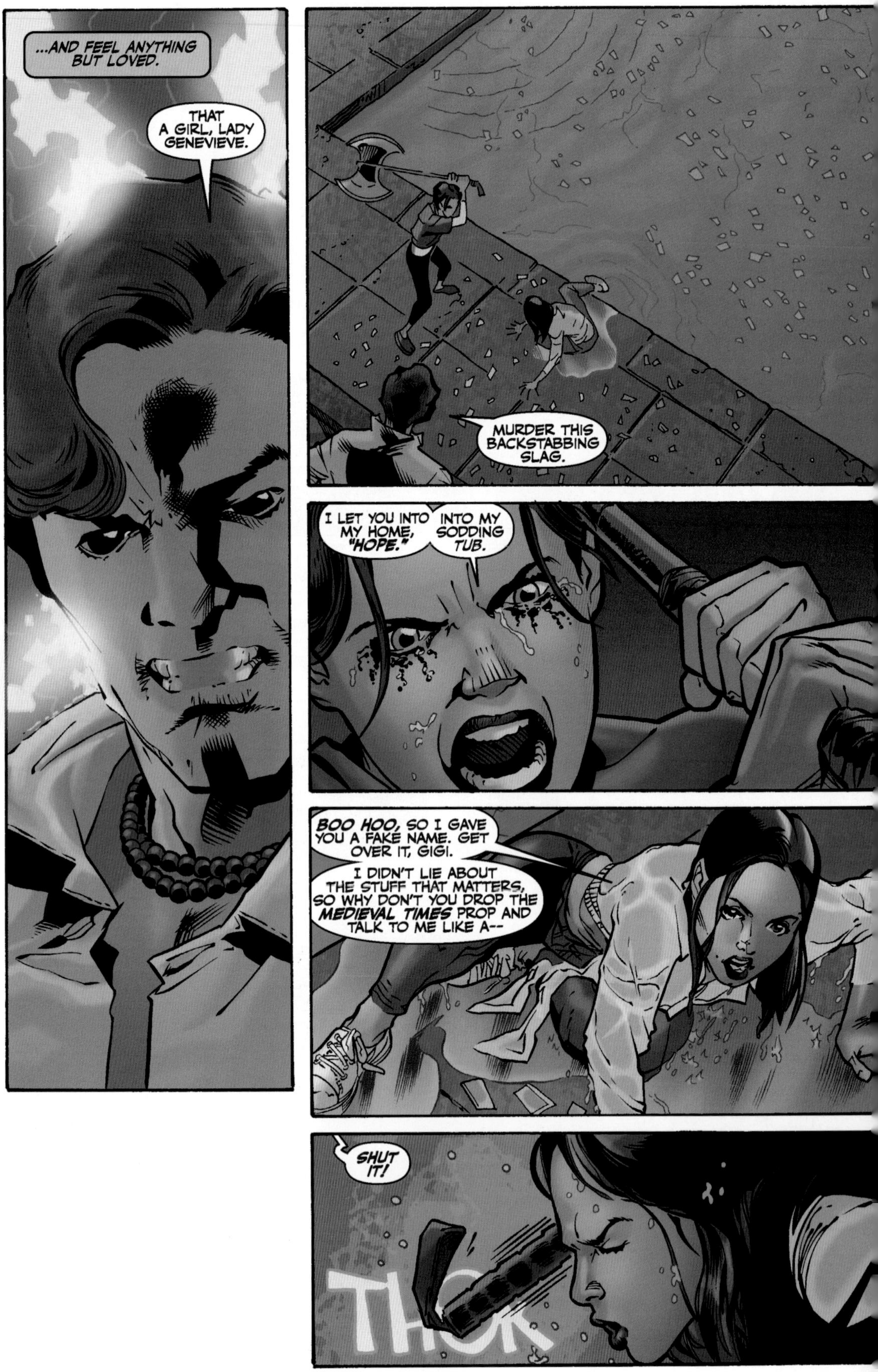
...AND FEEL ANYTHING BUT LOVED.
THAT A GIRL, LADY GENEVIEVE.
MURDER THIS BACKSTABBING SLAG.
I LET YOU INTO MY HOME, *"HOPE."*
INTO MY SODDING *TUB.*
BOO HOO, SO I GAVE YOU A FAKE NAME. GET OVER IT, GIGI.
I DIDN'T LIE ABOUT THE STUFF THAT MATTERS, SO WHY DON'T YOU DROP THE *MEDIEVAL TIMES* PROP AND TALK TO ME LIKE A--
SHUT IT!
THOK

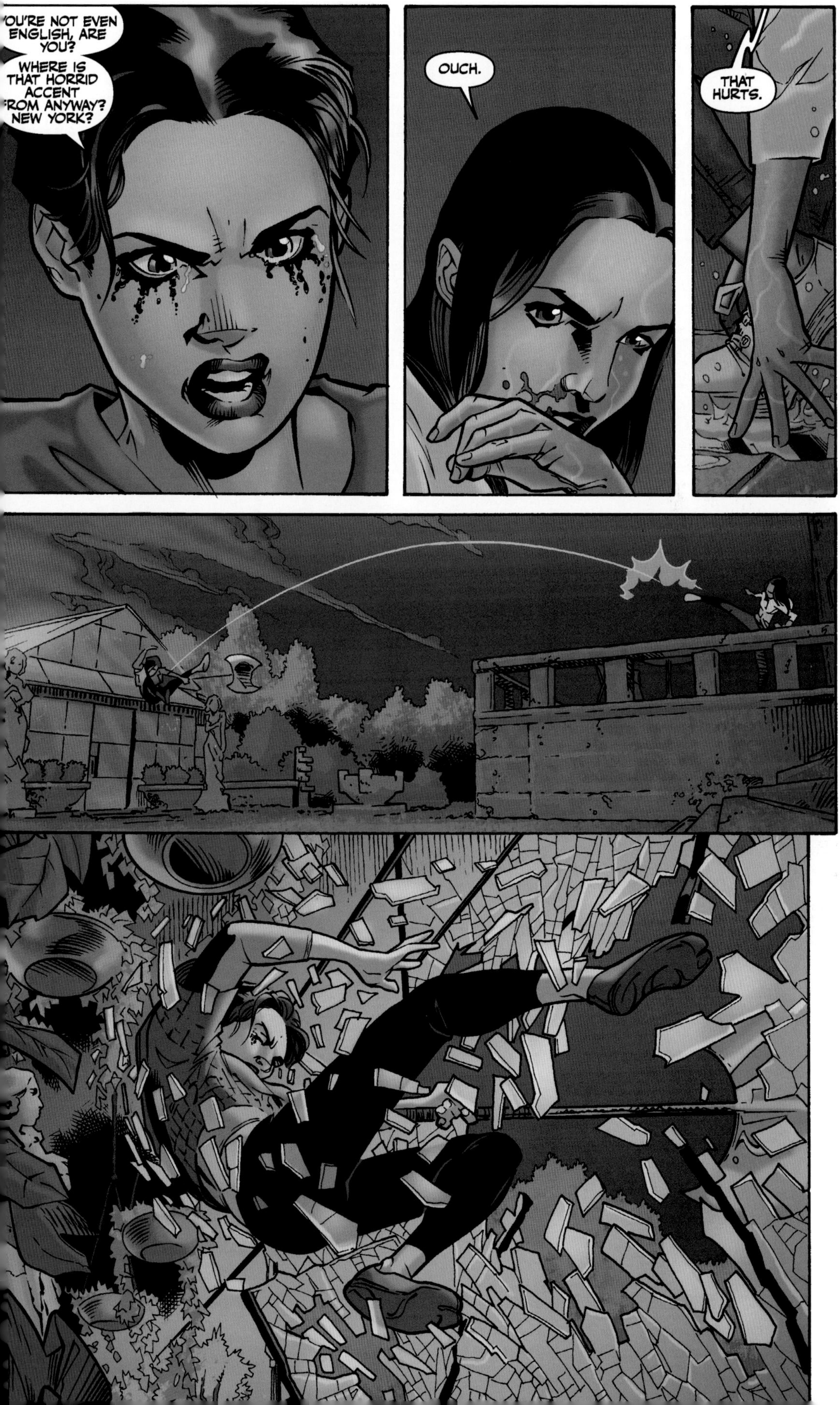
YOU'RE NOT EVEN ENGLISH, ARE YOU?
WHERE IS THAT HORRID ACCENT FROM ANYWAY? NEW YORK?
OUCH.
THAT HURTS.

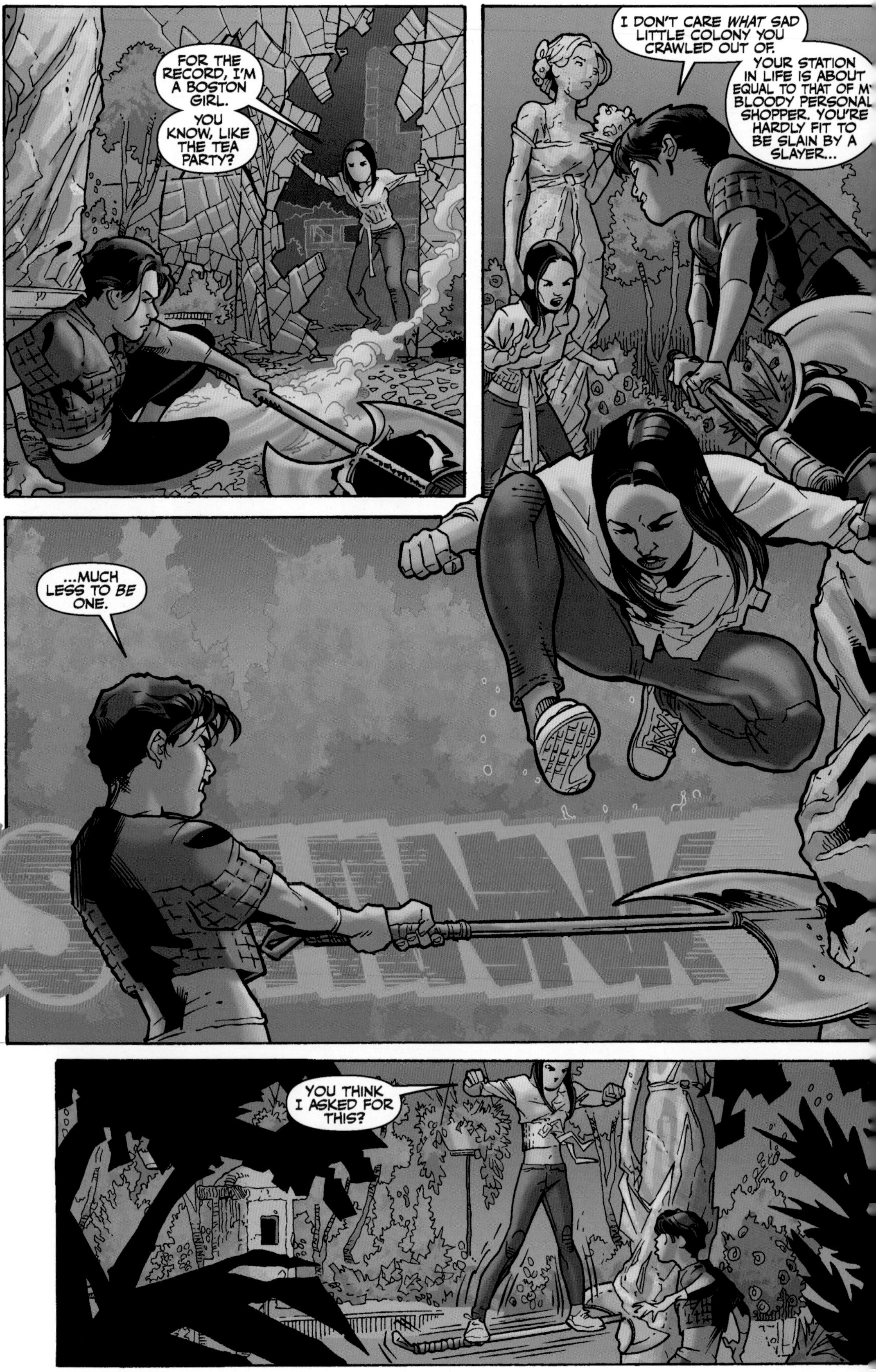
FOR THE RECORD, I'M A BOSTON GIRL.
YOU KNOW, LIKE THE TEA PARTY?
I DON'T CARE *WHAT* SAD LITTLE COLONY YOU CRAWLED OUT OF.
YOUR STATION IN LIFE IS ABOUT EQUAL TO THAT OF MY BLOODY PERSONAL SHOPPER. YOU'RE HARDLY FIT TO BE SLAIN BY A SLAYER...
...MUCH LESS TO *BE* ONE.
YOU THINK I ASKED FOR THIS?

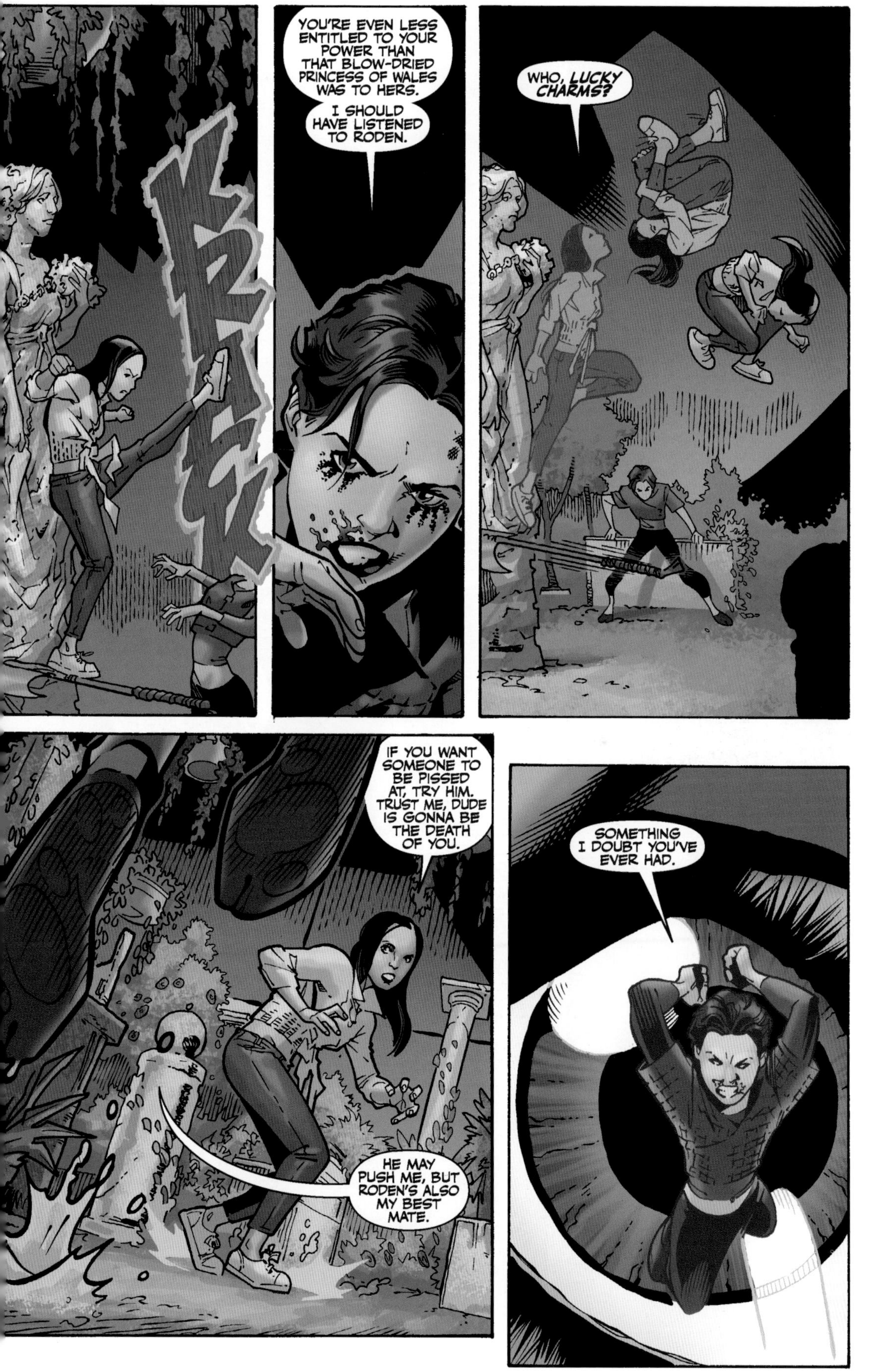
YOU'RE EVEN LESS ENTITLED TO YOUR POWER THAN THAT BLOW-DRIED PRINCESS OF WALES WAS TO HERS.
I SHOULD HAVE LISTENED TO RODEN.
WHO, LUCKY CHARMS?
IF YOU WANT SOMEONE TO BE PISSED AT, TRY HIM. TRUST ME, DUDE IS GONNA BE THE DEATH OF YOU.
HE MAY PUSH ME, BUT RODEN'S ALSO MY BEST MATE.
SOMETHING I DOUBT YOU'VE EVER HAD.

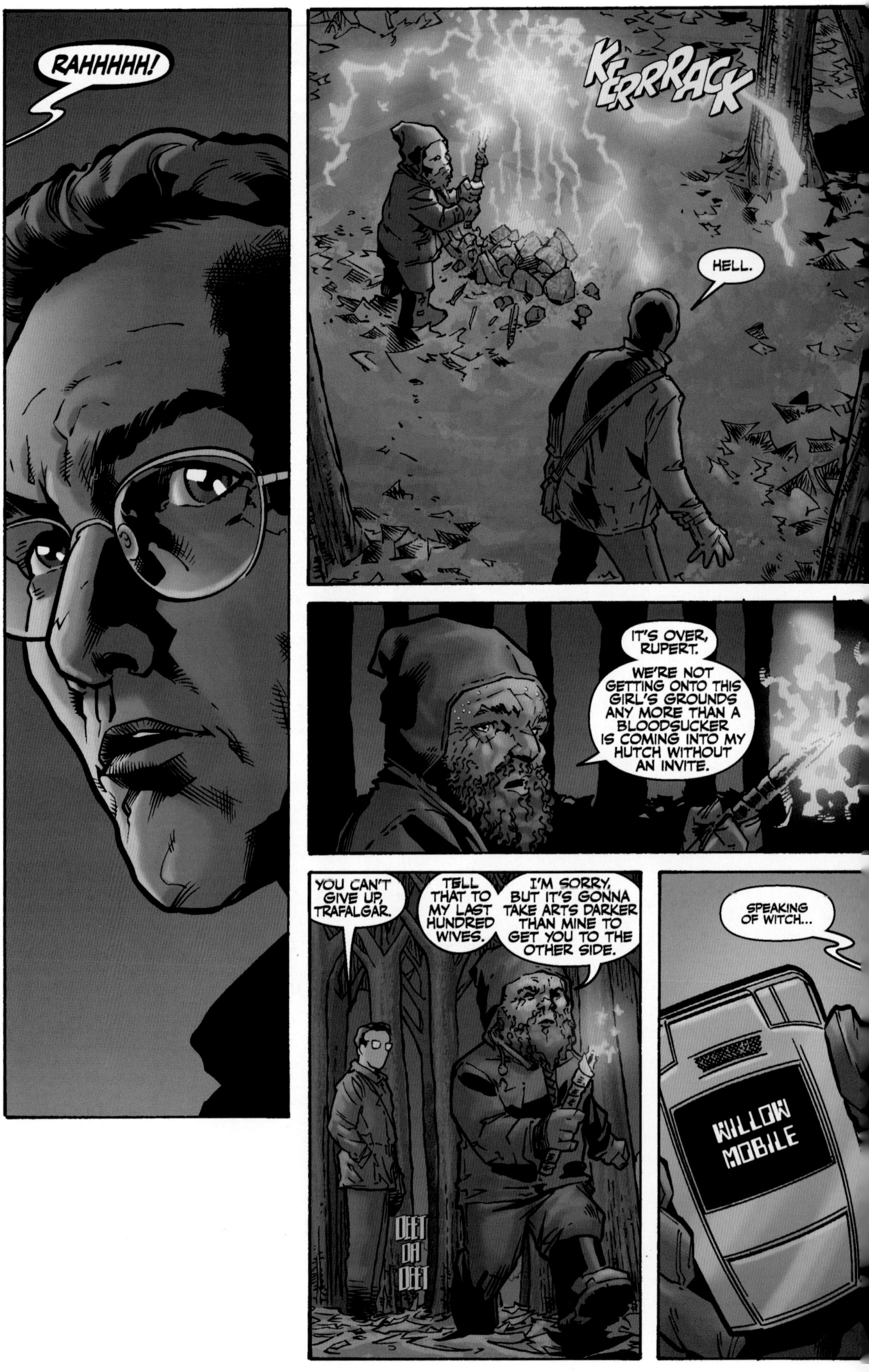
RAHHHHH!
KERRRACK
HELL.
IT'S OVER, RUPERT.
WE'RE NOT GETTING ONTO THIS GIRL'S GROUNDS ANY MORE THAN A BLOODSUCKER IS COMING INTO MY HUTCH WITHOUT AN INVITE.
YOU CAN'T GIVE UP, TRAFALGAR.
TELL THAT TO MY LAST HUNDRED WIVES.
I'M SORRY, BUT IT'S GONNA TAKE ARTS DARKER THAN MINE TO GET YOU TO THE OTHER SIDE.
DEET DA DEET
SPEAKING OF WITCH...
WILLOW MOBILE

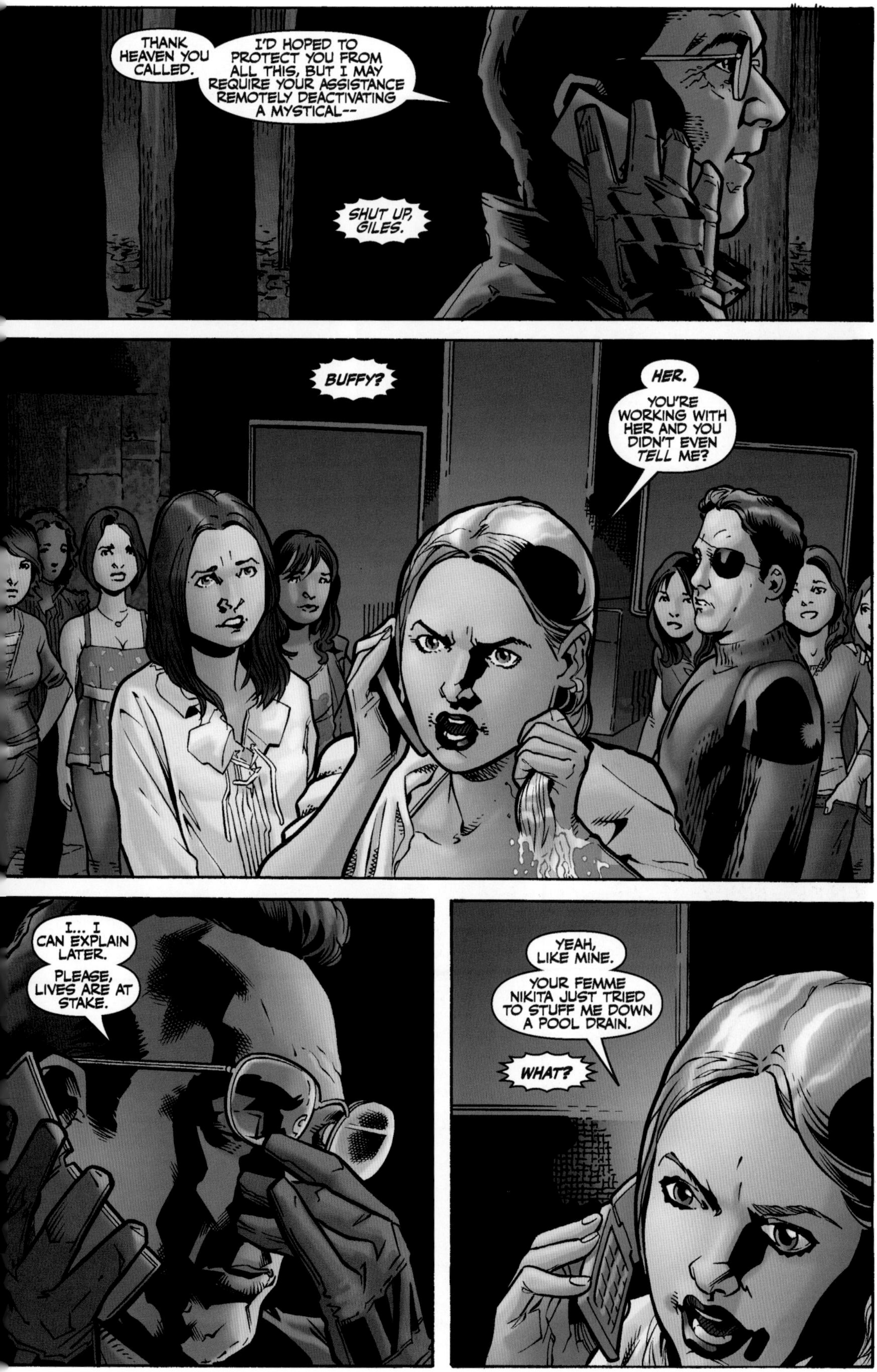
THANK HEAVEN YOU CALLED.
I'D HOPED TO PROTECT YOU FROM ALL THIS, BUT I MAY REQUIRE YOUR ASSISTANCE REMOTELY DEACTIVATING A MYSTICAL--
SHUT UP, GILES.
BUFFY?
HER.
YOU'RE WORKING WITH HER AND YOU DIDN'T EVEN TELL ME?
I... I CAN EXPLAIN LATER.
PLEASE, LIVES ARE AT STAKE.
YEAH, LIKE MINE.
YOUR FEMME NIKITA JUST TRIED TO STUFF ME DOWN A POOL DRAIN.
WHAT?

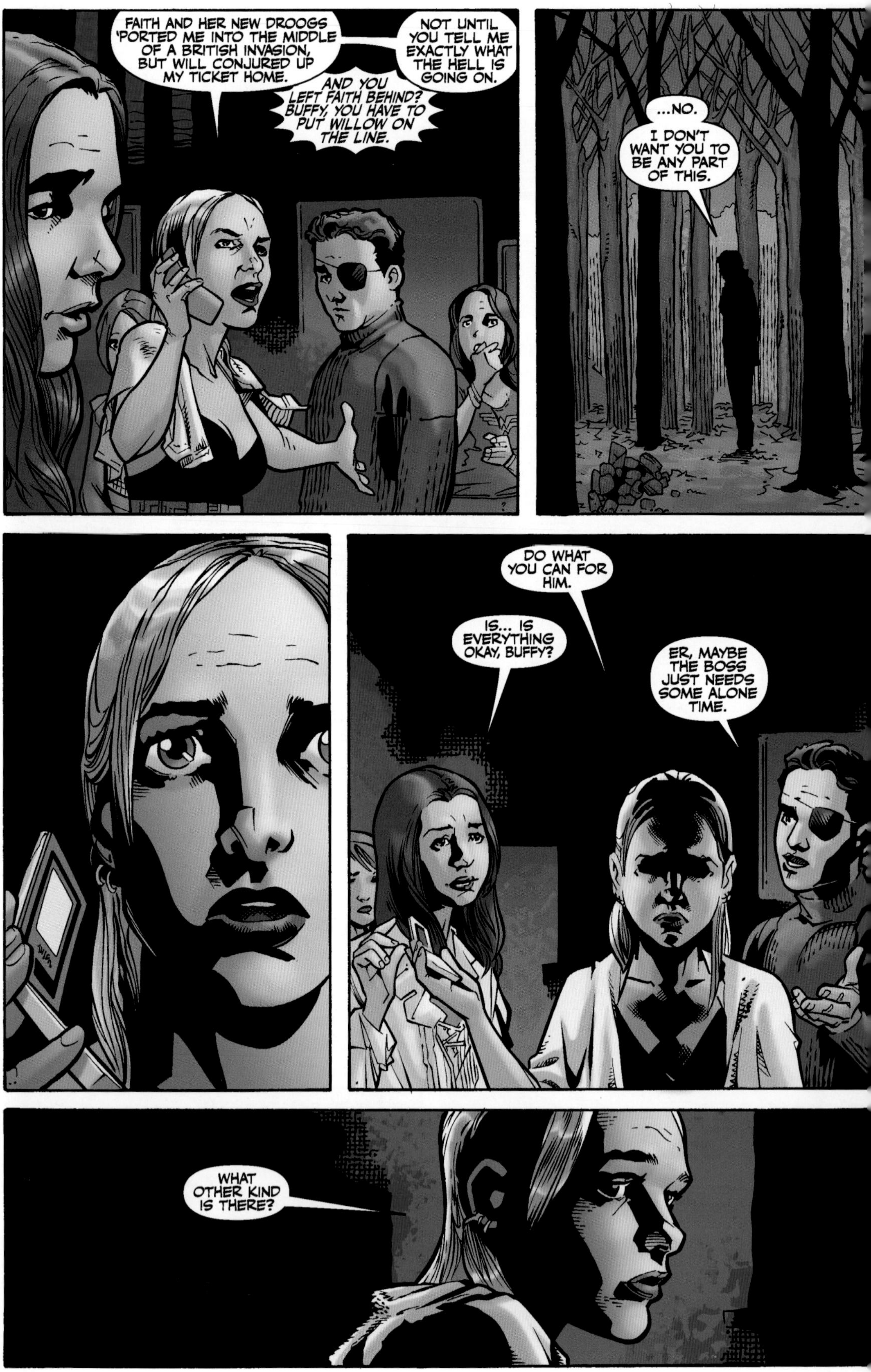
FAITH AND HER NEW DROOGS 'PORTED ME INTO THE MIDDLE OF A BRITISH INVASION, BUT WILL CONJURED UP MY TICKET HOME.
NOT UNTIL YOU TELL ME EXACTLY WHAT THE HELL IS GOING ON.
AND YOU LEFT FAITH BEHIND? BUFFY, YOU HAVE TO PUT WILLOW ON THE LINE.
...NO.
I DON'T WANT YOU TO BE ANY PART OF THIS.
DO WHAT YOU CAN FOR HIM.
IS... IS EVERYTHING OKAY, BUFFY?
ER, MAYBE THE BOSS JUST NEEDS SOME ALONE TIME.
WHAT OTHER KIND IS THERE?

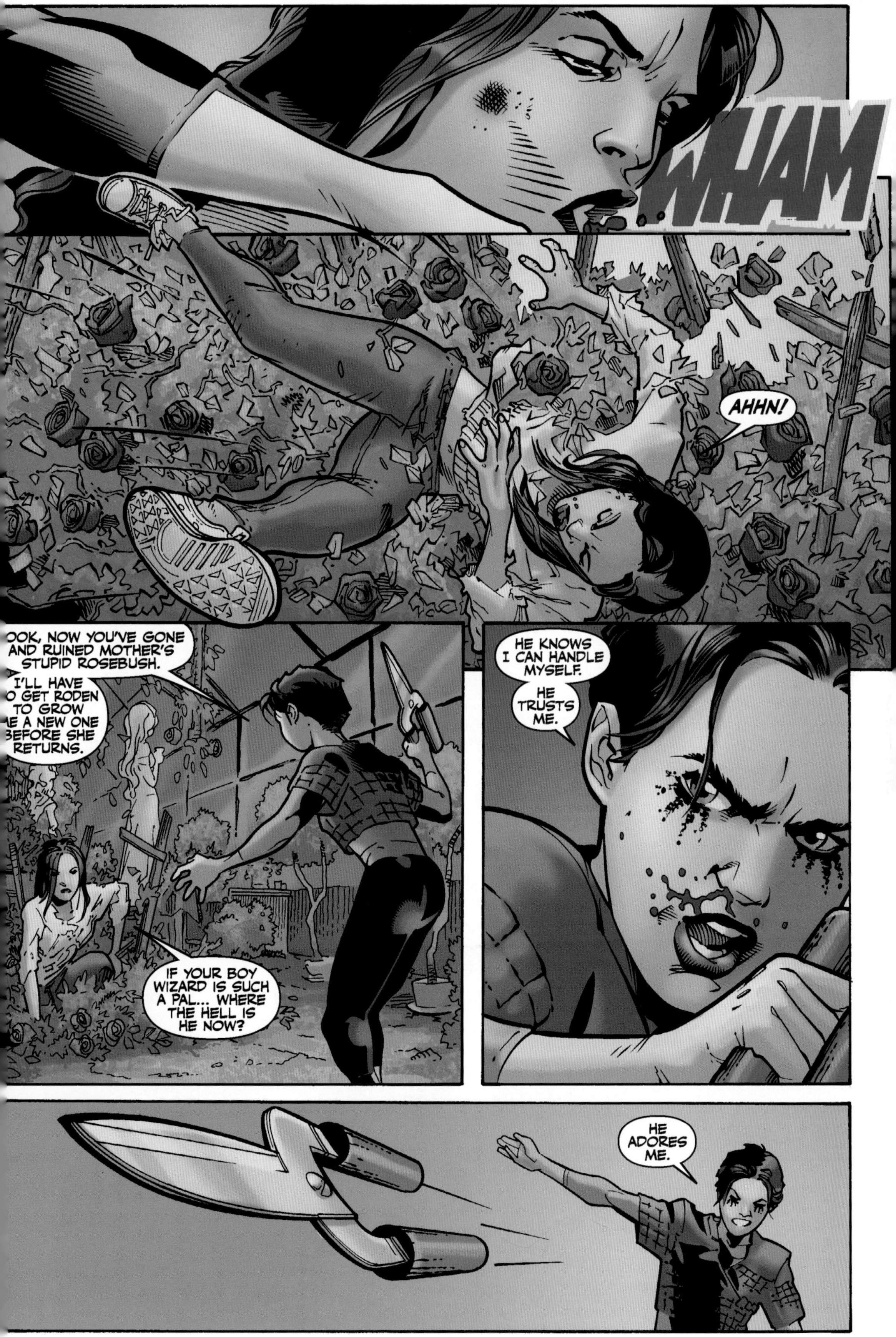
WHAM
AHHN!
OOK, NOW YOU'VE GONE AND RUINED MOTHER'S STUPID ROSEBUSH.
I'LL HAVE O GET RODEN TO GROW E A NEW ONE BEFORE SHE RETURNS.
IF YOUR BOY WIZARD IS SUCH A PAL... WHERE THE HELL IS HE NOW?
HE KNOWS I CAN HANDLE MYSELF.
HE TRUSTS ME.
HE ADORES ME.

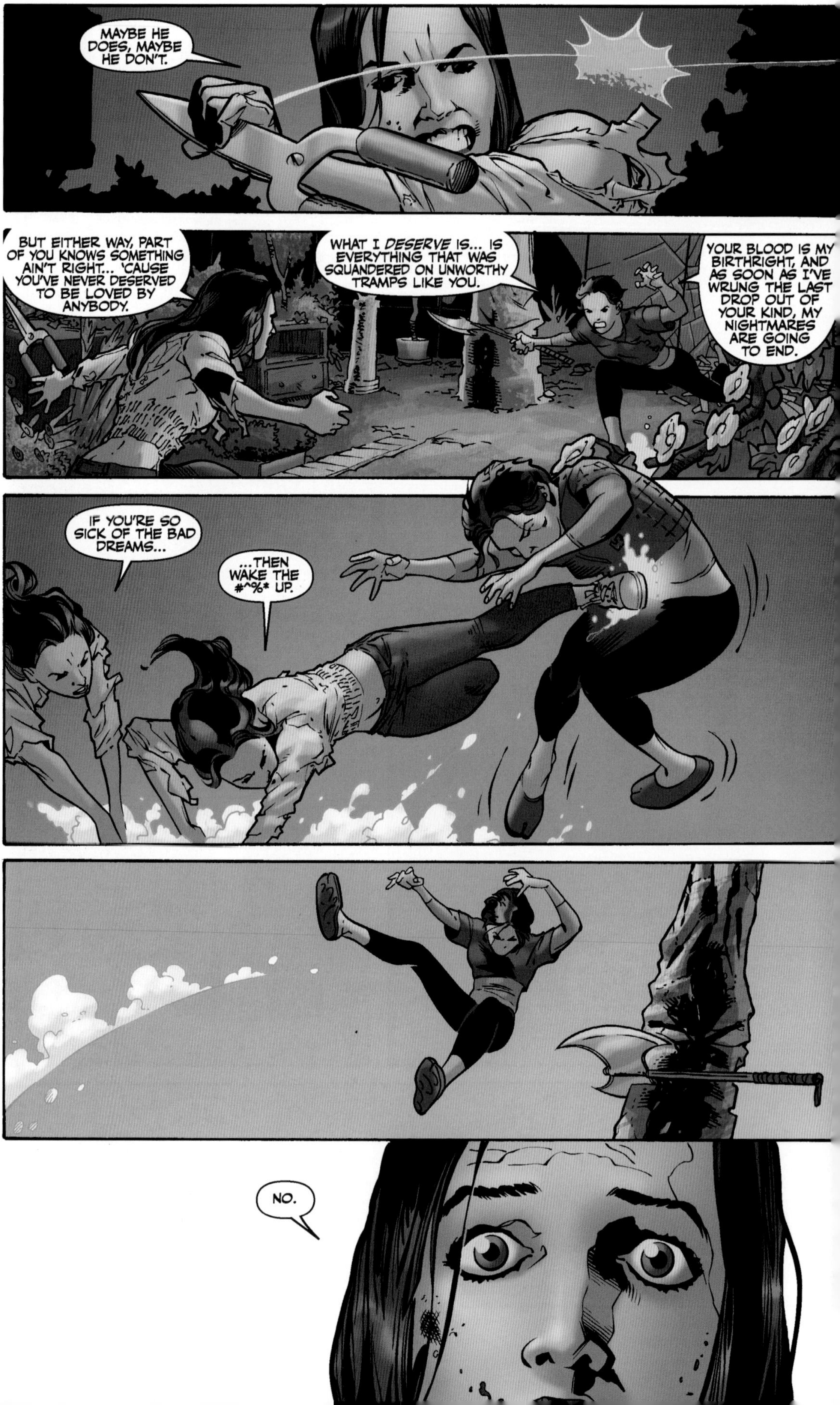
MAYBE HE DOES, MAYBE HE DON'T.
BUT EITHER WAY, PART OF YOU KNOWS SOMETHING AIN'T RIGHT... 'CAUSE YOU'VE NEVER DESERVED TO BE LOVED BY ANYBODY.
WHAT I DESERVE IS... IS EVERYTHING THAT WAS SQUANDERED ON UNWORTHY TRAMPS LIKE YOU.
YOUR BLOOD IS MY BIRTHRIGHT, AND AS SOON AS I'VE WRUNG THE LAST DROP OUT OF YOUR KIND, MY NIGHTMARES ARE GOING TO END.
IF YOU'RE SO SICK OF THE BAD DREAMS...
...THEN WAKE THE #^%* UP.
NO.

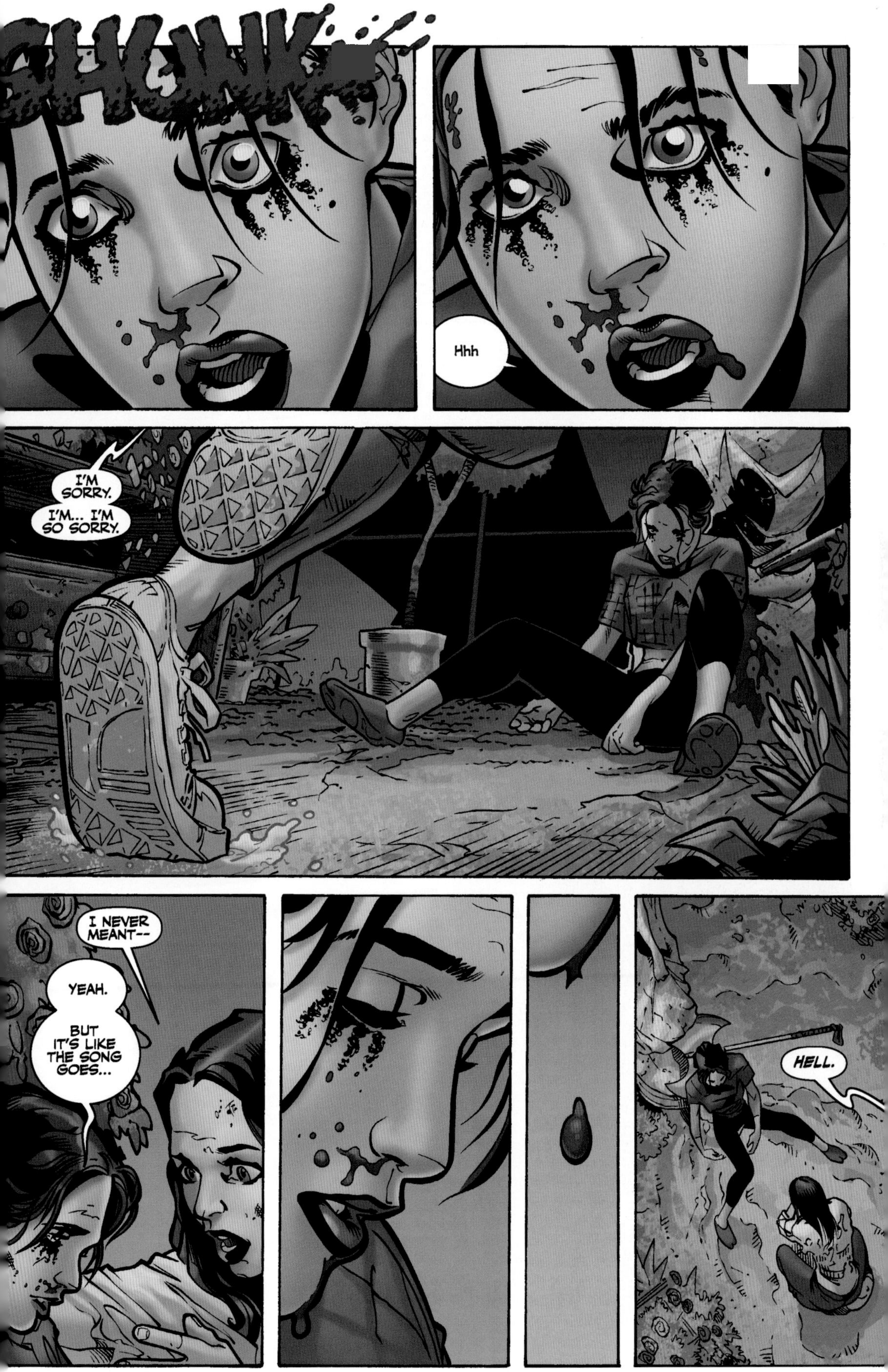
Hhh
I'M SORRY. I'M... I'M SO SORRY.
I NEVER MEANT--
YEAH.
BUT IT'S LIKE THE SONG GOES...
HELL.

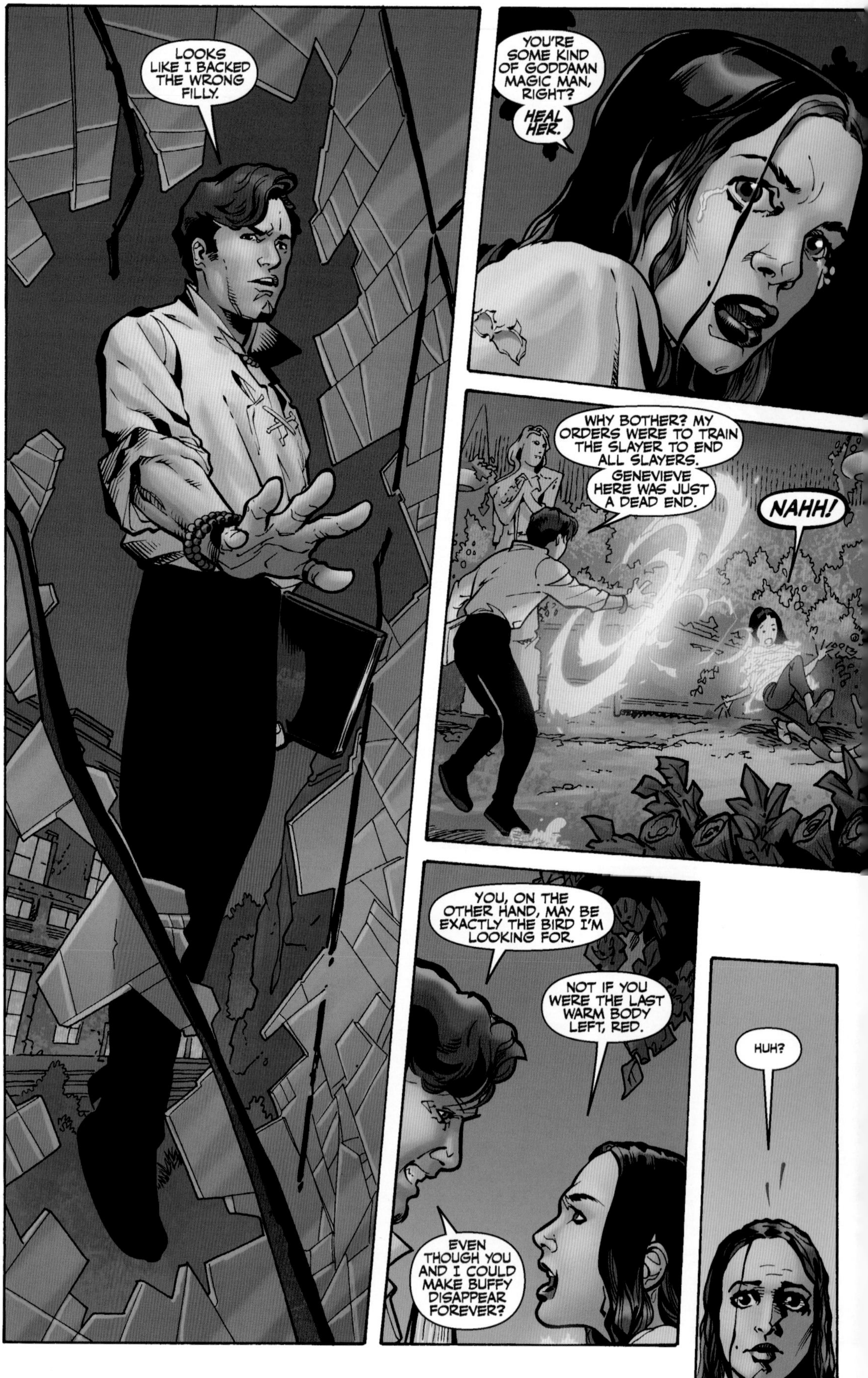
LOOKS LIKE I BACKED THE WRONG FILLY.
YOU'RE SOME KIND OF GODDAMN MAGIC MAN, RIGHT?
HEAL HER.
WHY BOTHER? MY ORDERS WERE TO TRAIN THE SLAYER TO END ALL SLAYERS. GENEVIEVE HERE WAS JUST A DEAD END.
NAHH!
YOU, ON THE OTHER HAND, MAY BE EXACTLY THE BIRD I'M LOOKING FOR.
NOT IF YOU WERE THE LAST WARM BODY LEFT, RED.
EVEN THOUGH YOU AND I COULD MAKE BUFFY DISAPPEAR FOREVER?
HUH?

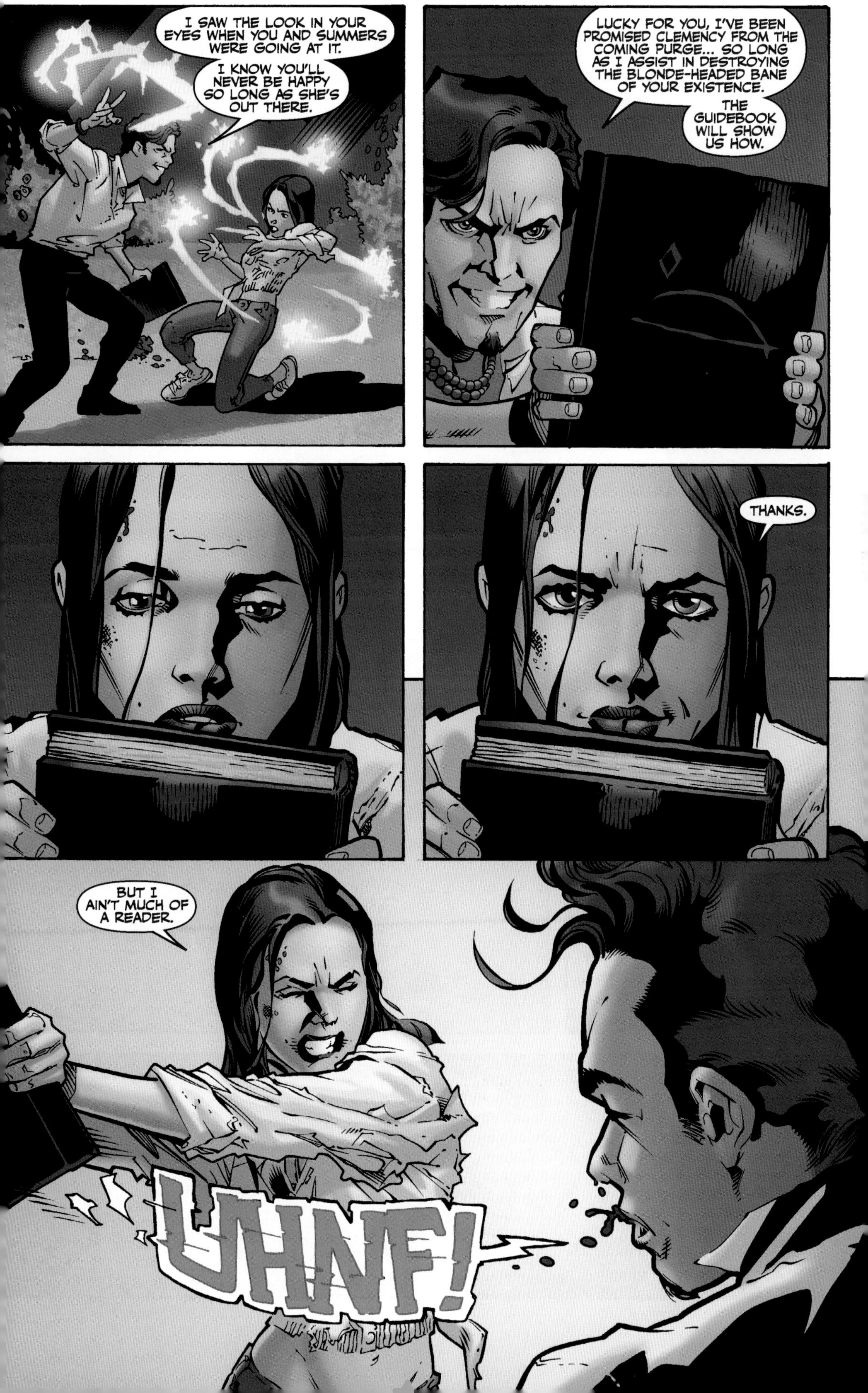
I SAW THE LOOK IN YOUR EYES WHEN YOU AND SUMMERS WERE GOING AT IT.
I KNOW YOU'LL NEVER BE HAPPY SO LONG AS SHE'S OUT THERE.
LUCKY FOR YOU, I'VE BEEN PROMISED CLEMENCY FROM THE COMING PURGE... SO LONG AS I ASSIST IN DESTROYING THE BLONDE-HEADED BANE OF YOUR EXISTENCE.
THE GUIDEBOOK WILL SHOW US HOW.
THANKS.
BUT I AIN'T MUCH OF A READER.
UHNF!

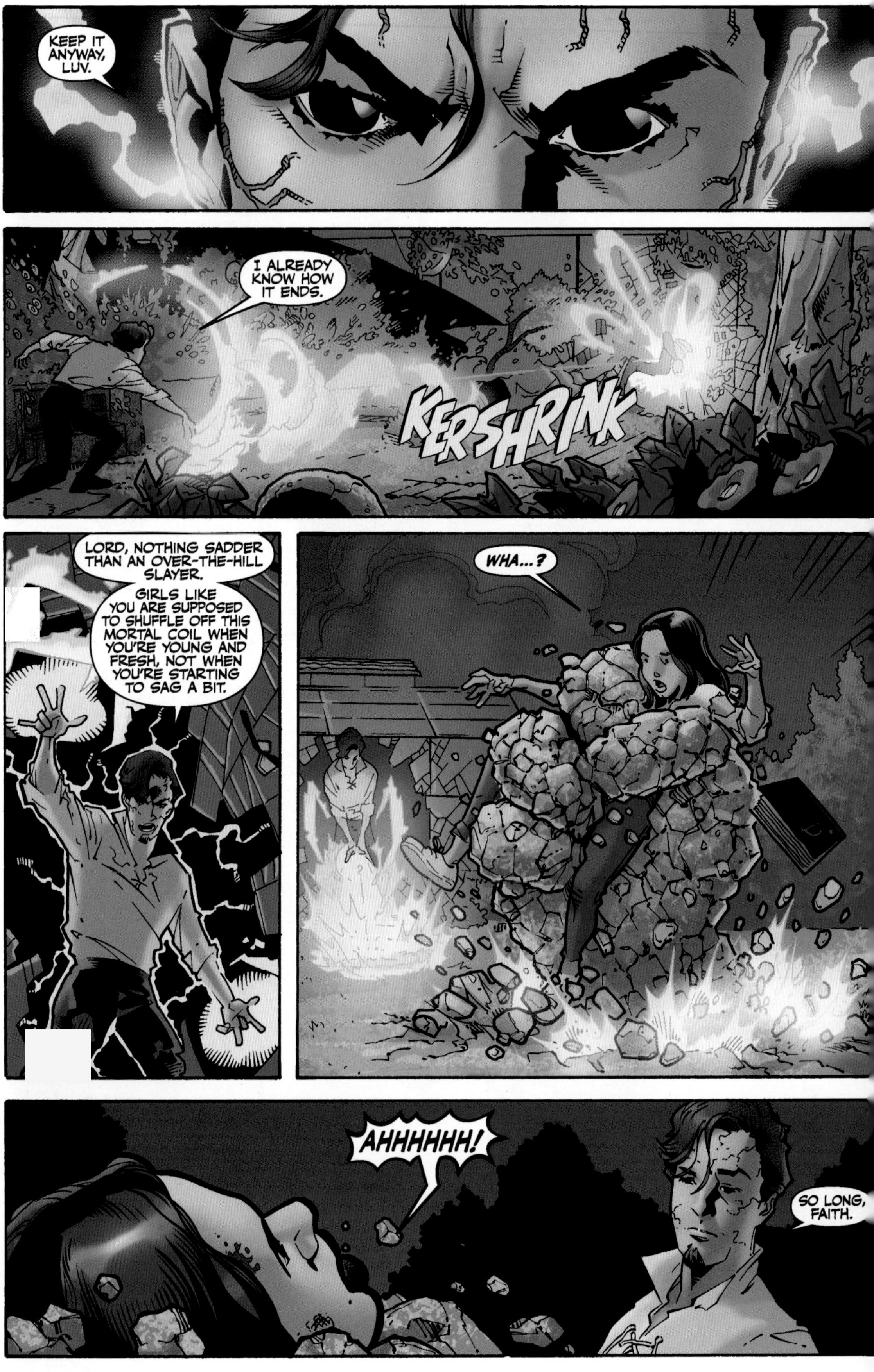
KEEP IT ANYWAY, LUV.
I ALREADY KNOW HOW IT ENDS.
KERSHRINK
LORD, NOTHING SADDER THAN AN OVER-THE-HILL SLAYER.
GIRLS LIKE YOU ARE SUPPOSED TO SHUFFLE OFF THIS MORTAL COIL WHEN YOU'RE YOUNG AND FRESH, NOT WHEN YOU'RE STARTING TO SAG A BIT.
WHA...?
AHHHHHH!
SO LONG, FAITH.

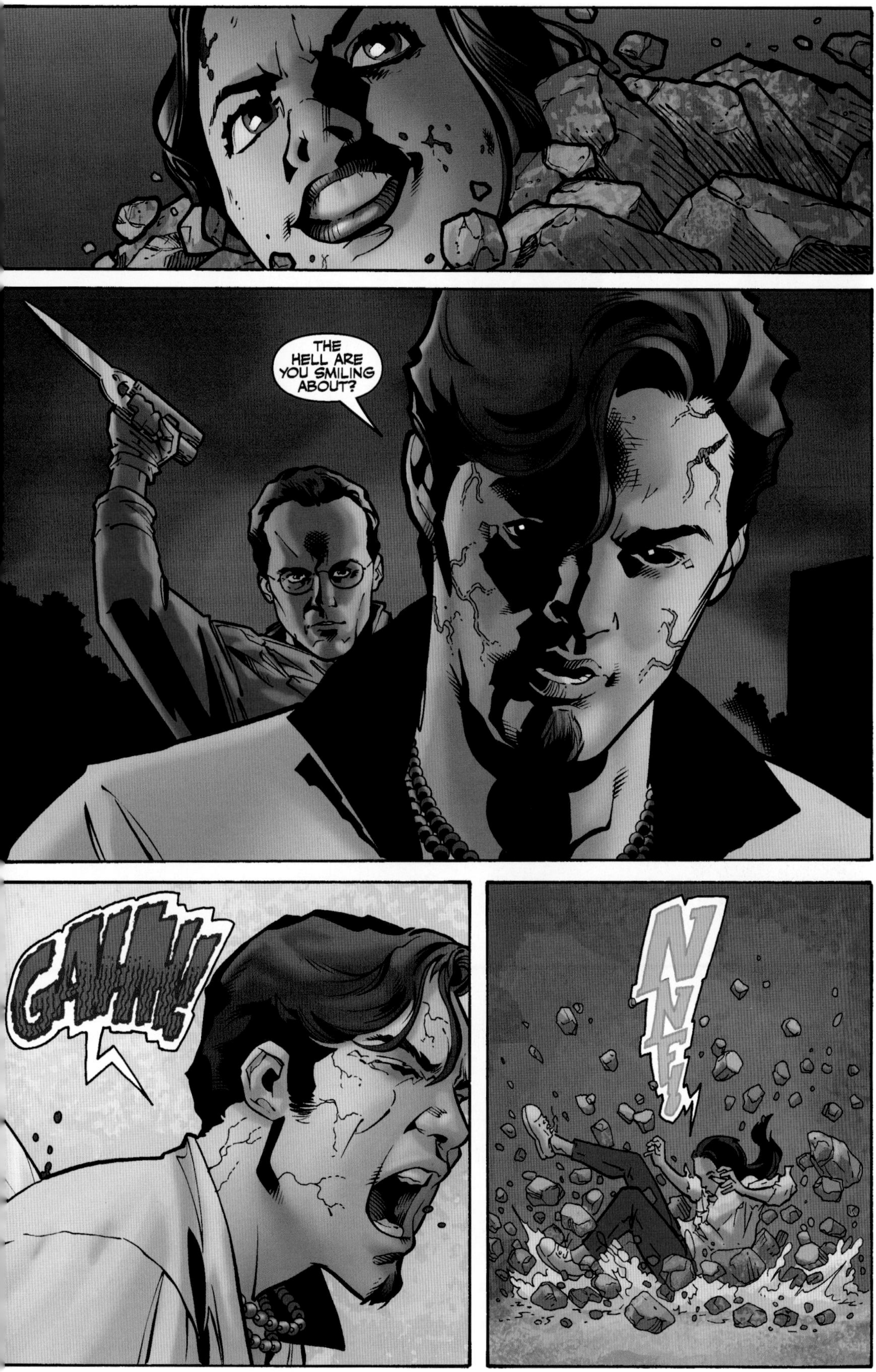
THE HELL ARE YOU SMILING ABOUT?
GAHH!
NNF!

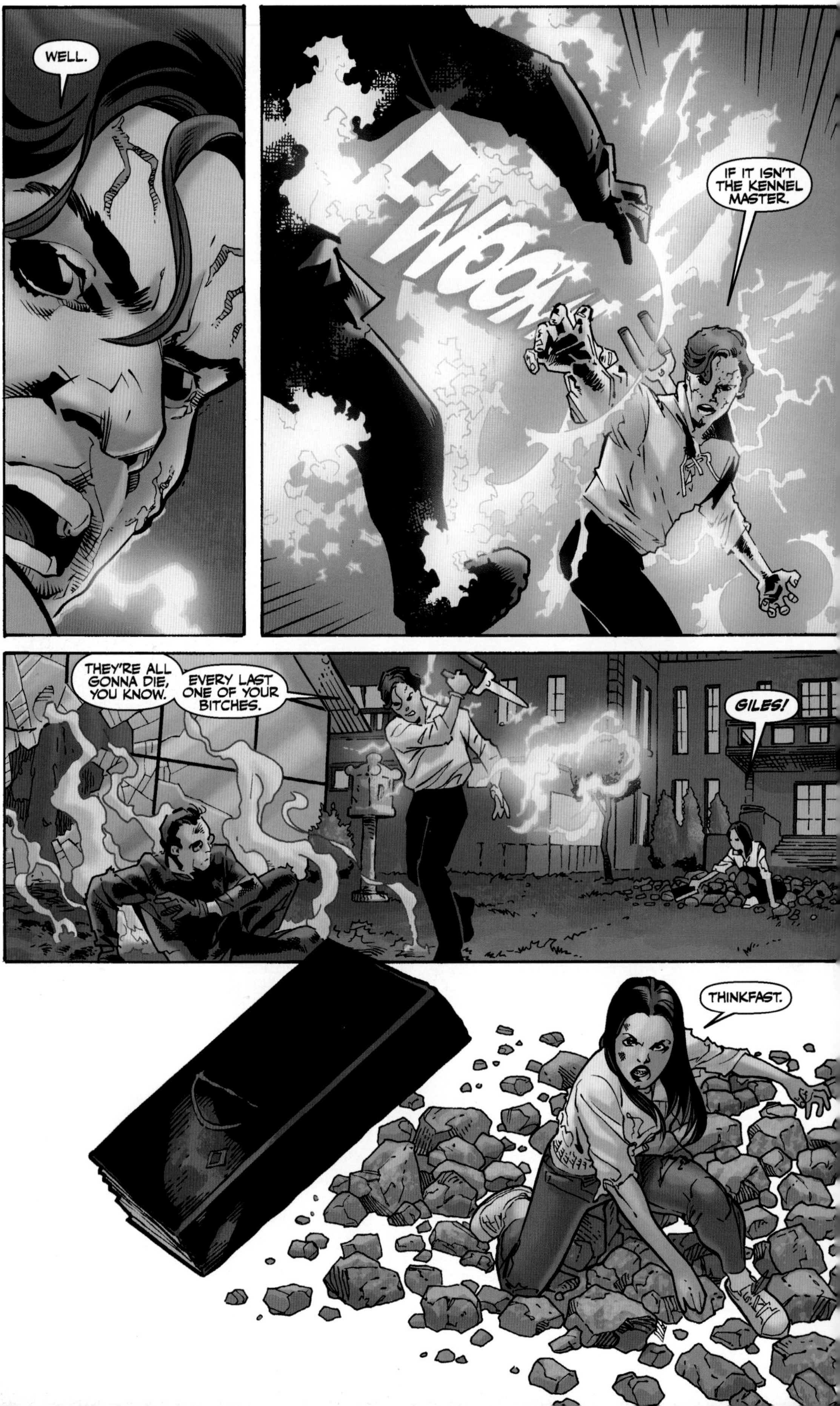
WELL.
FWOOM
IF IT ISN'T THE KENNEL MASTER.
THEY'RE ALL GONNA DIE, YOU KNOW.
EVERY LAST ONE OF YOUR BITCHES.
GILES!
THINKFAST.

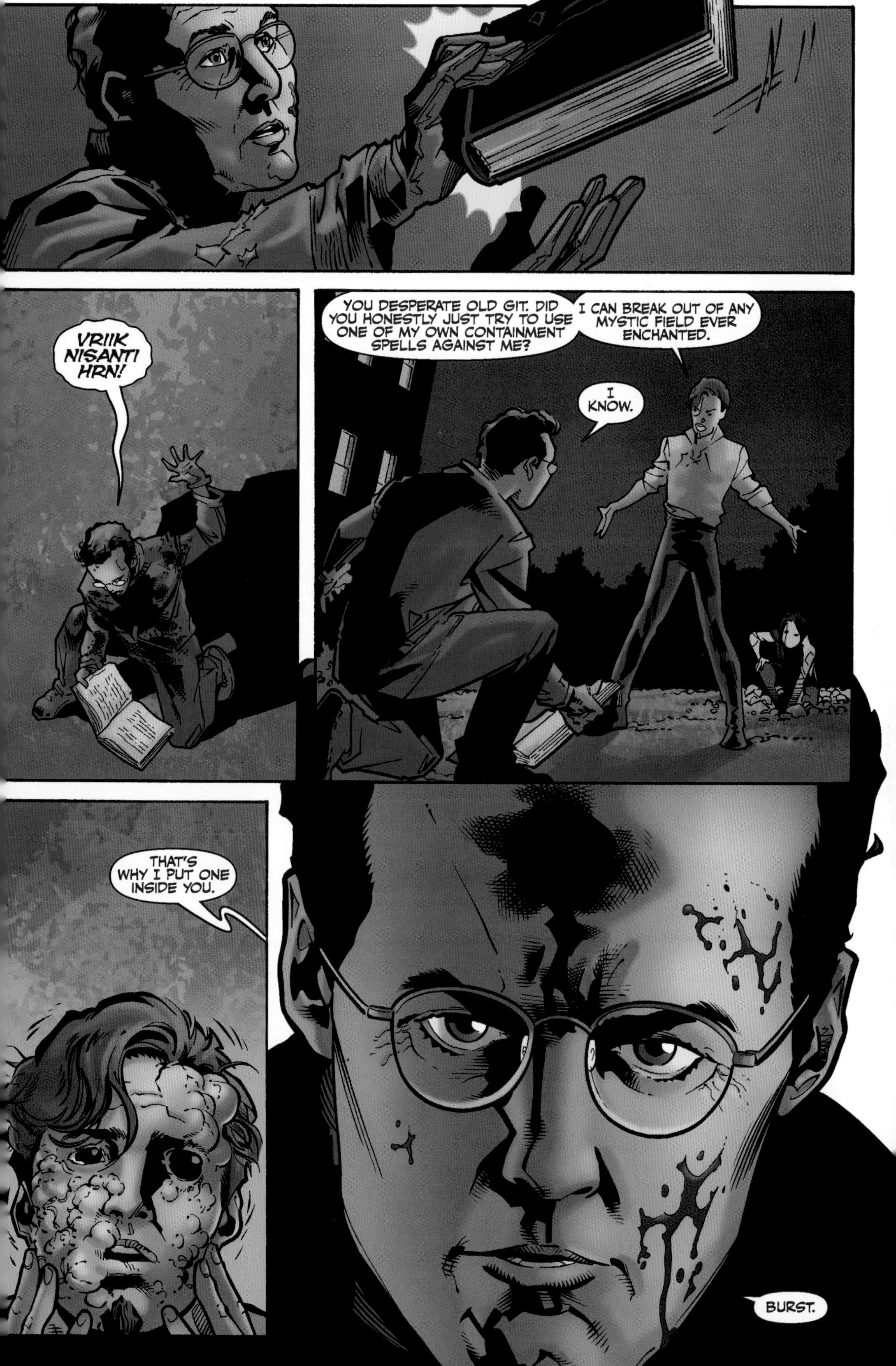
VRIIK NISANTI HRN!
YOU DESPERATE OLD GIT. DID YOU HONESTLY JUST TRY TO USE ONE OF MY OWN CONTAINMENT SPELLS AGAINST ME?
I CAN BREAK OUT OF ANY MYSTIC FIELD EVER ENCHANTED.
I KNOW.
THAT'S WHY I PUT ONE INSIDE YOU.
BURST.

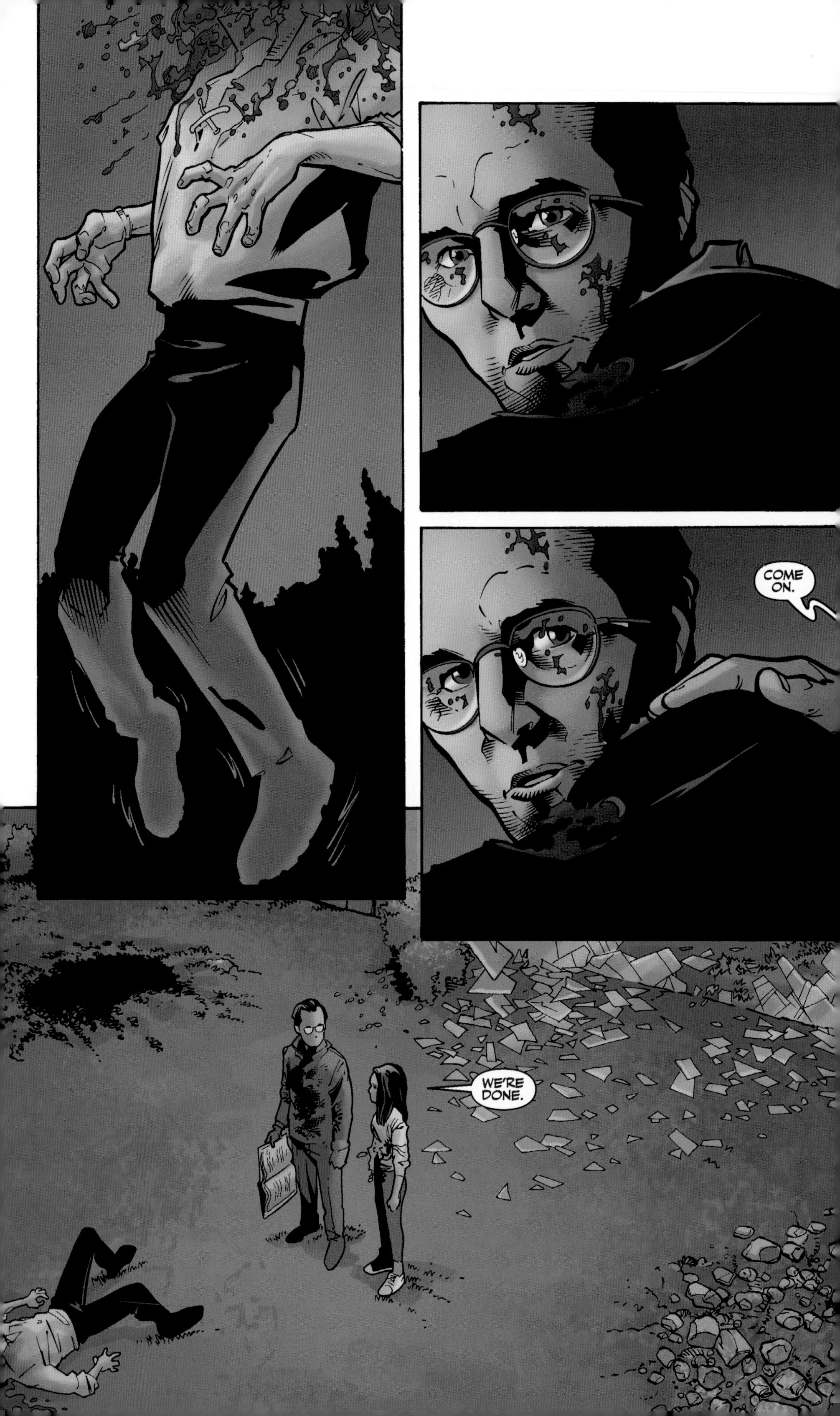
COME ON.
WE'RE DONE.

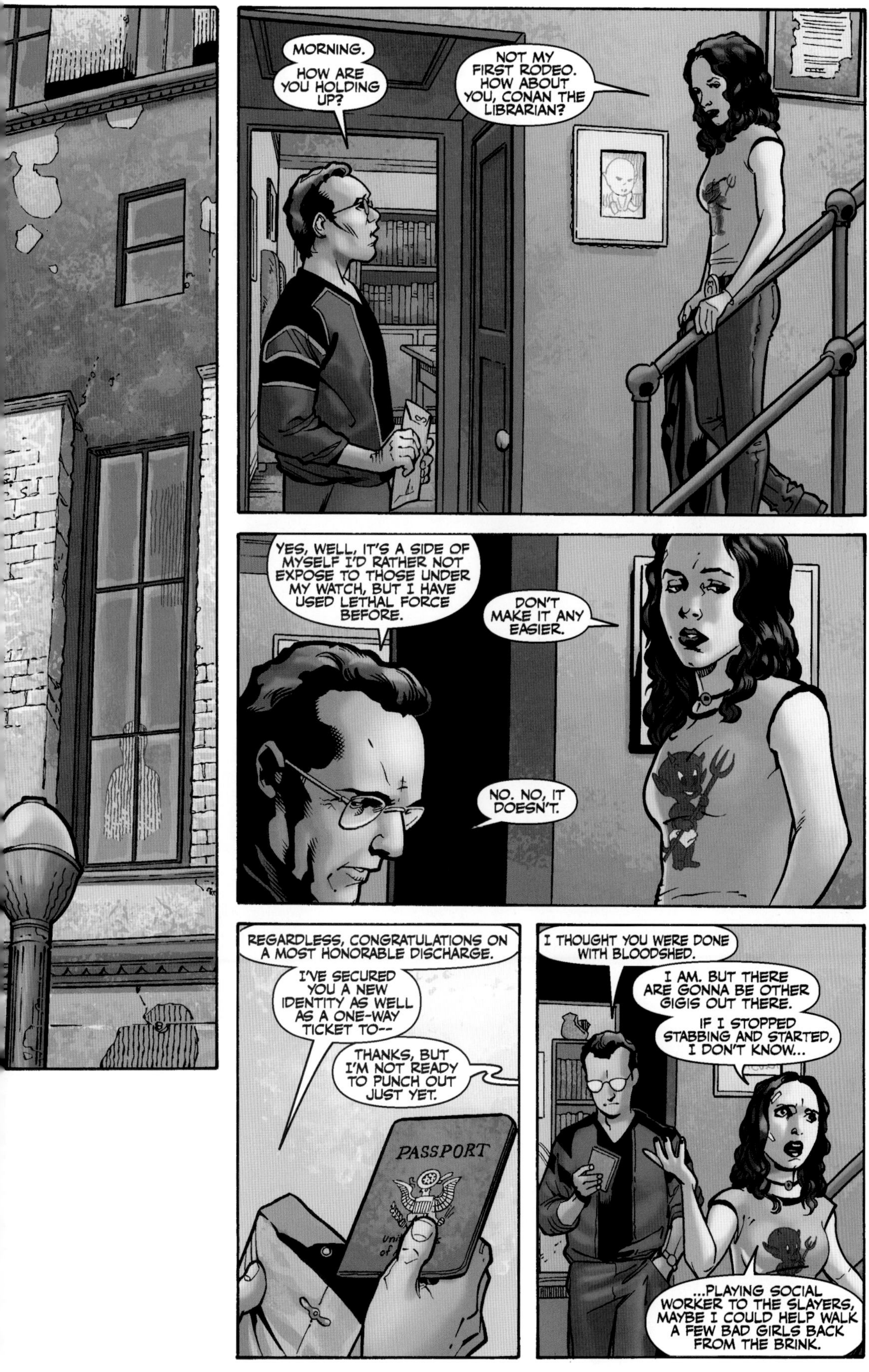
MORNING.
HOW ARE YOU HOLDING UP?
NOT MY FIRST RODEO. HOW ABOUT YOU, CONAN THE LIBRARIAN?
YES, WELL, IT'S A SIDE OF MYSELF I'D RATHER NOT EXPOSE TO THOSE UNDER MY WATCH, BUT I HAVE USED LETHAL FORCE BEFORE.
DON'T MAKE IT ANY EASIER.
NO. NO, IT DOESN'T.
REGARDLESS, CONGRATULATIONS ON A MOST HONORABLE DISCHARGE.
I'VE SECURED YOU A NEW IDENTITY AS WELL AS A ONE-WAY TICKET TO--
THANKS, BUT I'M NOT READY TO PUNCH OUT JUST YET.
PASSPORT
I THOUGHT YOU WERE DONE WITH BLOODSHED.
I AM. BUT THERE ARE GONNA BE OTHER GIGIS OUT THERE.
IF I STOPPED STABBING AND STARTED, I DON'T KNOW...
...PLAYING SOCIAL WORKER TO THE SLAYERS, MAYBE I COULD HELP WALK A FEW BAD GIRLS BACK FROM THE BRINK.

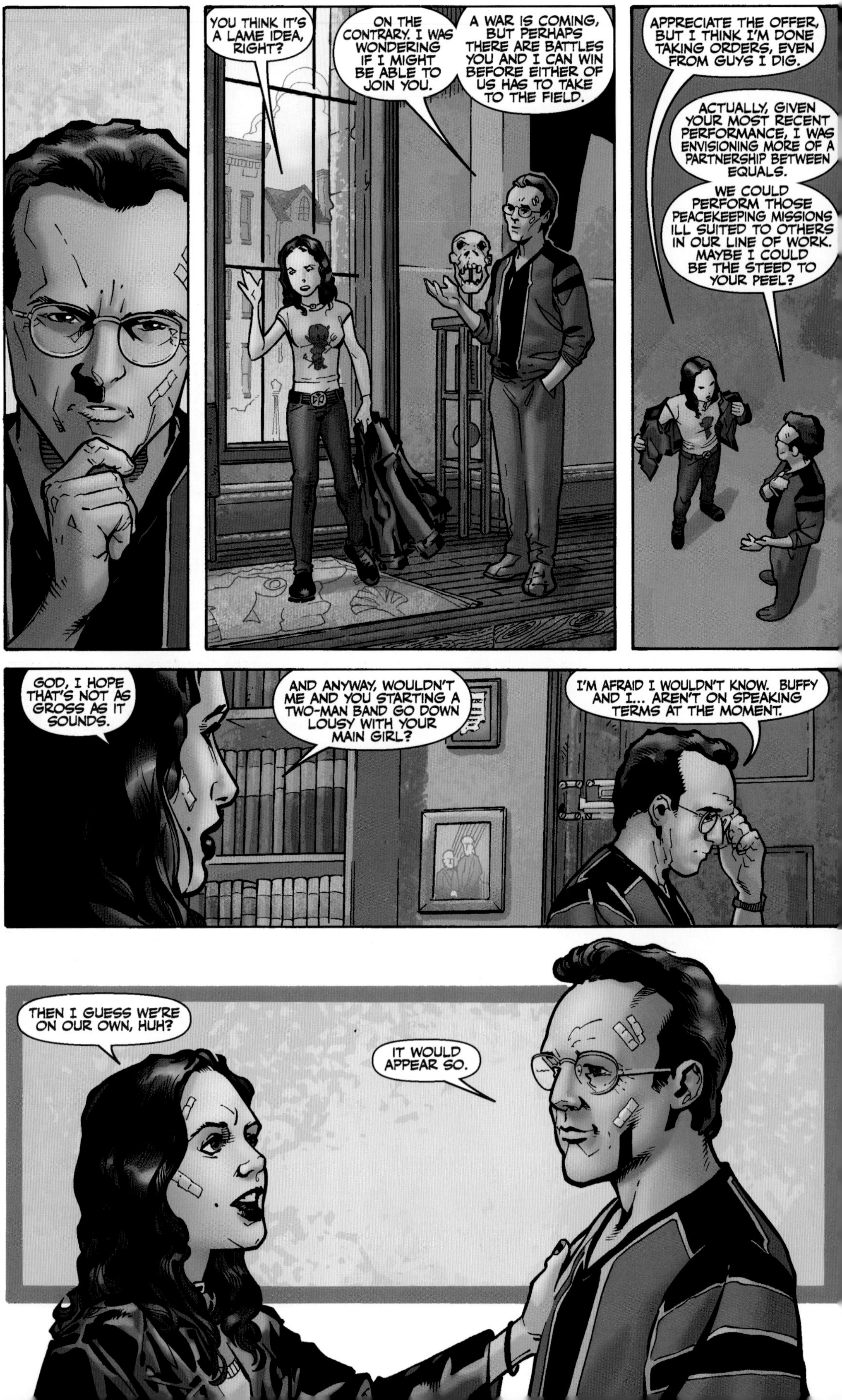
YOU THINK IT'S A LAME IDEA, RIGHT?
ON THE CONTRARY. I WAS WONDERING IF I MIGHT BE ABLE TO JOIN YOU.
A WAR IS COMING, BUT PERHAPS THERE ARE BATTLES YOU AND I CAN WIN BEFORE EITHER OF US HAS TO TAKE TO THE FIELD.
APPRECIATE THE OFFER, BUT I THINK I'M DONE TAKING ORDERS, EVEN FROM GUYS I DIG.
ACTUALLY, GIVEN YOUR MOST RECENT PERFORMANCE, I WAS ENVISIONING MORE OF A PARTNERSHIP BETWEEN EQUALS.
WE COULD PERFORM THOSE PEACEKEEPING MISSIONS ILL SUITED TO OTHERS IN OUR LINE OF WORK. MAYBE I COULD BE THE STEED TO YOUR PEEL?
GOD, I HOPE THAT'S NOT AS GROSS AS IT SOUNDS.
AND ANYWAY, WOULDN'T ME AND YOU STARTING A TWO-MAN BAND GO DOWN LOUSY WITH YOUR MAIN GIRL?
I'M AFRAID I WOULDN'T KNOW. BUFFY AND I... AREN'T ON SPEAKING TERMS AT THE MOMENT.
THEN I GUESS WE'RE ON OUR OWN, HUH?
IT WOULD APPEAR SO.

"BUT PERHAPS WE CAN BE ON OUR OWN TOGETHER."

TWILIGHT? YOU THERE?

"I HUMBLY REQUEST YOUR AUDIENCE" AND ALL THAT CRAP.

I BEAR YOUR MARK. NOW GIVE ME MY DAMN AUDIENCE!

CALM YOURSELF, LIEUTENANT MOLTER.

YOU'RE NOT GONNA BE WALKING ON AIR WHEN YOU HEAR WHAT I HAVE TO SAY. OUR MAN ON THE INSIDE CONFIRMS THAT SUMMERS IS STILL ALIVE. YOUR GOONS FAILED.

RODEN AND GENEVIEVE WERE NOT MY MINIONS... THEY WERE MY TARGETS.

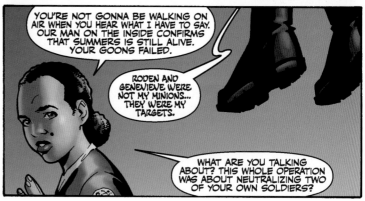

WHAT ARE YOU TALKING ABOUT? THIS WHOLE OPERATION WAS ABOUT NEUTRALIZING TWO OF YOUR OWN SOLDIERS?

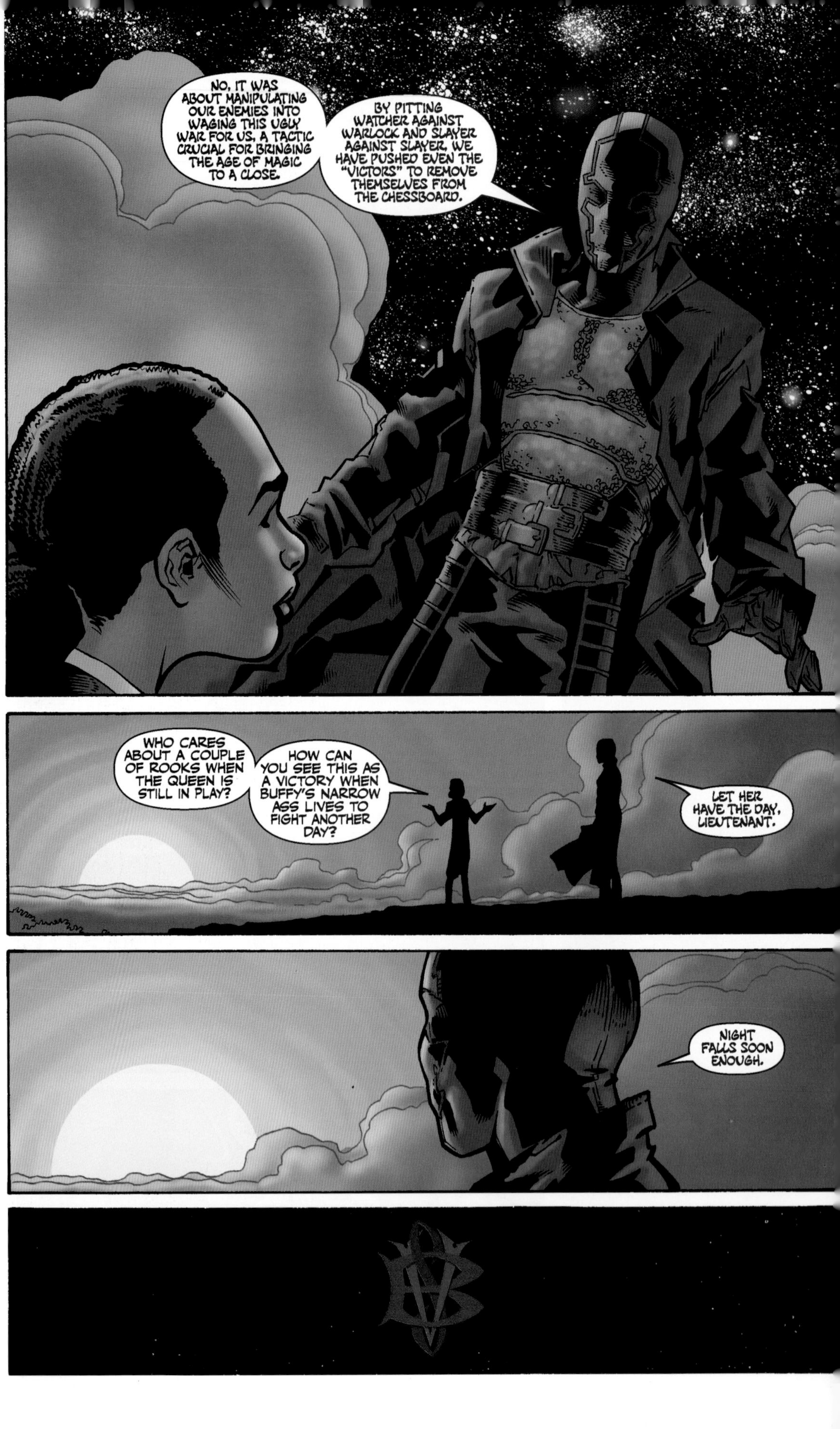

NO, IT WAS ABOUT MANIPULATING OUR ENEMIES INTO WAGING THIS UGLY WAR FOR US, A TACTIC CRUCIAL FOR BRINGING THE AGE OF MAGIC TO A CLOSE.
BY PITTING WATCHER AGAINST WARLOCK AND SLAYER AGAINST SLAYER, WE HAVE PUSHED EVEN THE "VICTORS" TO REMOVE THEMSELVES FROM THE CHESSBOARD.
WHO CARES ABOUT A COUPLE OF ROOKS WHEN THE QUEEN IS STILL IN PLAY?
HOW CAN YOU SEE THIS AS A VICTORY WHEN BUFFY'S NARROW ASS LIVES TO FIGHT ANOTHER DAY?
LET HER HAVE THE DAY, LIEUTENANT.
NIGHT FALLS SOON ENOUGH.

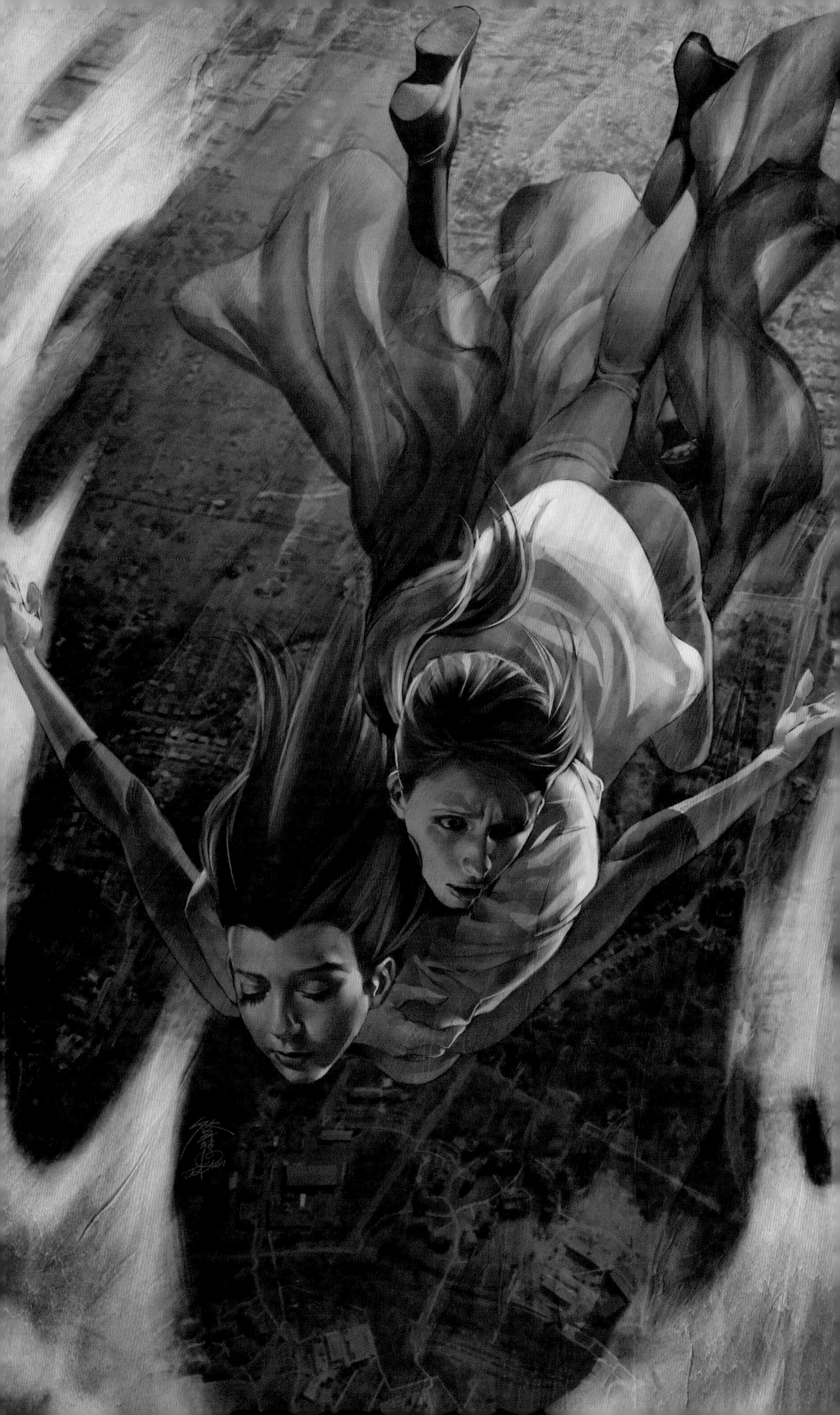

ANYWHERE BUT HERE

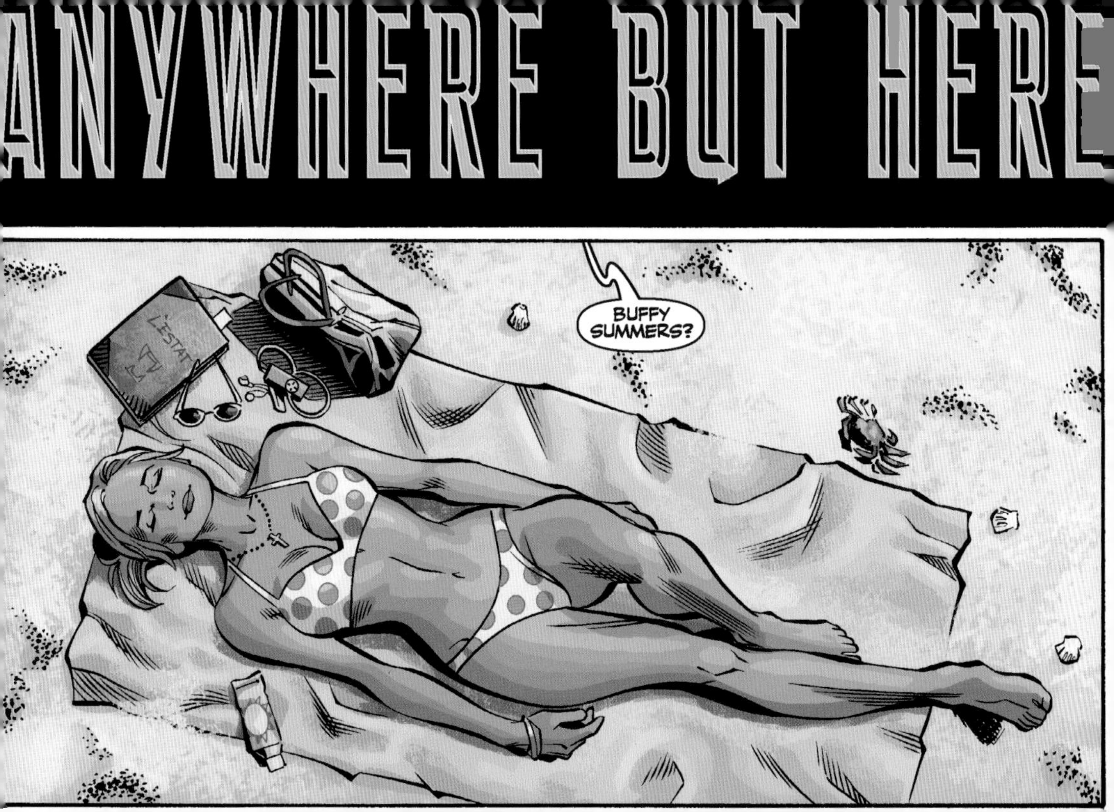
BUFFY SUMMERS?

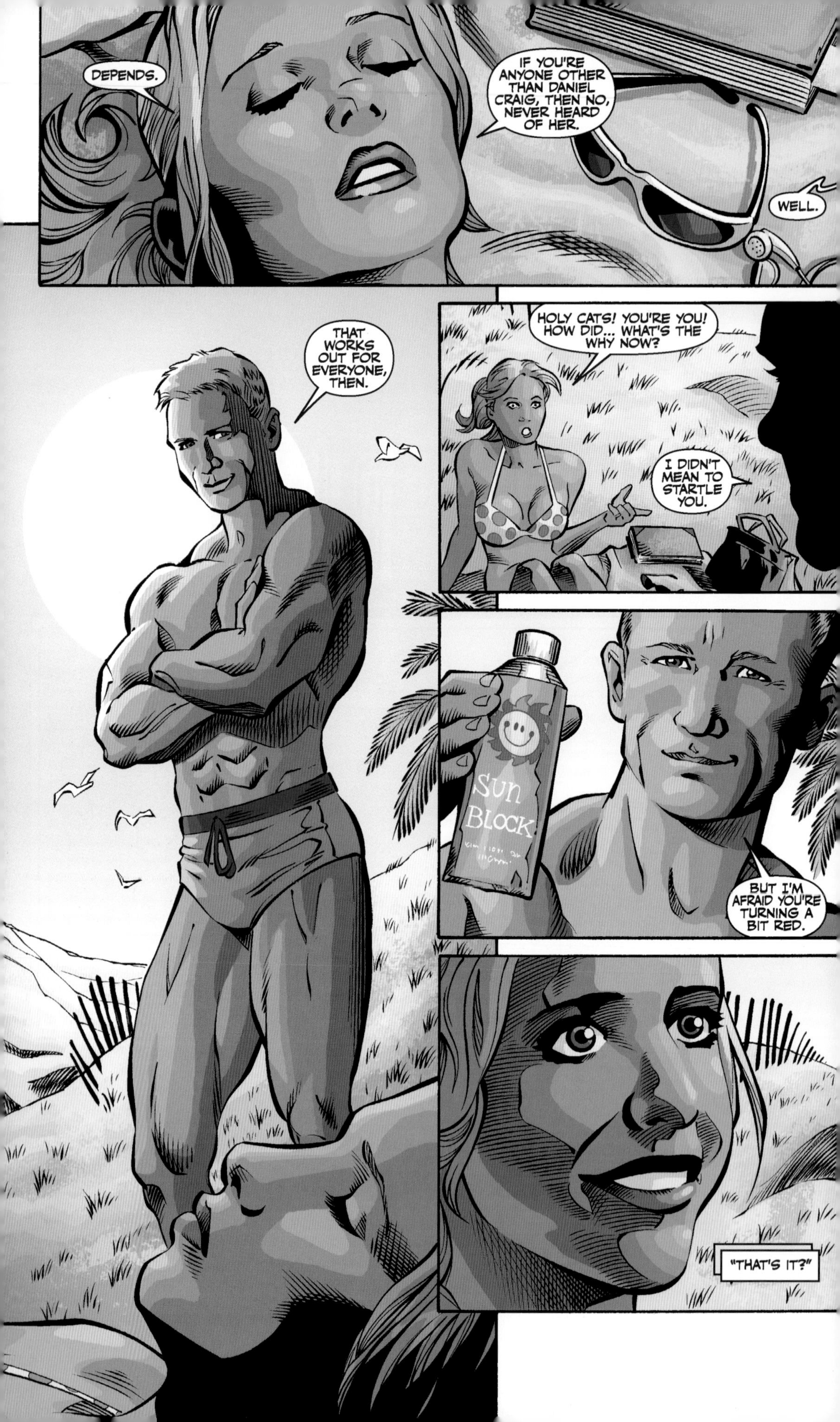
DEPENDS.
IF YOU'RE ANYONE OTHER THAN DANIEL CRAIG, THEN NO, NEVER HEARD OF HER.
WELL.
THAT WORKS OUT FOR EVERYONE, THEN.
HOLY CATS! YOU'RE YOU! HOW DID... WHAT'S THE WHY NOW?
I DIDN'T MEAN TO STARTLE YOU.
SUN BLOCK
BUT I'M AFRAID YOU'RE TURNING A BIT RED.
"THAT'S IT?"

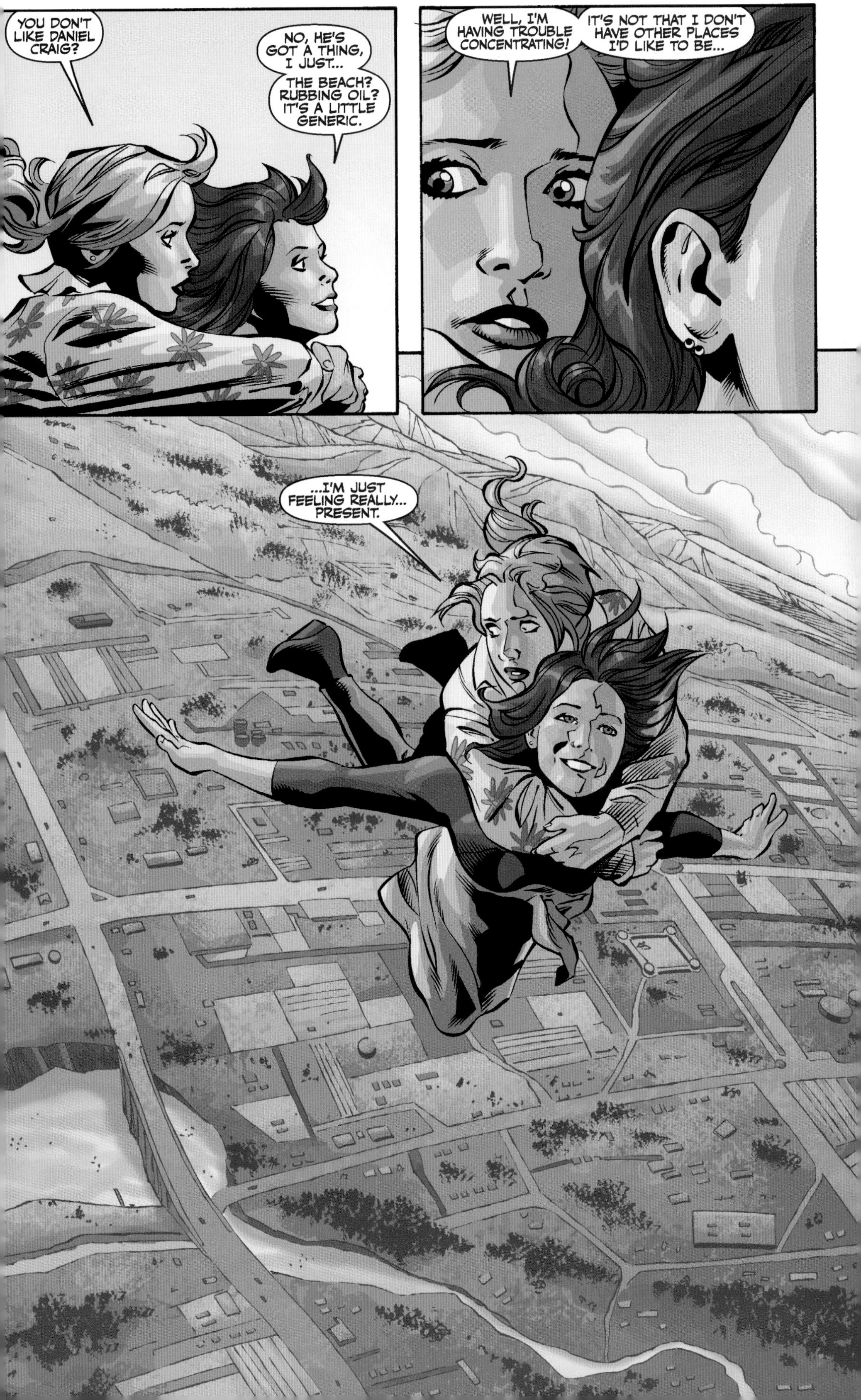
YOU DON'T LIKE DANIEL CRAIG?
NO, HE'S GOT A THING, I JUST...
THE BEACH? RUBBING OIL? IT'S A LITTLE GENERIC.
WELL, I'M HAVING TROUBLE CONCENTRATING!
IT'S NOT THAT I DON'T HAVE OTHER PLACES I'D LIKE TO BE...
...I'M JUST FEELING REALLY... PRESENT.

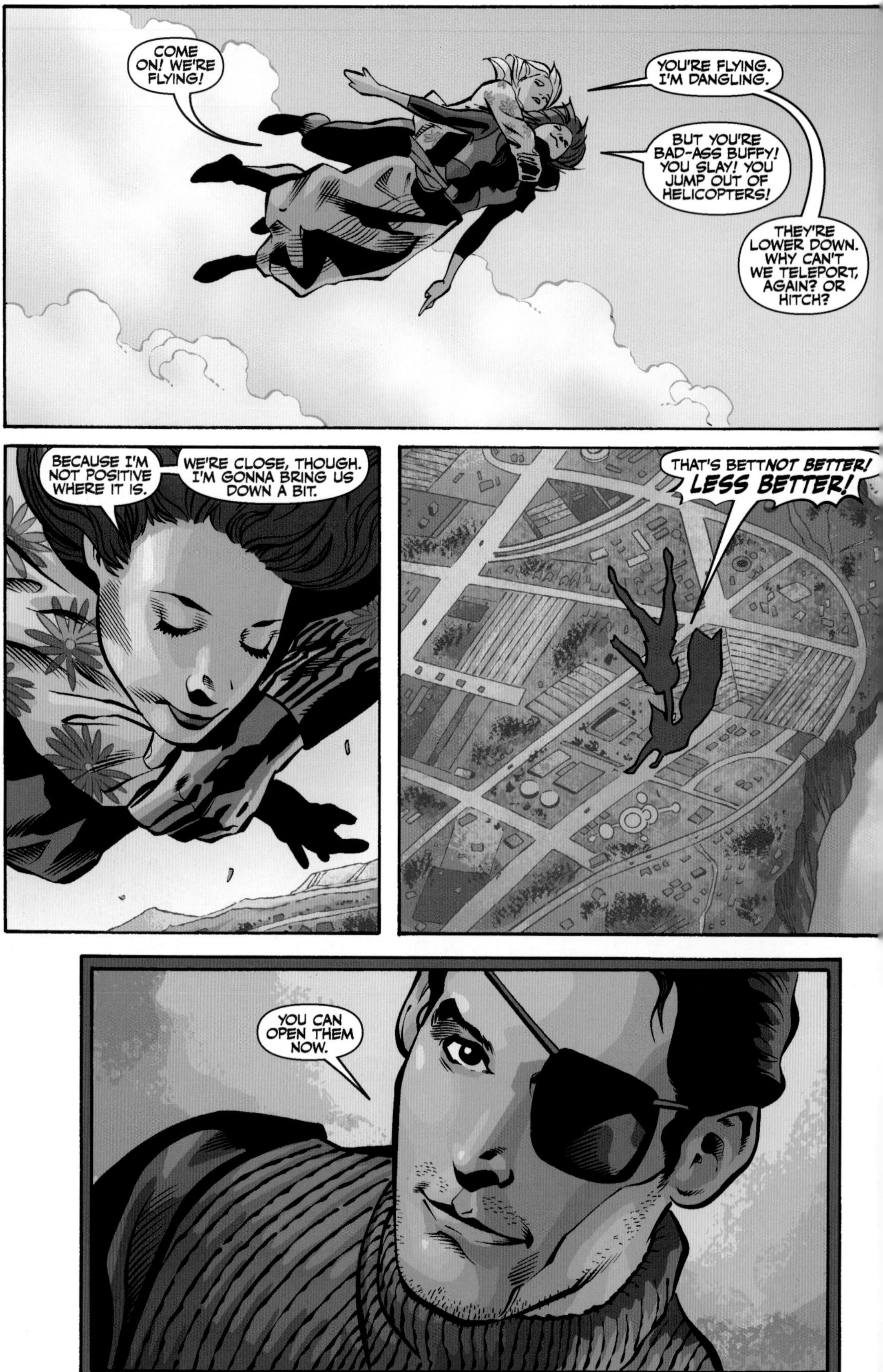
COME ON! WE'RE FLYING!
YOU'RE FLYING. I'M DANGLING.
BUT YOU'RE BAD-ASS BUFFY! YOU SLAY! YOU JUMP OUT OF HELICOPTERS!
THEY'RE LOWER DOWN. WHY CAN'T WE TELEPORT, AGAIN? OR HITCH?
BECAUSE I'M NOT POSITIVE WHERE IT IS.
WE'RE CLOSE, THOUGH. I'M GONNA BRING US DOWN A BIT.
THAT'S BETTNOT BETTER! LESS BETTER!
YOU CAN OPEN THEM NOW.

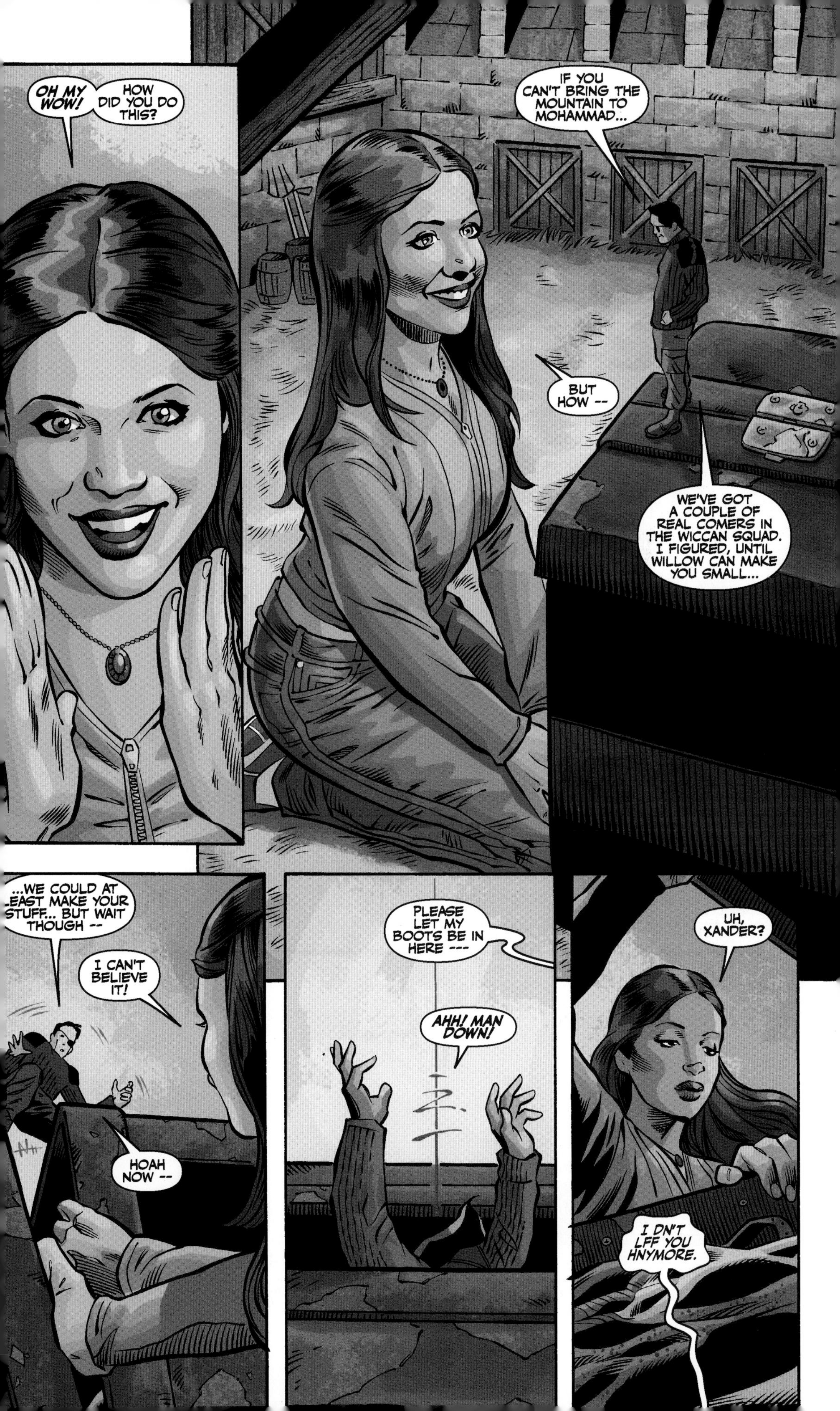
OH MY WOW!
HOW DID YOU DO THIS?
IF YOU CAN'T BRING THE MOUNTAIN TO MOHAMMAD...
BUT HOW --
WE'VE GOT A COUPLE OF REAL COMERS IN THE WICCAN SQUAD. I FIGURED, UNTIL WILLOW CAN MAKE YOU SMALL...
...WE COULD AT LEAST MAKE YOUR STUFF... BUT WAIT THOUGH --
I CAN'T BELIEVE IT!
HOAH NOW --
PLEASE LET MY BOOTS BE IN HERE ---
AHH! MAN DOWN!
UH, XANDER?
I DN'T LFF YOU HNYMORE.

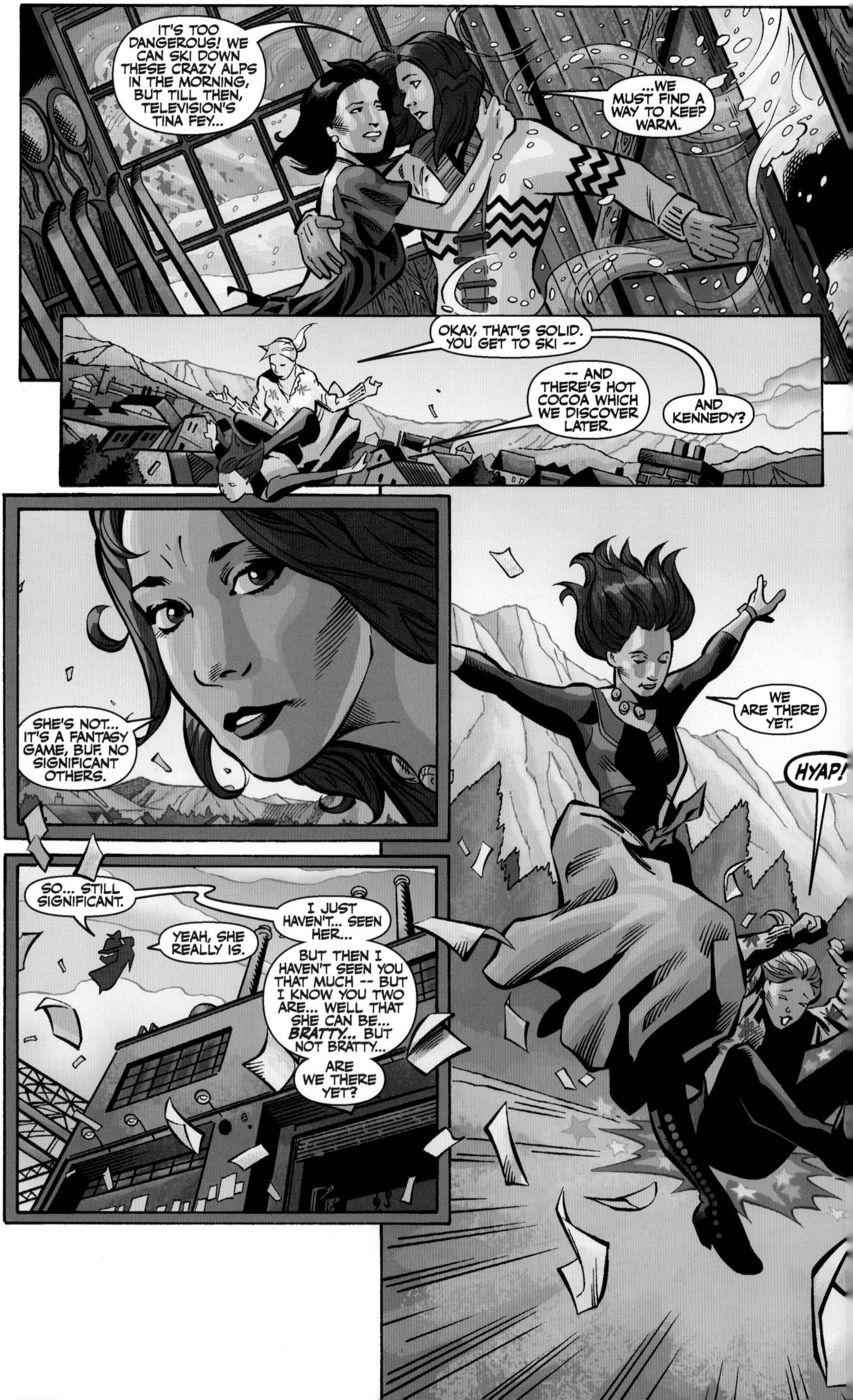
IT'S TOO DANGEROUS! WE CAN SKI DOWN THESE CRAZY ALPS IN THE MORNING, BUT TILL THEN, TELEVISION'S TINA FEY...
...WE MUST FIND A WAY TO KEEP WARM.
OKAY, THAT'S SOLID. YOU GET TO SKI --
-- AND THERE'S HOT COCOA WHICH WE DISCOVER LATER.
AND KENNEDY?
SHE'S NOT... IT'S A FANTASY GAME, BUF. NO SIGNIFICANT OTHERS.
SO... STILL SIGNIFICANT.
YEAH, SHE REALLY IS.
I JUST HAVEN'T... SEEN HER...
BUT THEN I HAVEN'T SEEN YOU THAT MUCH -- BUT I KNOW YOU TWO ARE... WELL THAT SHE CAN BE... BRATTY... BUT NOT BRATTY...
ARE WE THERE YET?
WE ARE THERE YET.
HYAP!

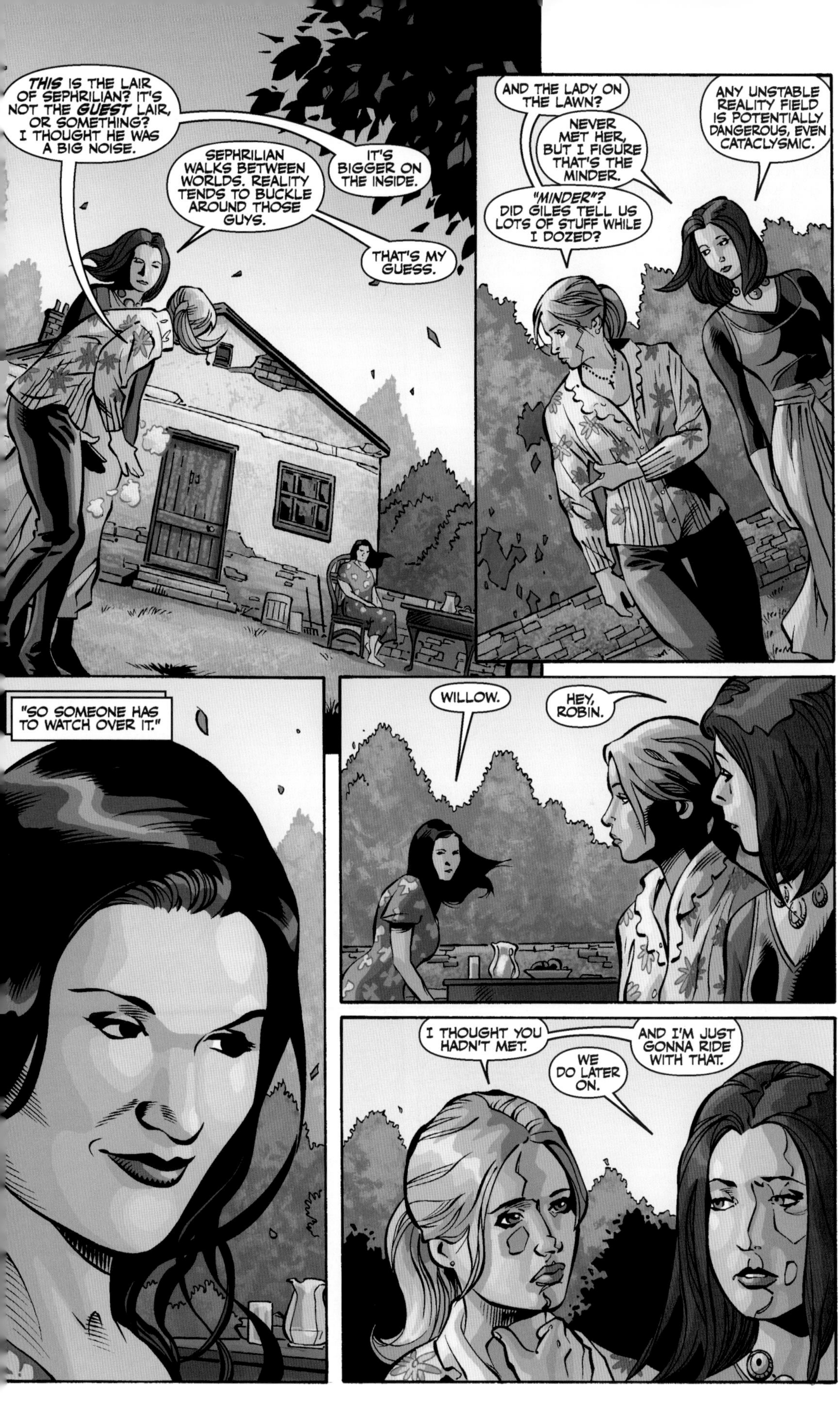

THIS IS THE LAIR OF SEPHRILIAN? IT'S NOT THE *GUEST* LAIR, OR SOMETHING? I THOUGHT HE WAS A BIG NOISE.
IT'S BIGGER ON THE INSIDE.
SEPHRILIAN WALKS BETWEEN WORLDS. REALITY TENDS TO BUCKLE AROUND THOSE GUYS.
THAT'S MY GUESS.
AND THE LADY ON THE LAWN?
NEVER MET HER, BUT I FIGURE THAT'S THE MINDER.
"MINDER"? DID GILES TELL US LOTS OF STUFF WHILE I DOZED?
ANY UNSTABLE REALITY FIELD IS POTENTIALLY DANGEROUS, EVEN CATACLYSMIC.
"SO SOMEONE HAS TO WATCH OVER IT."
WILLOW.
HEY, ROBIN.
I THOUGHT YOU HADN'T MET.
WE DO LATER ON.
AND I'M JUST GONNA RIDE WITH THAT.

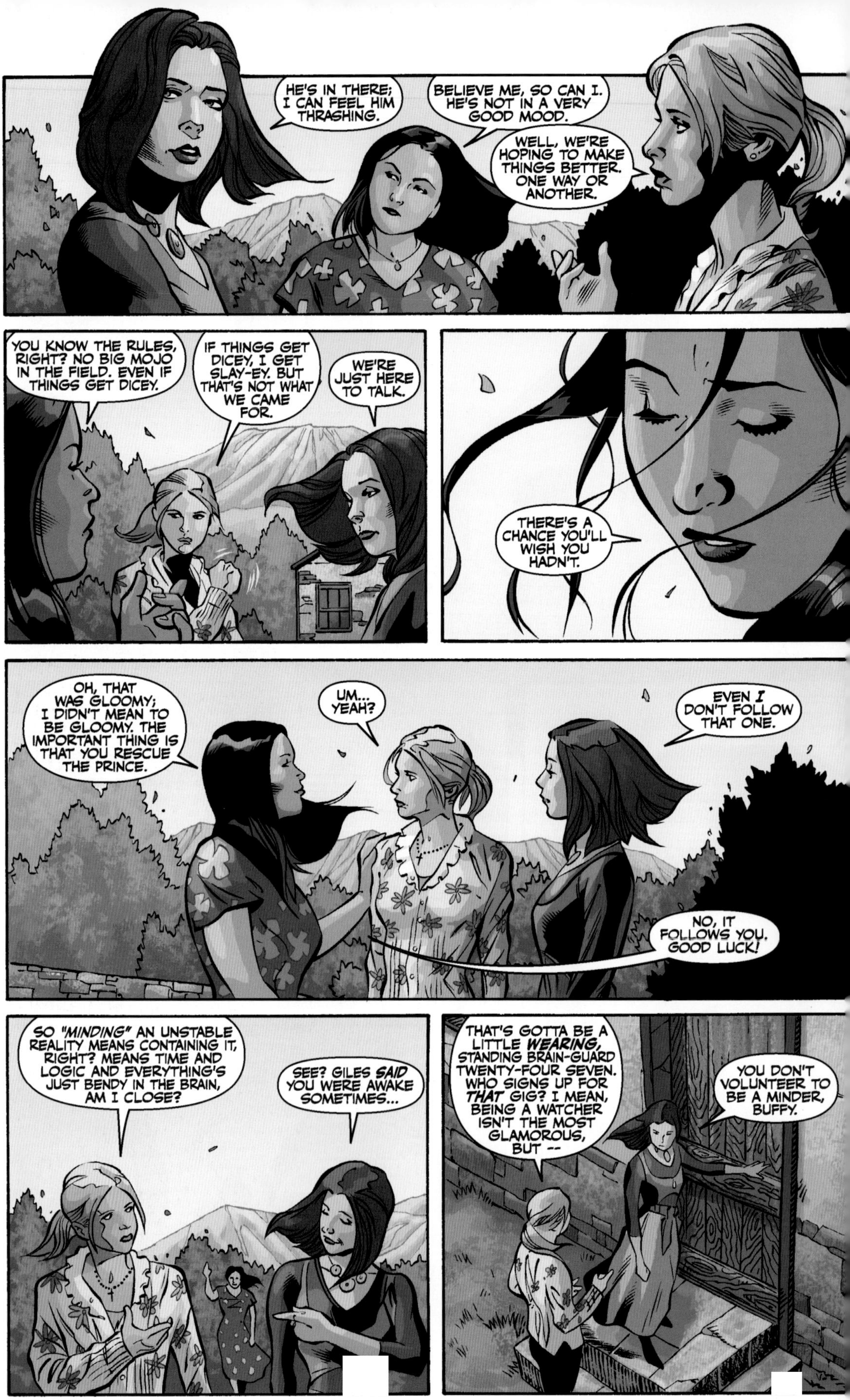
HE'S IN THERE; I CAN FEEL HIM THRASHING.
BELIEVE ME, SO CAN I. HE'S NOT IN A VERY GOOD MOOD.
WELL, WE'RE HOPING TO MAKE THINGS BETTER. ONE WAY OR ANOTHER.
YOU KNOW THE RULES, RIGHT? NO BIG MOJO IN THE FIELD. EVEN IF THINGS GET DICEY.
IF THINGS GET DICEY, I GET SLAY-EY. BUT THAT'S NOT WHAT WE CAME FOR.
WE'RE JUST HERE TO TALK.
THERE'S A CHANCE YOU'LL WISH YOU HADN'T.
OH, THAT WAS GLOOMY; I DIDN'T MEAN TO BE GLOOMY. THE IMPORTANT THING IS THAT YOU RESCUE THE PRINCE.
UM... YEAH?
EVEN *I* DON'T FOLLOW THAT ONE.
NO, IT FOLLOWS YOU. GOOD LUCK!
SO "*MINDING*" AN UNSTABLE REALITY MEANS CONTAINING IT, RIGHT? MEANS TIME AND LOGIC AND EVERYTHING'S JUST BENDY IN THE BRAIN, AM I CLOSE?
SEE? GILES *SAID* YOU WERE AWAKE SOMETIMES...
THAT'S GOTTA BE A LITTLE *WEARING*, STANDING BRAIN-GUARD TWENTY-FOUR SEVEN. WHO SIGNS UP FOR *THAT* GIG? I MEAN, BEING A WATCHER ISN'T THE MOST GLAMOROUS, BUT --
YOU DON'T VOLUNTEER TO BE A MINDER, BUFFY.

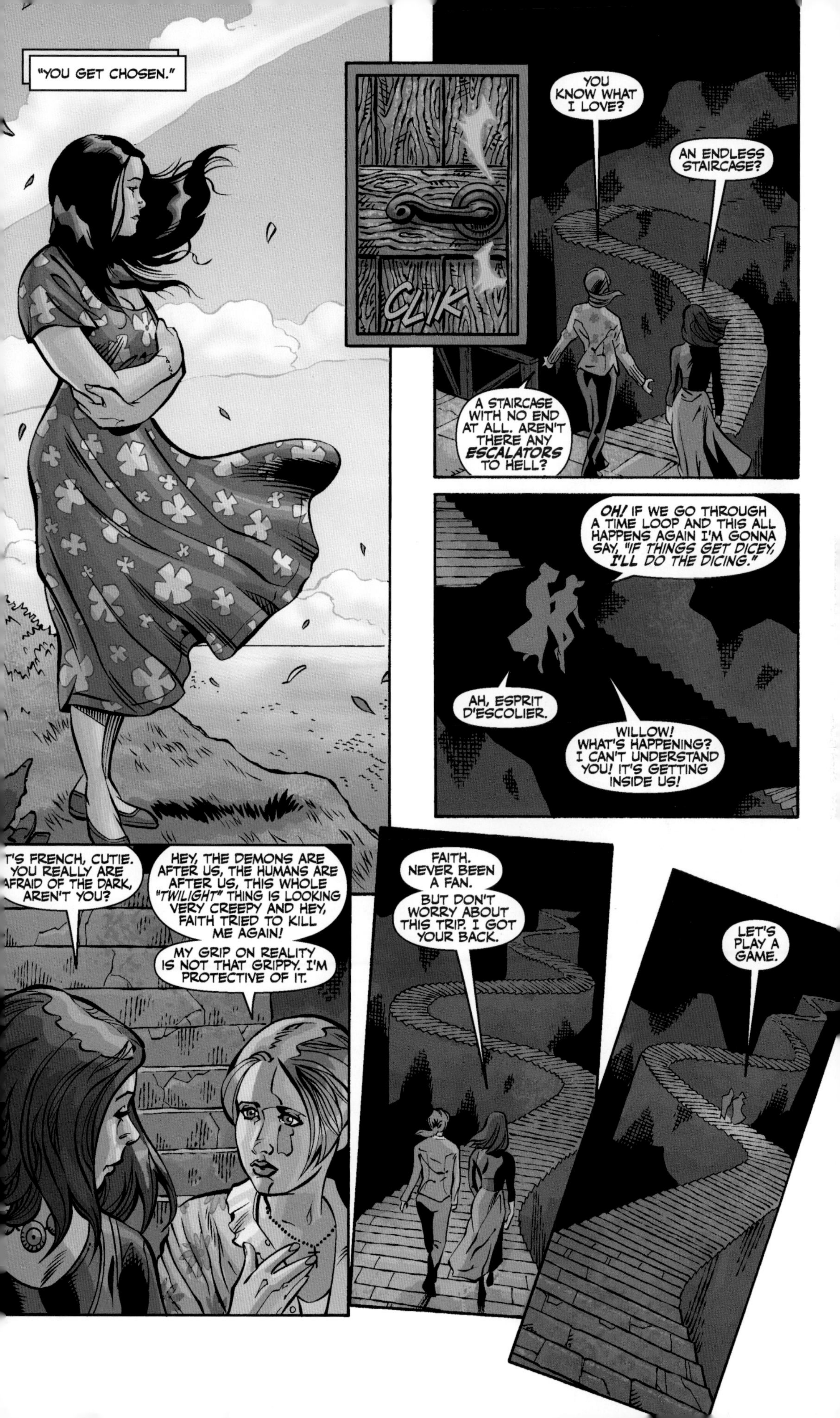
"YOU GET CHOSEN."
CLIK
YOU KNOW WHAT I LOVE?
AN ENDLESS STAIRCASE?
A STAIRCASE WITH NO END AT ALL. AREN'T THERE ANY ESCALATORS TO HELL?
OH! IF WE GO THROUGH A TIME LOOP AND THIS ALL HAPPENS AGAIN I'M GONNA SAY, "IF THINGS GET DICEY, I'LL DO THE DICING."
AH, ESPRIT D'ESCOLIER.
WILLOW! WHAT'S HAPPENING? I CAN'T UNDERSTAND YOU! IT'S GETTING INSIDE US!
T'S FRENCH, CUTIE. YOU REALLY ARE AFRAID OF THE DARK, AREN'T YOU?
HEY, THE DEMONS ARE AFTER US, THE HUMANS ARE AFTER US, THIS WHOLE "TWILIGHT" THING IS LOOKING VERY CREEPY AND HEY, FAITH TRIED TO KILL ME AGAIN!
MY GRIP ON REALITY IS NOT THAT GRIPPY. I'M PROTECTIVE OF IT.
FAITH. NEVER BEEN A FAN.
BUT DON'T WORRY ABOUT THIS TRIP. I GOT YOUR BACK.
LET'S PLAY A GAME.

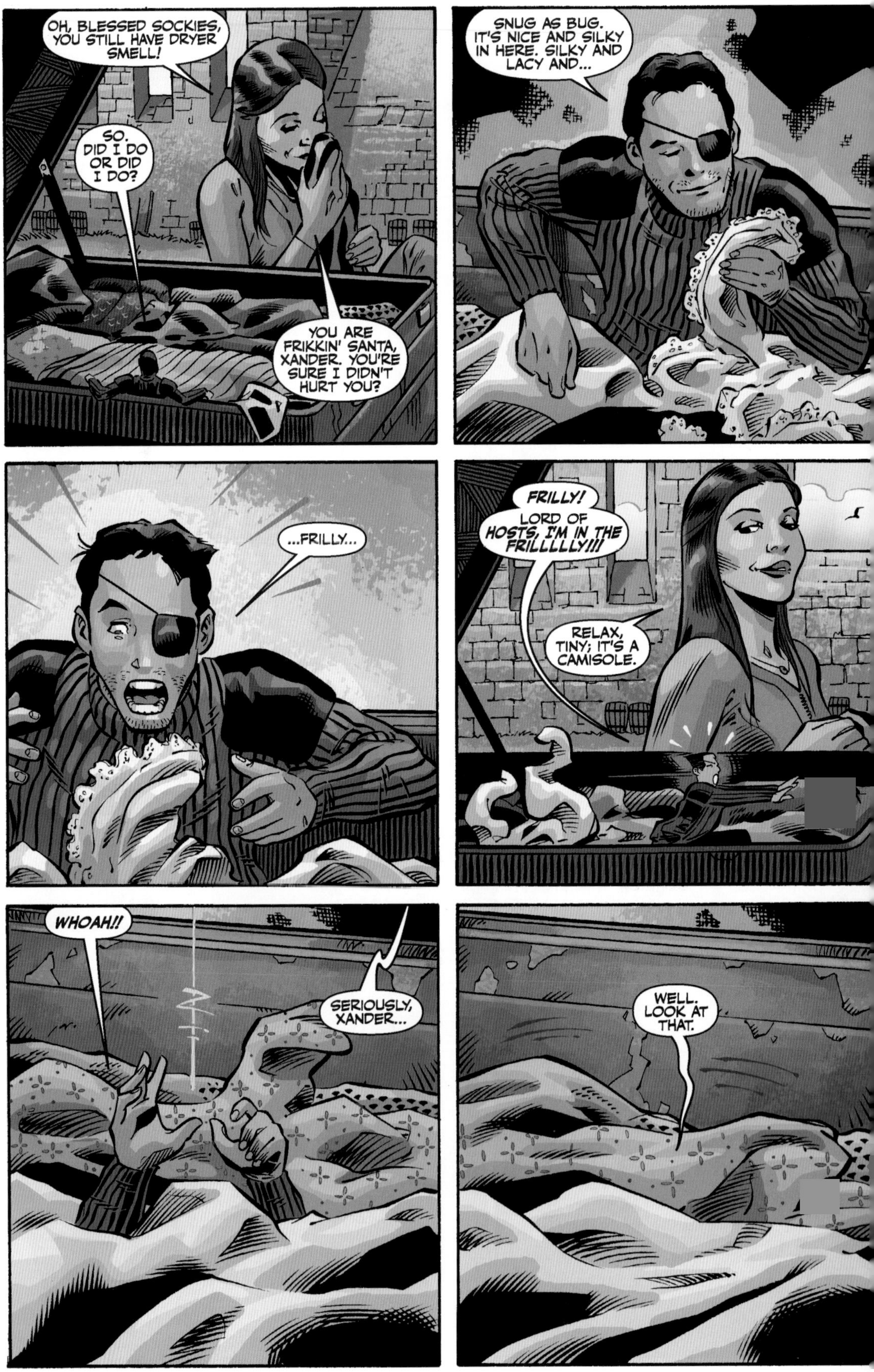
OH, BLESSED SOCKIES, YOU STILL HAVE DRYER SMELL!
SO. DID I DO OR DID I DO?
YOU ARE FRIKKIN' SANTA, XANDER. YOU'RE SURE I DIDN'T HURT YOU?
SNUG AS BUG. IT'S NICE AND SILKY IN HERE. SILKY AND LACY AND...
...FRILLY...
FRILLY! LORD OF HOSTS, I'M IN THE FRILLLLLLY!!!
RELAX, TINY; IT'S A CAMISOLE.
WHOAH!!
SERIOUSLY, XANDER...
WELL. LOOK AT THAT.

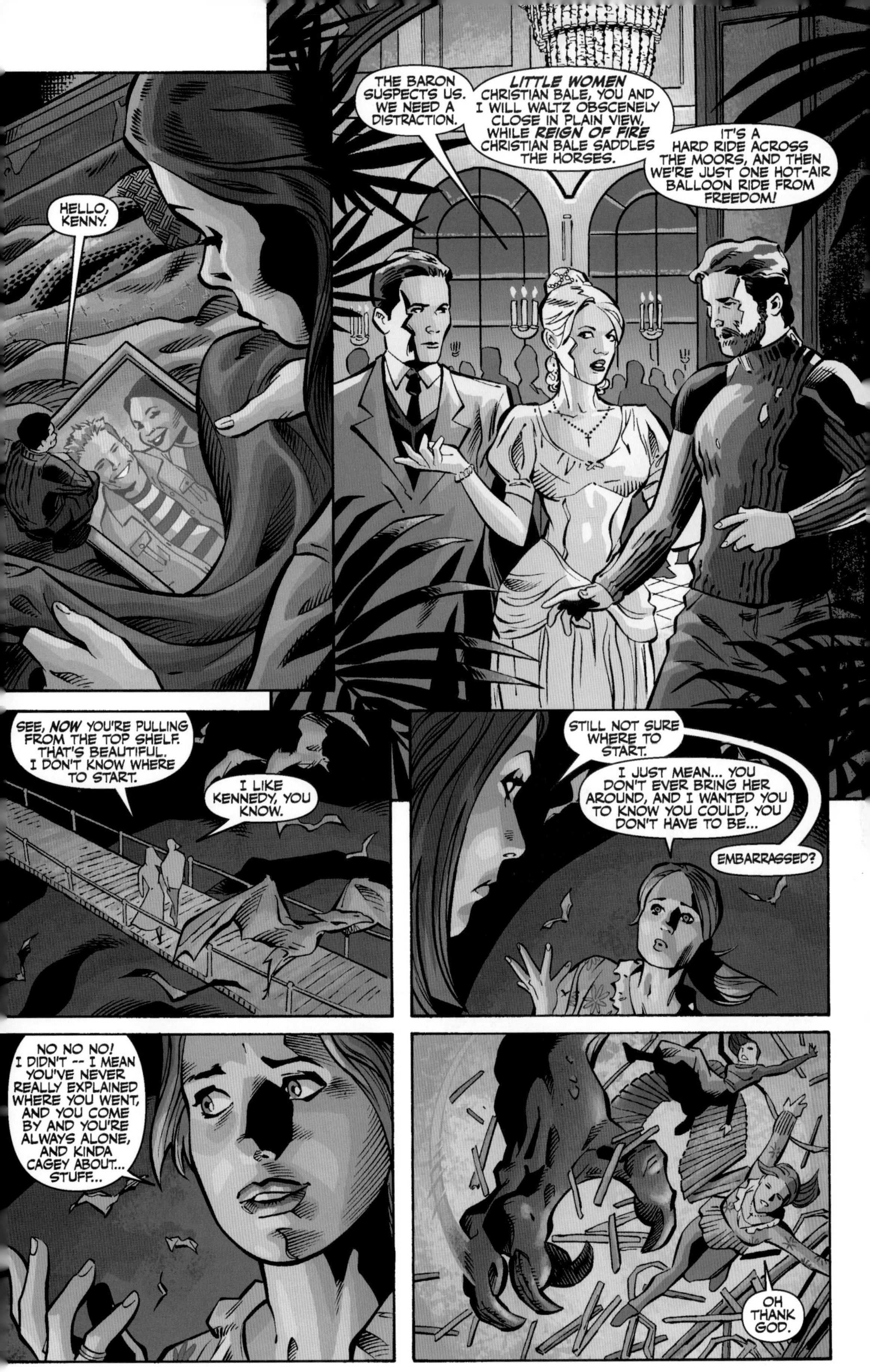
HELLO, KENNY.
THE BARON SUSPECTS US. WE NEED A DISTRACTION.
LITTLE WOMEN CHRISTIAN BALE, YOU AND I WILL WALTZ OBSCENELY CLOSE IN PLAIN VIEW, WHILE REIGN OF FIRE CHRISTIAN BALE SADDLES THE HORSES.
IT'S A HARD RIDE ACROSS THE MOORS, AND THEN WE'RE JUST ONE HOT-AIR BALLOON RIDE FROM FREEDOM!
SEE, NOW YOU'RE PULLING FROM THE TOP SHELF. THAT'S BEAUTIFUL. I DON'T KNOW WHERE TO START.
I LIKE KENNEDY, YOU KNOW.
STILL NOT SURE WHERE TO START.
I JUST MEAN... YOU DON'T EVER BRING HER AROUND, AND I WANTED YOU TO KNOW YOU COULD, YOU DON'T HAVE TO BE...
EMBARRASSED?
NO NO NO! I DIDN'T -- I MEAN YOU'VE NEVER REALLY EXPLAINED WHERE YOU WENT, AND YOU COME BY AND YOU'RE ALWAYS ALONE, AND KINDA CAGEY ABOUT... STUFF...
OH THANK GOD.

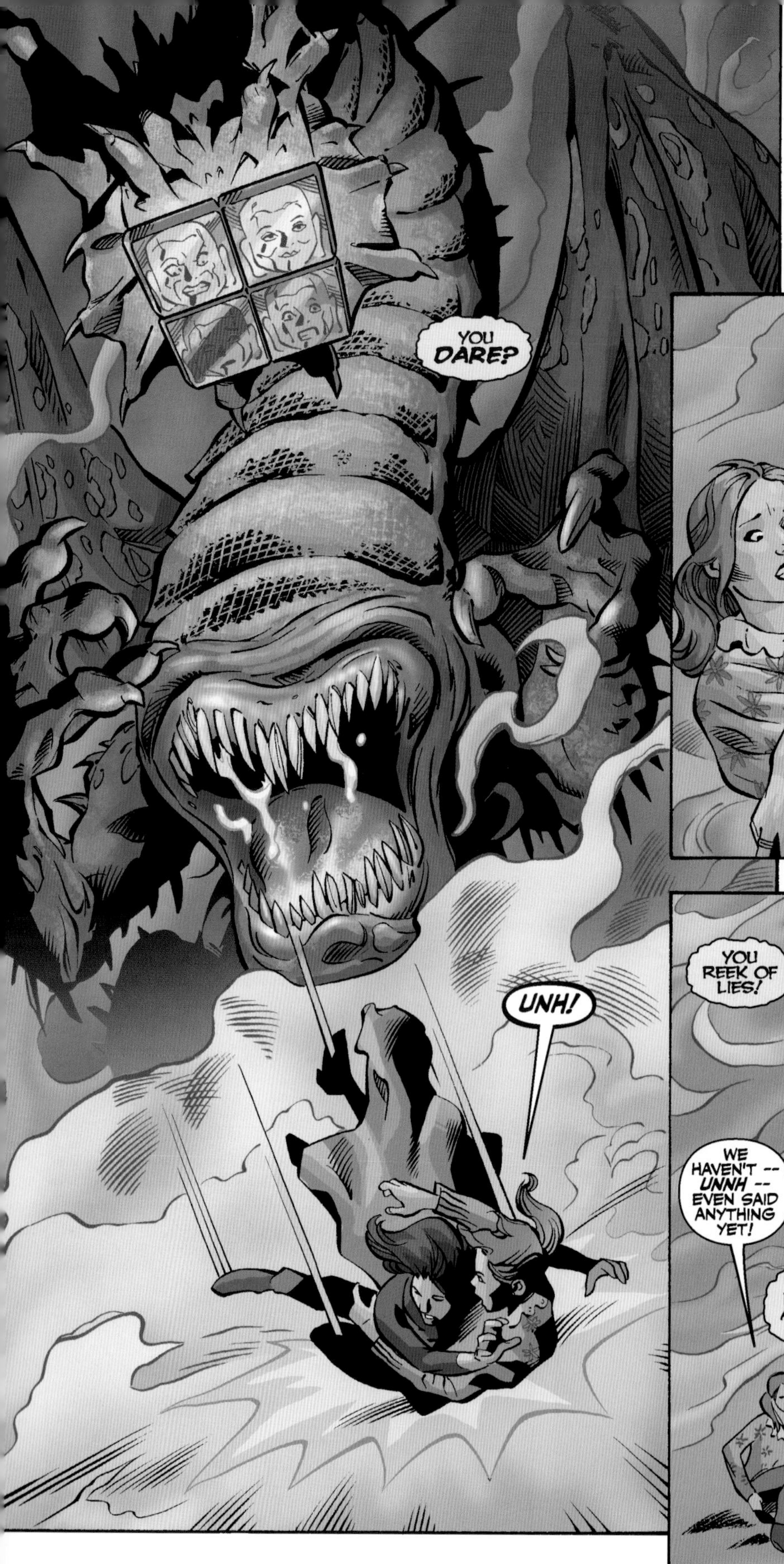
YOU *DARE?*
UNH!

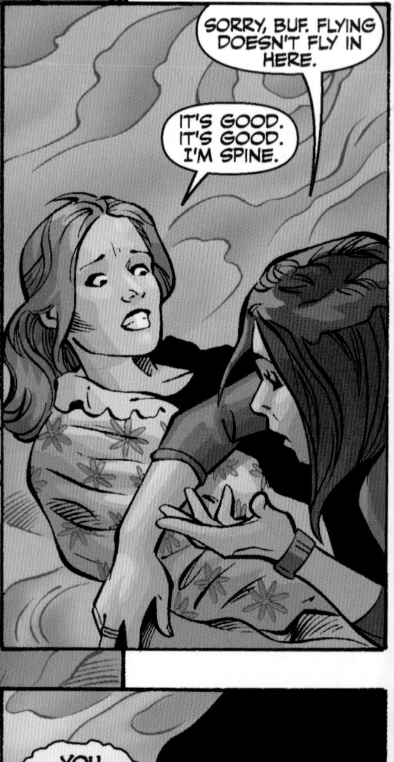
SORRY, BUF. FLYING DOESN'T FLY IN HERE.
IT'S GOOD. IT'S GOOD. I'M SPINE.

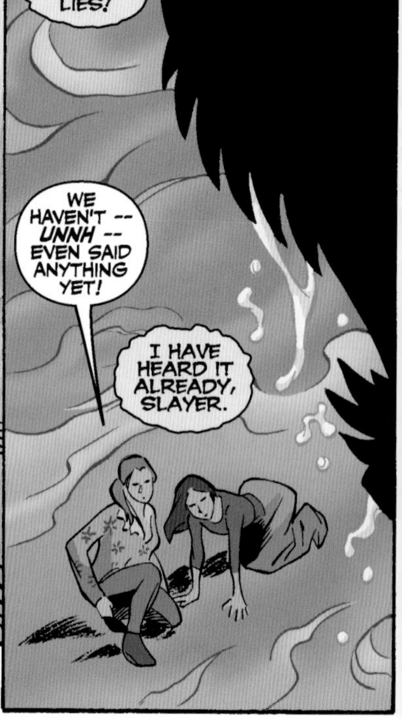
YOU REEK OF LIES!
WE HAVEN'T -- *UNNH* -- EVEN SAID ANYTHING YET!
I HAVE HEARD IT ALREADY, SLAYER.

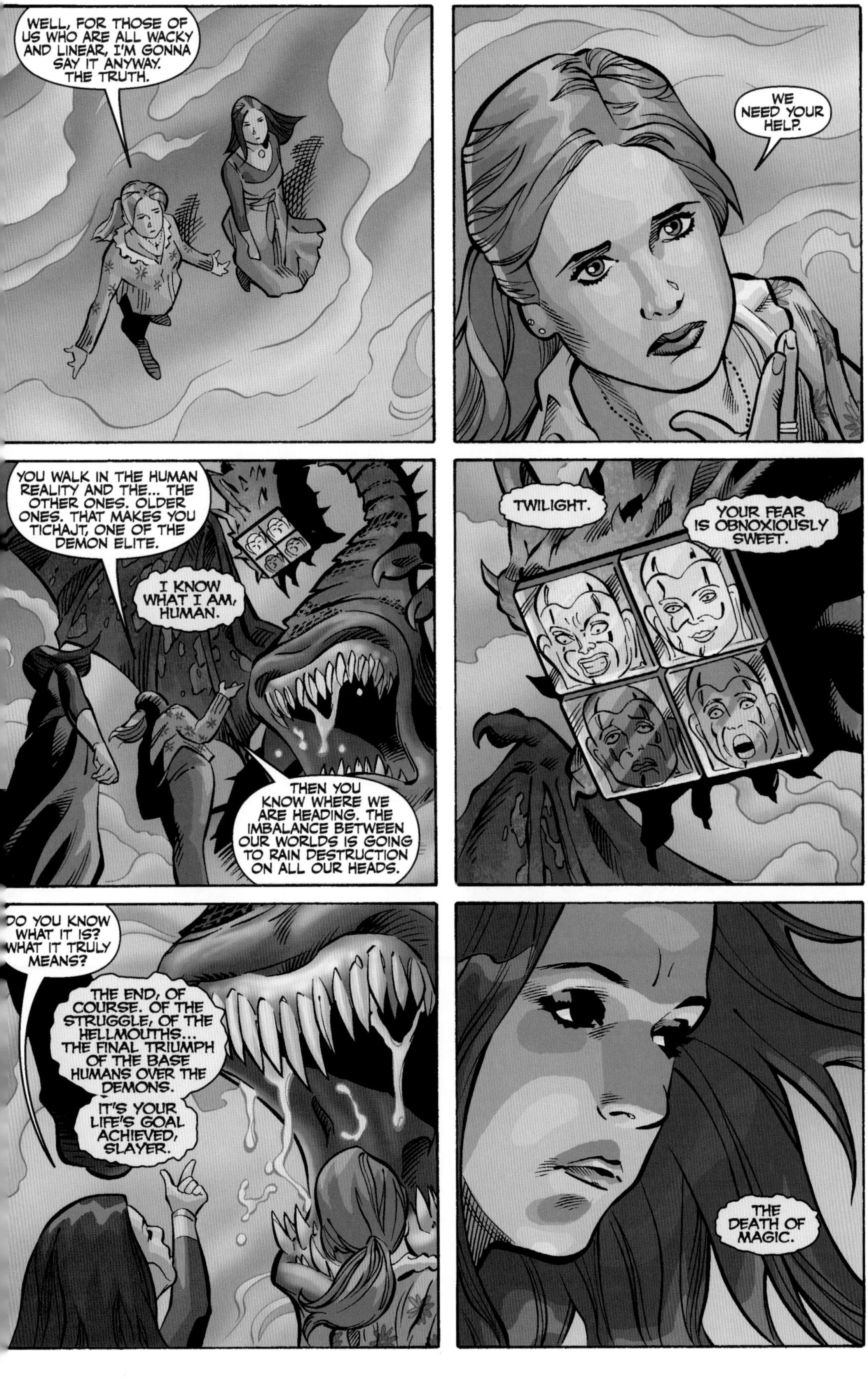
WELL, FOR THOSE OF US WHO ARE ALL WACKY AND LINEAR, I'M GONNA SAY IT ANYWAY. THE TRUTH.
WE NEED YOUR HELP.
YOU WALK IN THE HUMAN REALITY AND THE... THE OTHER ONES. OLDER ONES. THAT MAKES YOU TICHAJT, ONE OF THE DEMON ELITE.
I KNOW WHAT I AM, HUMAN.
THEN YOU KNOW WHERE WE ARE HEADING. THE IMBALANCE BETWEEN OUR WORLDS IS GOING TO RAIN DESTRUCTION ON ALL OUR HEADS.
TWILIGHT.
YOUR FEAR IS OBNOXIOUSLY SWEET.
DO YOU KNOW WHAT IT IS? WHAT IT TRULY MEANS?
THE END, OF COURSE. OF THE STRUGGLE, OF THE HELLMOUTHS... THE FINAL TRIUMPH OF THE BASE HUMANS OVER THE DEMONS.
IT'S YOUR LIFE'S GOAL ACHIEVED, SLAYER.
THE DEATH OF MAGIC.

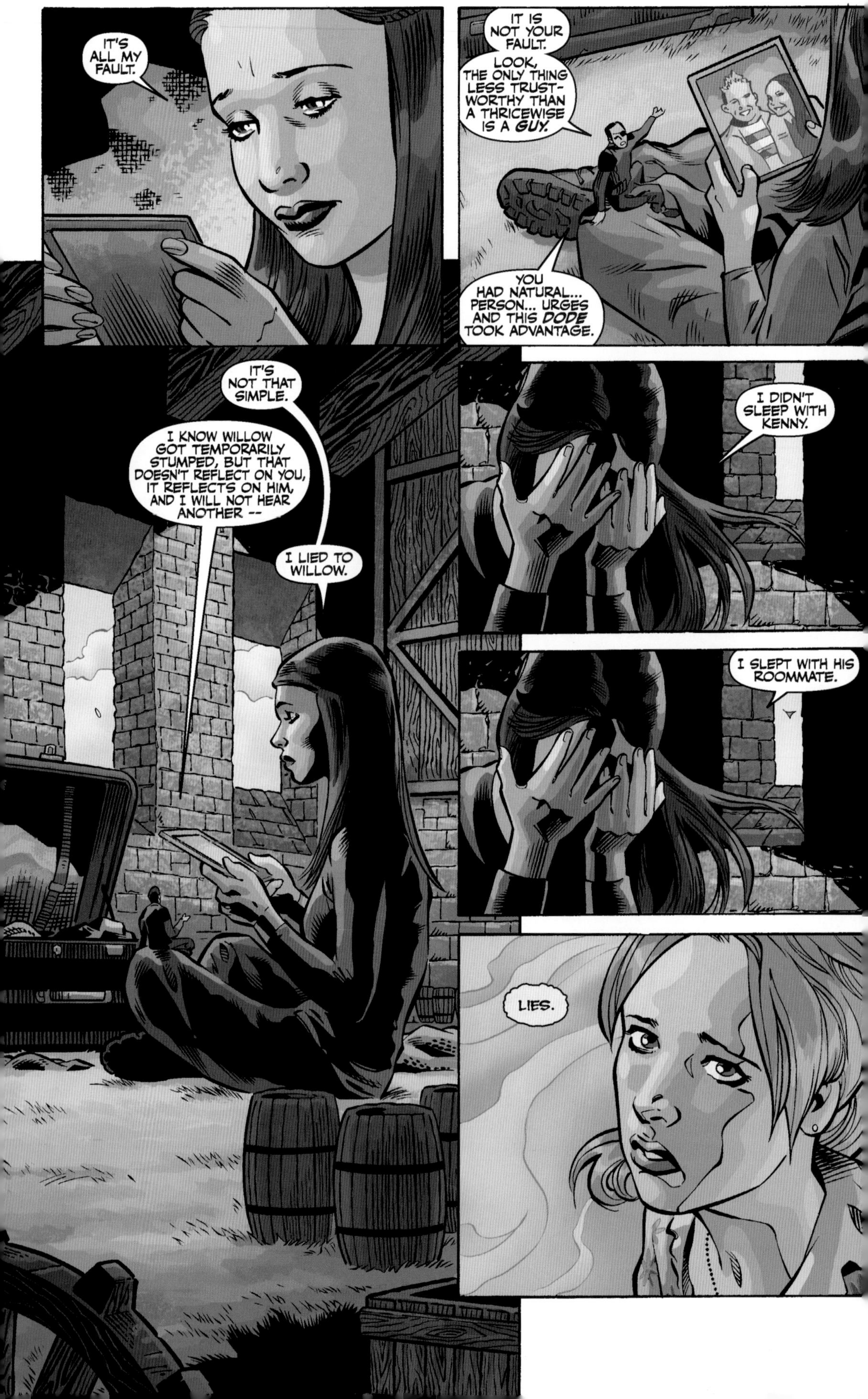
IT'S ALL MY FAULT.
IT IS NOT YOUR FAULT.
LOOK, THE ONLY THING LESS TRUST-WORTHY THAN A THRICEWISE IS A *GUY.*
YOU HAD NATURAL... PERSON... URGES AND THIS *DODE* TOOK ADVANTAGE.
IT'S NOT THAT SIMPLE.
I KNOW WILLOW GOT TEMPORARILY STUMPED, BUT THAT DOESN'T REFLECT ON YOU, IT REFLECTS ON HIM, AND I WILL NOT HEAR ANOTHER --
I LIED TO WILLOW.
I DIDN'T SLEEP WITH KENNY.
I SLEPT WITH HIS ROOMMATE.
LIES.

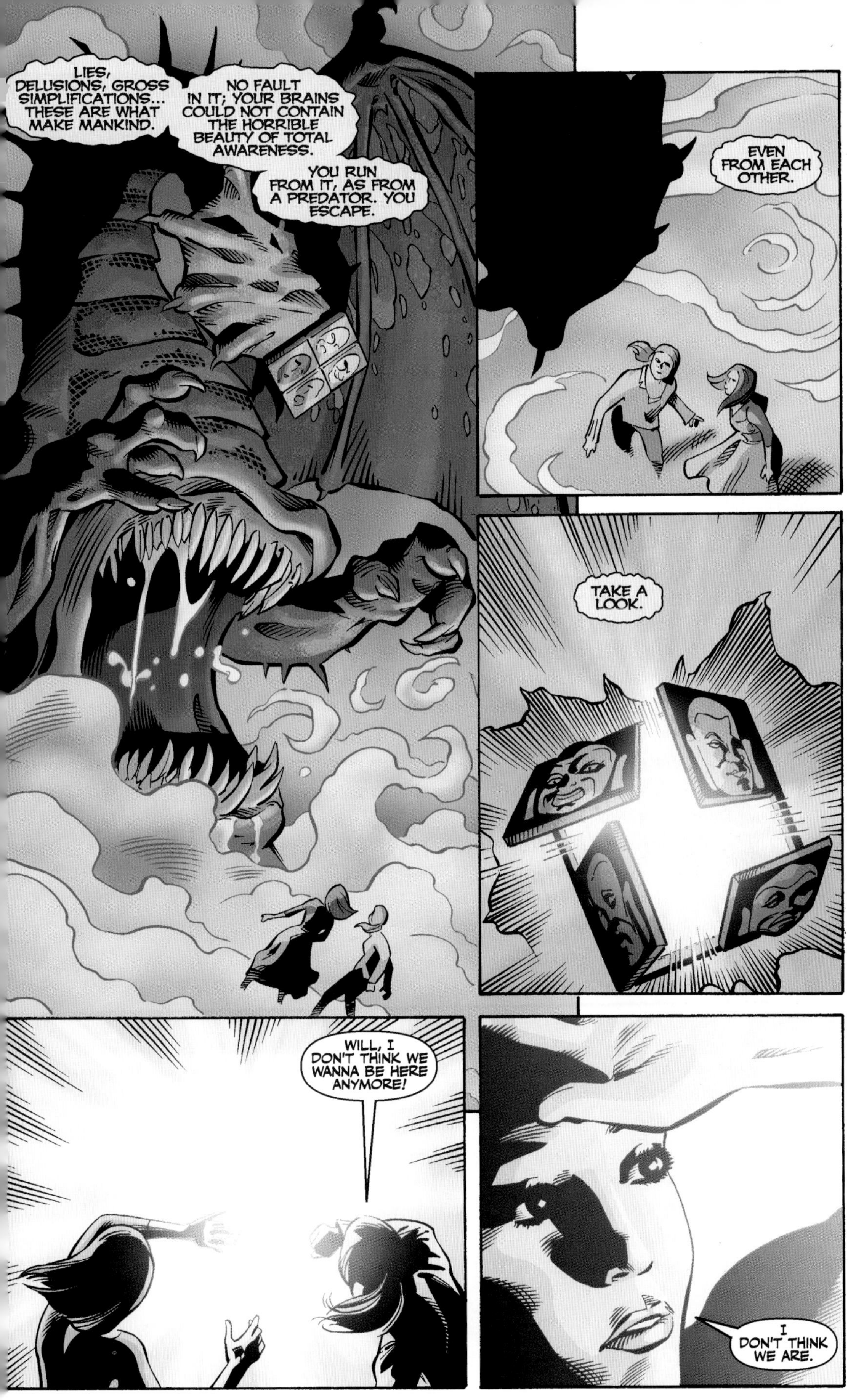
LIES, DELUSIONS, GROSS SIMPLIFICATIONS... THESE ARE WHAT MAKE MANKIND.
NO FAULT IN IT; YOUR BRAINS COULD NOT CONTAIN THE HORRIBLE BEAUTY OF TOTAL AWARENESS.
YOU RUN FROM IT, AS FROM A PREDATOR. YOU ESCAPE.
EVEN FROM EACH OTHER.
TAKE A LOOK.
WILL, I DON'T THINK WE WANNA BE HERE ANYMORE!
I DON'T THINK WE ARE.

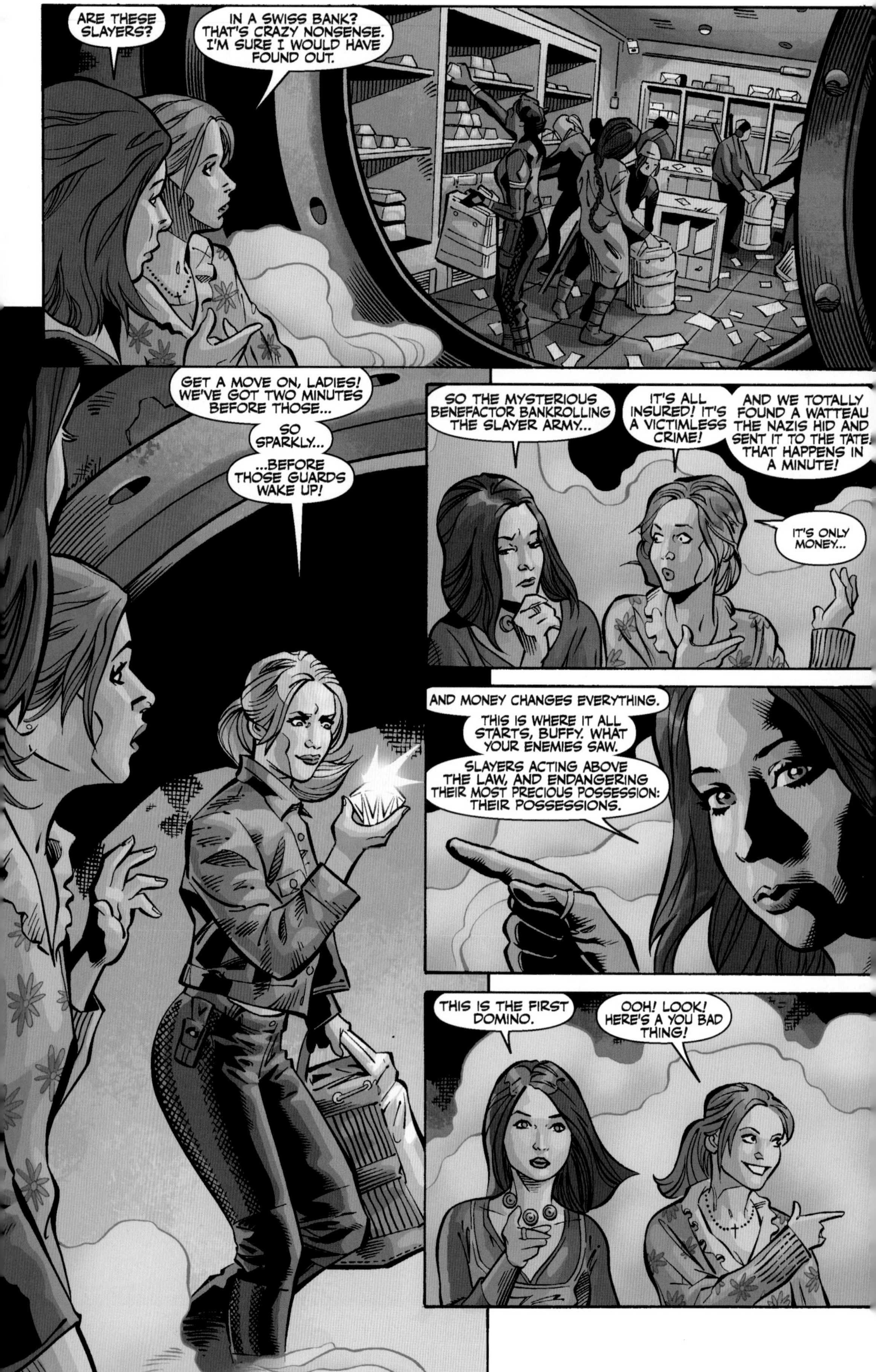
ARE THESE SLAYERS?
IN A SWISS BANK? THAT'S CRAZY NONSENSE. I'M SURE I WOULD HAVE FOUND OUT.
GET A MOVE ON, LADIES! WE'VE GOT TWO MINUTES BEFORE THOSE...
SO SPARKLY...
...BEFORE THOSE GUARDS WAKE UP!
SO THE MYSTERIOUS BENEFACTOR BANKROLLING THE SLAYER ARMY...
IT'S ALL INSURED! IT'S A VICTIMLESS CRIME!
AND WE TOTALLY FOUND A WATTEAU THE NAZIS HID AND SENT IT TO THE TATE. THAT HAPPENS IN A MINUTE!
IT'S ONLY MONEY...
AND MONEY CHANGES EVERYTHING.
THIS IS WHERE IT ALL STARTS, BUFFY. WHAT YOUR ENEMIES SAW.
SLAYERS ACTING ABOVE THE LAW, AND ENDANGERING THEIR MOST PRECIOUS POSSESSION: THEIR POSSESSIONS.
THIS IS THE FIRST DOMINO.
OOH! LOOK! HERE'S A YOU BAD THING!

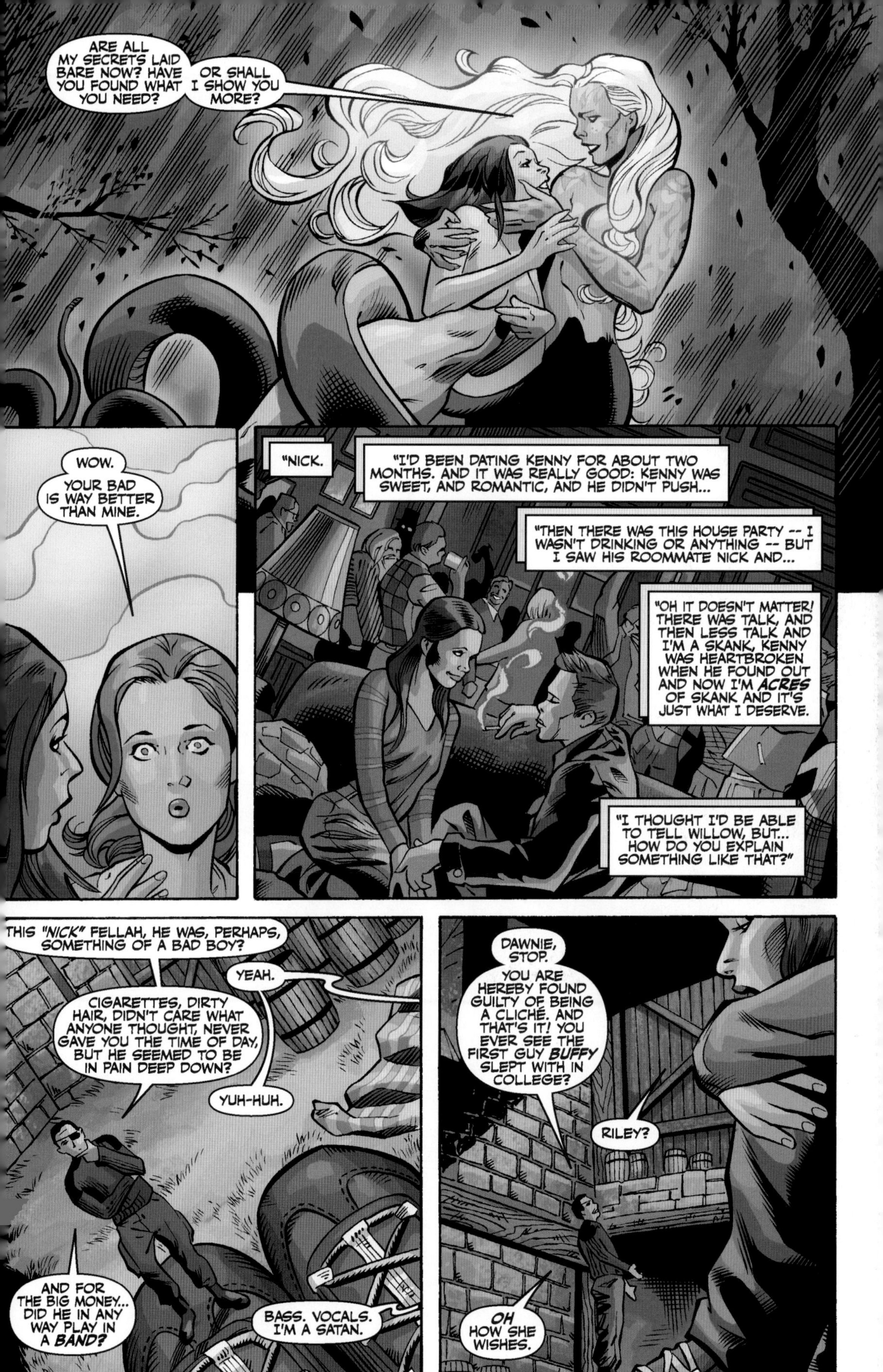
ARE ALL MY SECRETS LAID BARE NOW? HAVE YOU FOUND WHAT YOU NEED?
OR SHALL I SHOW YOU MORE?
WOW. YOUR BAD IS WAY BETTER THAN MINE.
"NICK.
"I'D BEEN DATING KENNY FOR ABOUT TWO MONTHS. AND IT WAS REALLY GOOD: KENNY WAS SWEET, AND ROMANTIC, AND HE DIDN'T PUSH...
"THEN THERE WAS THIS HOUSE PARTY -- I WASN'T DRINKING OR ANYTHING -- BUT I SAW HIS ROOMMATE NICK AND...
"OH IT DOESN'T MATTER! THERE WAS TALK, AND THEN LESS TALK AND I'M A SKANK, KENNY WAS HEARTBROKEN WHEN HE FOUND OUT AND NOW I'M *ACRES* OF SKANK AND IT'S JUST WHAT I DESERVE.
"I THOUGHT I'D BE ABLE TO TELL WILLOW, BUT... HOW DO YOU EXPLAIN SOMETHING LIKE THAT?"
THIS *"NICK"* FELLAH, HE WAS, PERHAPS, SOMETHING OF A BAD BOY?
YEAH.
CIGARETTES, DIRTY HAIR, DIDN'T CARE WHAT ANYONE THOUGHT, NEVER GAVE YOU THE TIME OF DAY, BUT HE SEEMED TO BE IN PAIN DEEP DOWN?
YUH-HUH.
AND FOR THE BIG MONEY... DID HE IN ANY WAY PLAY IN A *BAND?*
BASS. VOCALS. I'M A SATAN.
DAWNIE, STOP.
YOU ARE HEREBY FOUND GUILTY OF BEING A CLICHÉ. AND THAT'S IT! YOU EVER SEE THE FIRST GUY *BUFFY* SLEPT WITH IN COLLEGE?
RILEY?
OH HOW SHE WISHES.

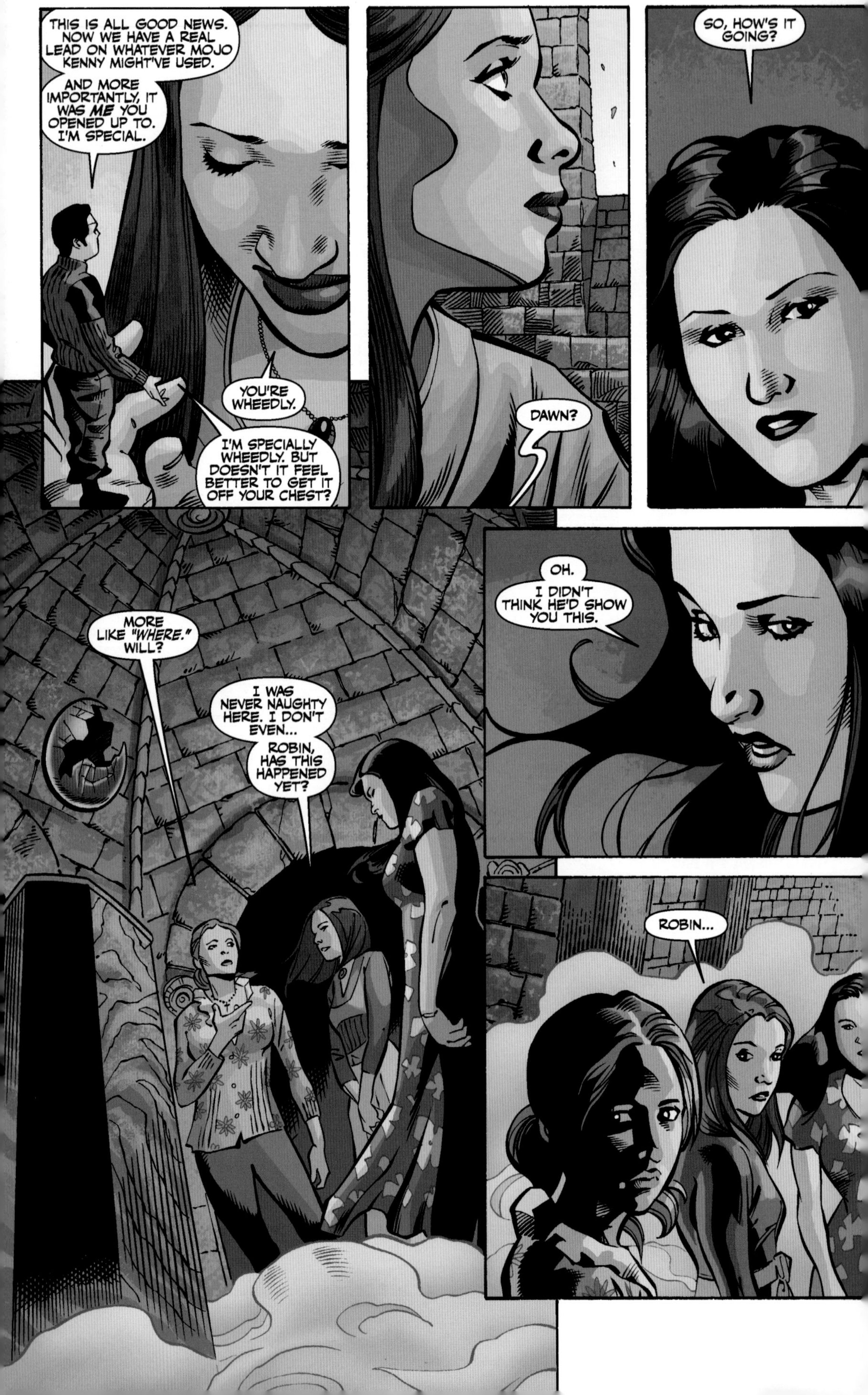
THIS IS ALL GOOD NEWS. NOW WE HAVE A REAL LEAD ON WHATEVER MOJO KENNY MIGHT'VE USED.
AND MORE IMPORTANTLY, IT WAS *ME* YOU OPENED UP TO. I'M SPECIAL.
YOU'RE WHEEDLY.
I'M SPECIALLY WHEEDLY. BUT DOESN'T IT FEEL BETTER TO GET IT OFF YOUR CHEST?
DAWN?
SO, HOW'S IT GOING?
MORE LIKE *"WHERE."* WILL?
I WAS NEVER NAUGHTY HERE. I DON'T EVEN...
ROBIN, HAS THIS HAPPENED YET?
OH.
I DIDN'T THINK HE'D SHOW YOU THIS.
ROBIN...

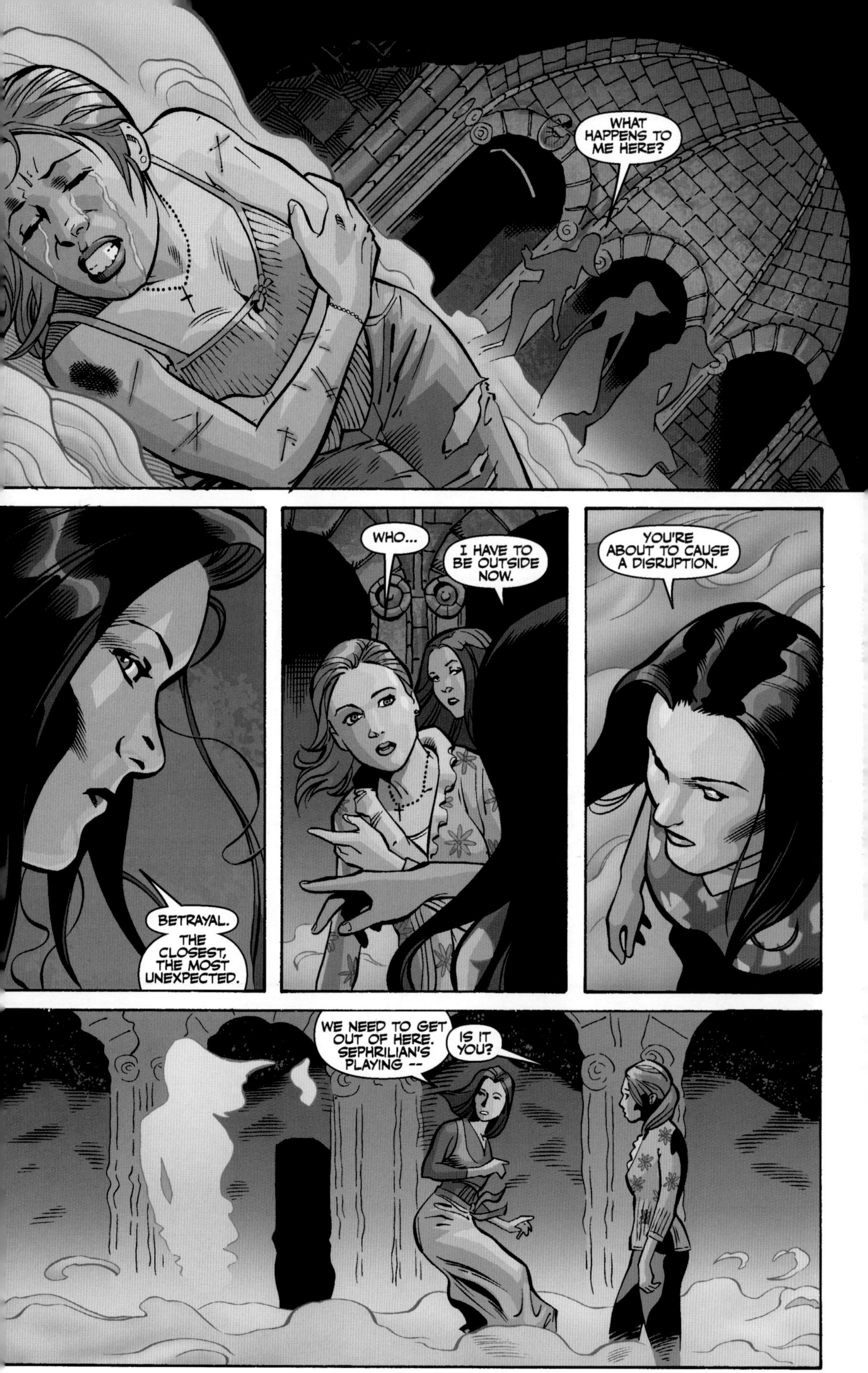
WHAT HAPPENS TO ME HERE?
BETRAYAL. THE CLOSEST, THE MOST UNEXPECTED.
WHO...
I HAVE TO BE OUTSIDE NOW.
YOU'RE ABOUT TO CAUSE A DISRUPTION.
WE NEED TO GET OUT OF HERE. SEPHRILIAN'S PLAYING --
IS IT YOU?

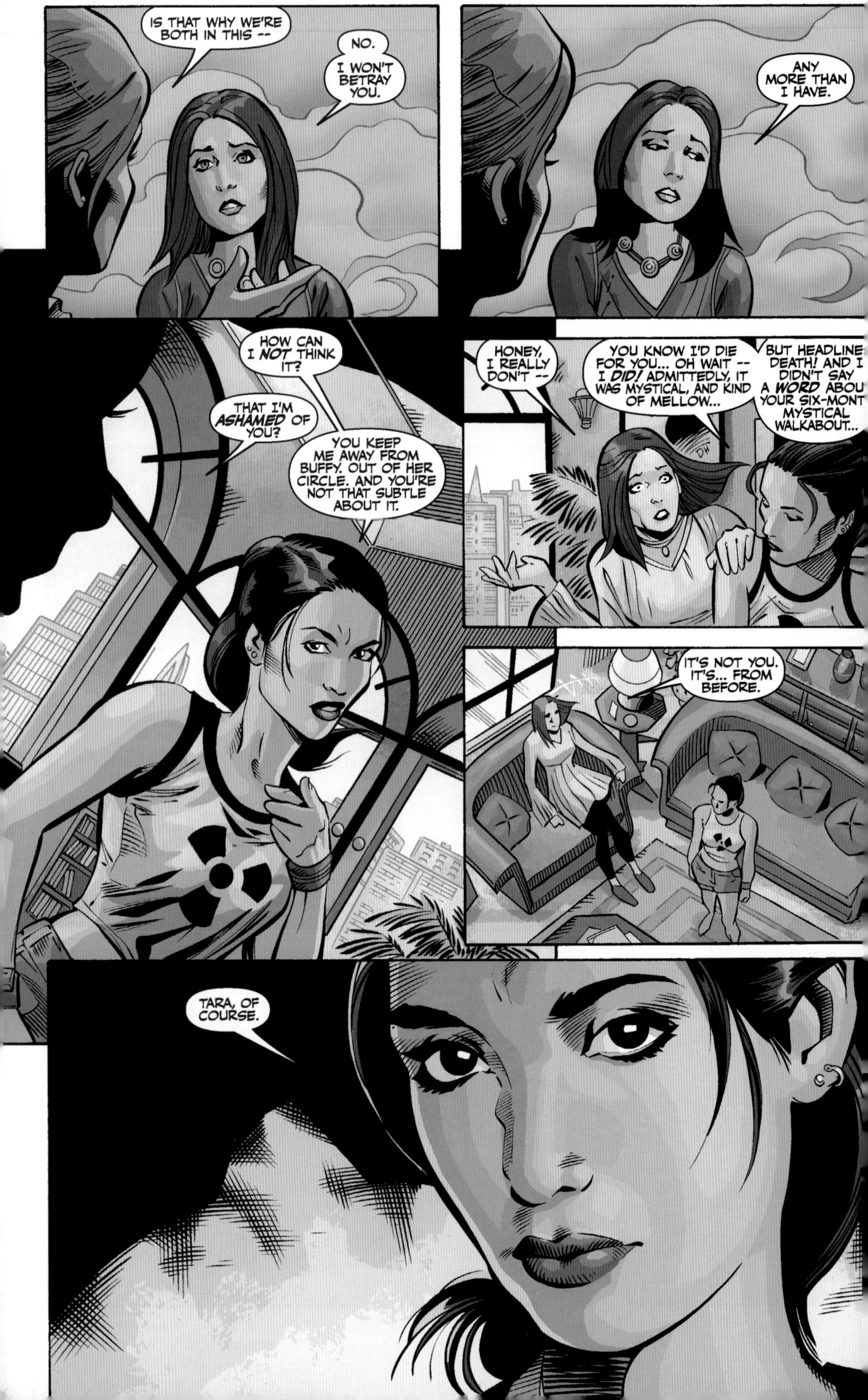
IS THAT WHY WE'RE BOTH IN THIS --
NO.
I WON'T BETRAY YOU.
ANY MORE THAN I HAVE.
HOW CAN I *NOT* THINK IT?
THAT I'M *ASHAMED* OF YOU?
YOU KEEP ME AWAY FROM BUFFY. OUT OF HER CIRCLE. AND YOU'RE NOT THAT SUBTLE ABOUT IT.
HONEY, I REALLY DON'T --
YOU KNOW I'D DIE FOR YOU... OH WAIT -- I *DID!* ADMITTEDLY, IT WAS MYSTICAL, AND KIND OF MELLOW...
BUT HEADLINE DEATH! AND I DIDN'T SAY A *WORD* ABOU YOUR SIX-MONT MYSTICAL WALKABOUT...
IT'S NOT YOU. IT'S... FROM BEFORE.
TARA, OF COURSE.

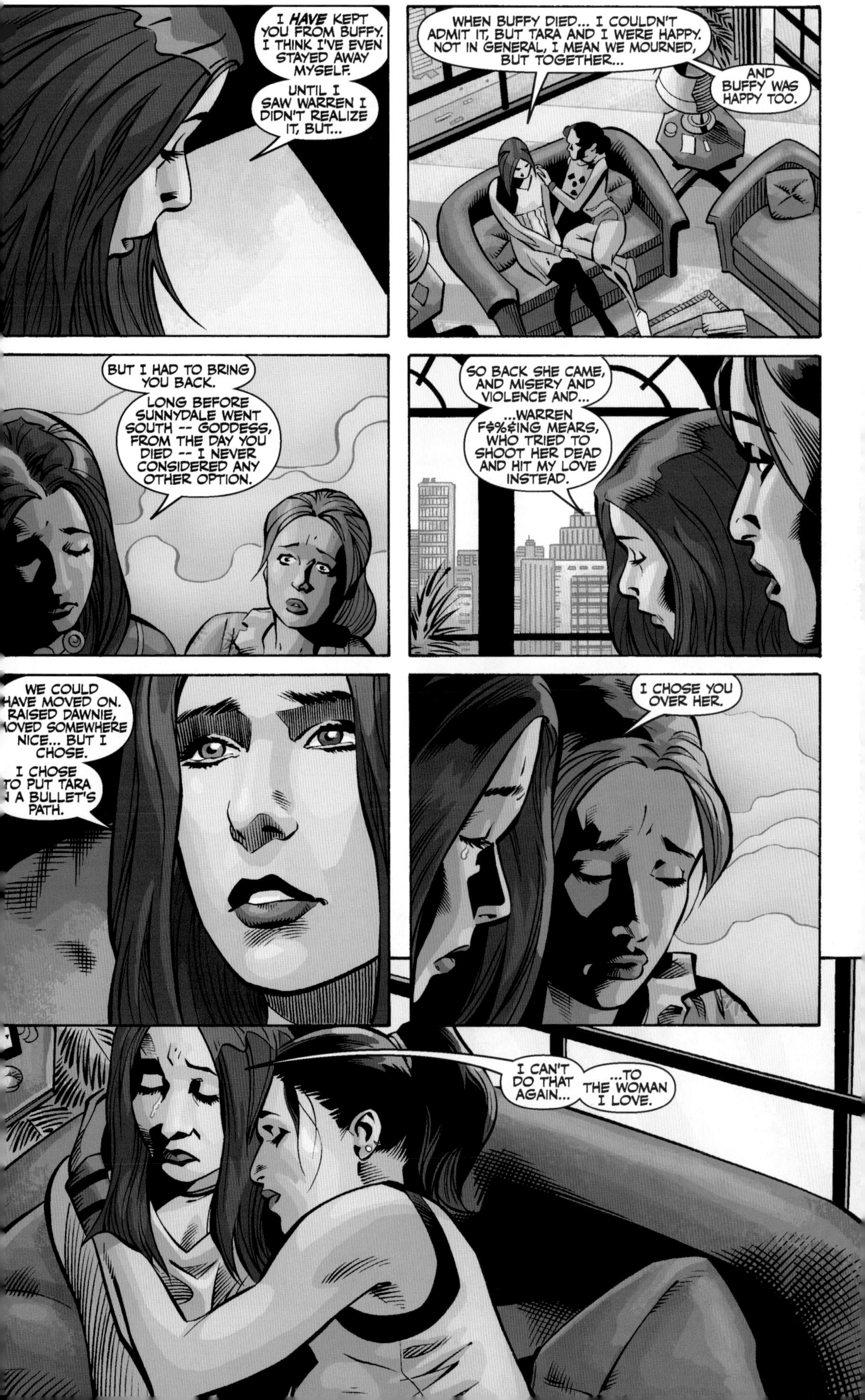
I *HAVE* KEPT YOU FROM BUFFY. I THINK I'VE EVEN STAYED AWAY MYSELF.
UNTIL I SAW WARREN I DIDN'T REALIZE IT, BUT...
WHEN BUFFY DIED... I COULDN'T ADMIT IT, BUT TARA AND I WERE HAPPY. NOT IN GENERAL, I MEAN WE MOURNED, BUT TOGETHER...
AND BUFFY WAS HAPPY TOO.
BUT I HAD TO BRING YOU BACK.
LONG BEFORE SUNNYDALE WENT SOUTH -- GODDESS, FROM THE DAY YOU DIED -- I NEVER CONSIDERED ANY OTHER OPTION.
SO BACK SHE CAME, AND MISERY AND VIOLENCE AND...
...WARREN F$%&ING MEARS, WHO TRIED TO SHOOT HER DEAD AND HIT MY LOVE INSTEAD.
WE COULD HAVE MOVED ON. RAISED DAWNIE, MOVED SOMEWHERE NICE... BUT I CHOSE.
I CHOSE TO PUT TARA IN A BULLET'S PATH.
I CHOSE YOU OVER HER.
I CAN'T DO THAT AGAIN...
...TO THE WOMAN I LOVE.

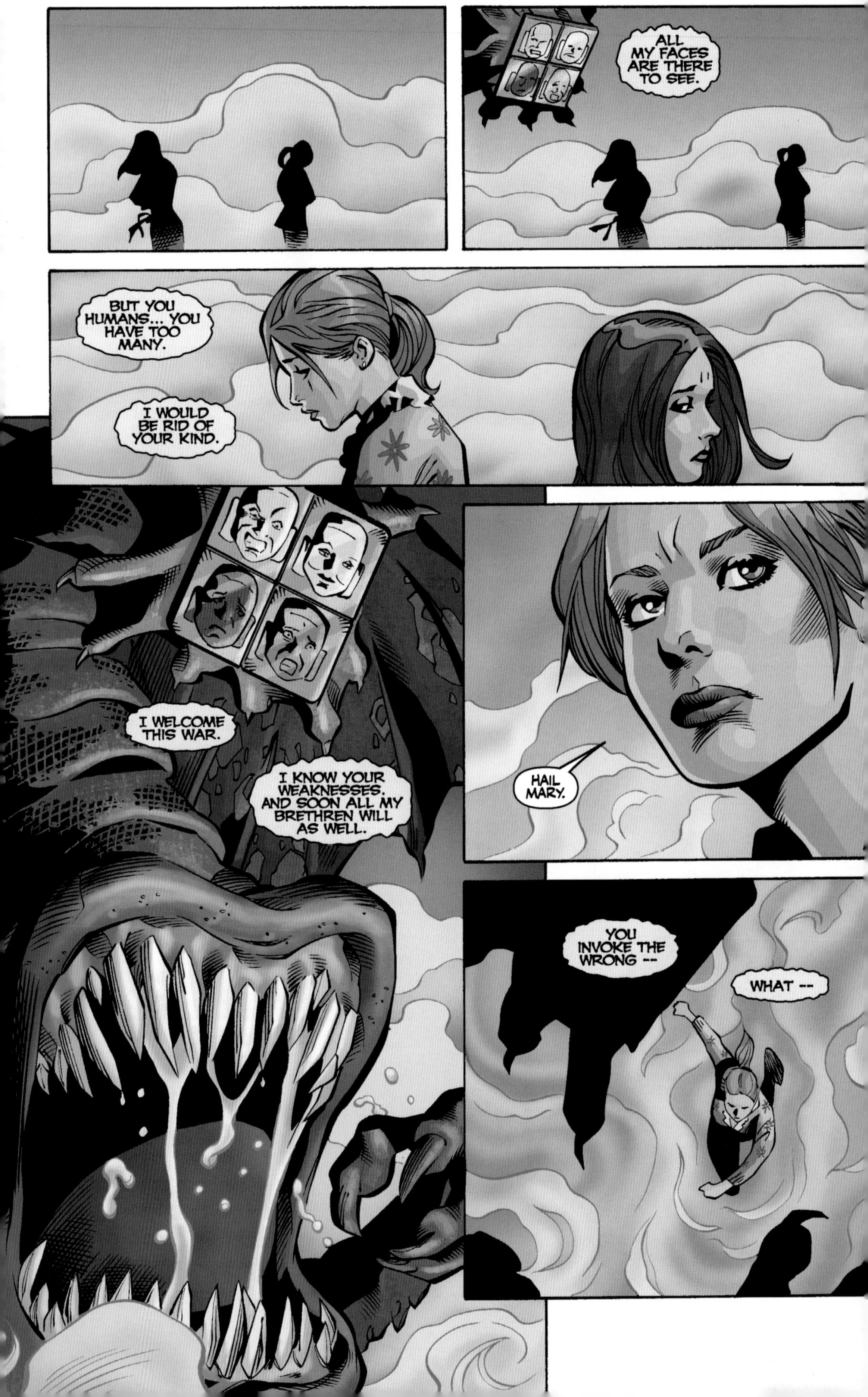
ALL MY FACES ARE THERE TO SEE.
BUT YOU HUMANS... YOU HAVE TOO MANY.
I WOULD BE RID OF YOUR KIND.
I WELCOME THIS WAR.
I KNOW YOUR WEAKNESSES. AND SOON ALL MY BRETHREN WILL AS WELL.
HAIL MARY.
YOU INVOKE THE WRONG --
WHAT --

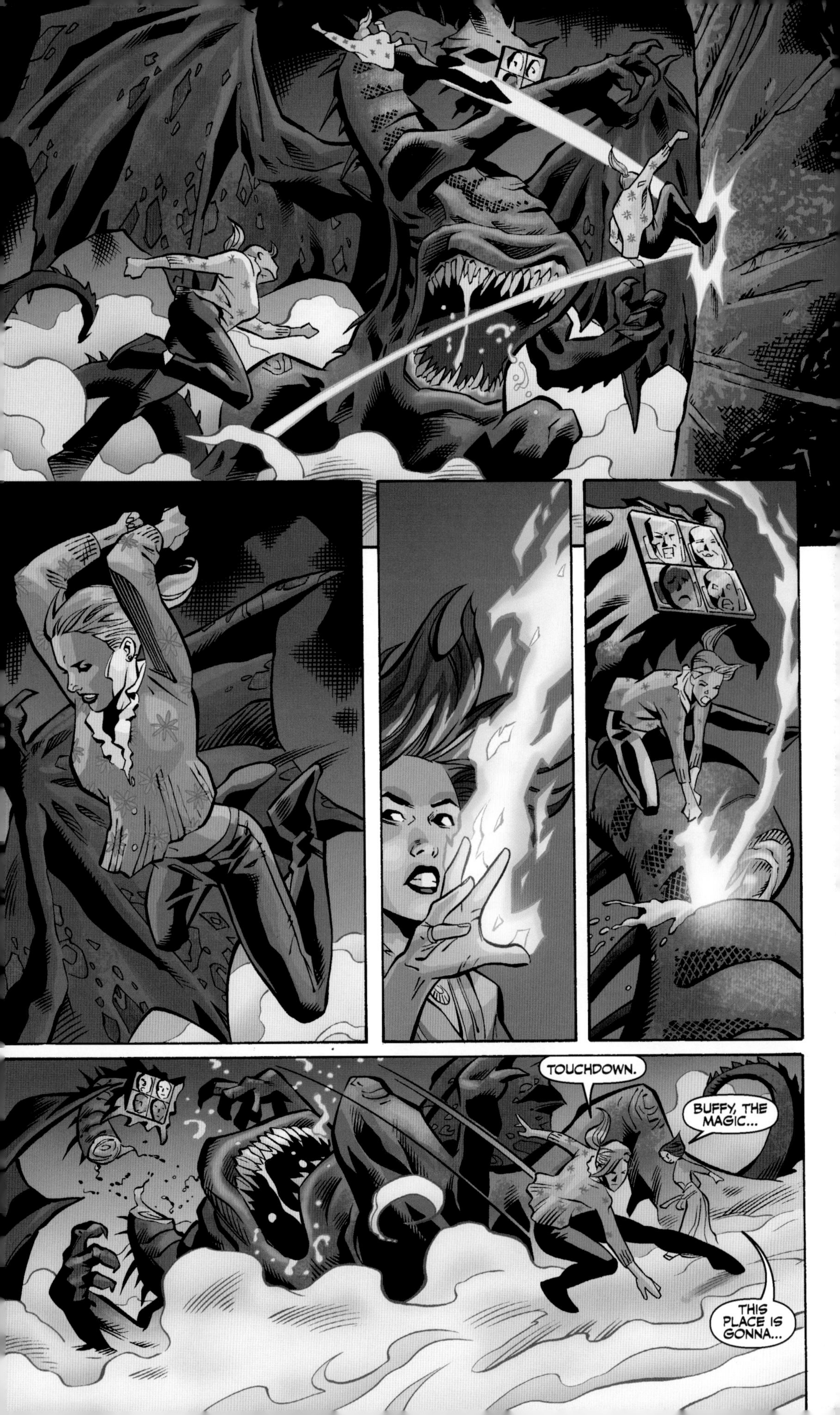
TOUCHDOWN.
BUFFY, THE MAGIC...
THIS PLACE IS GONNA...

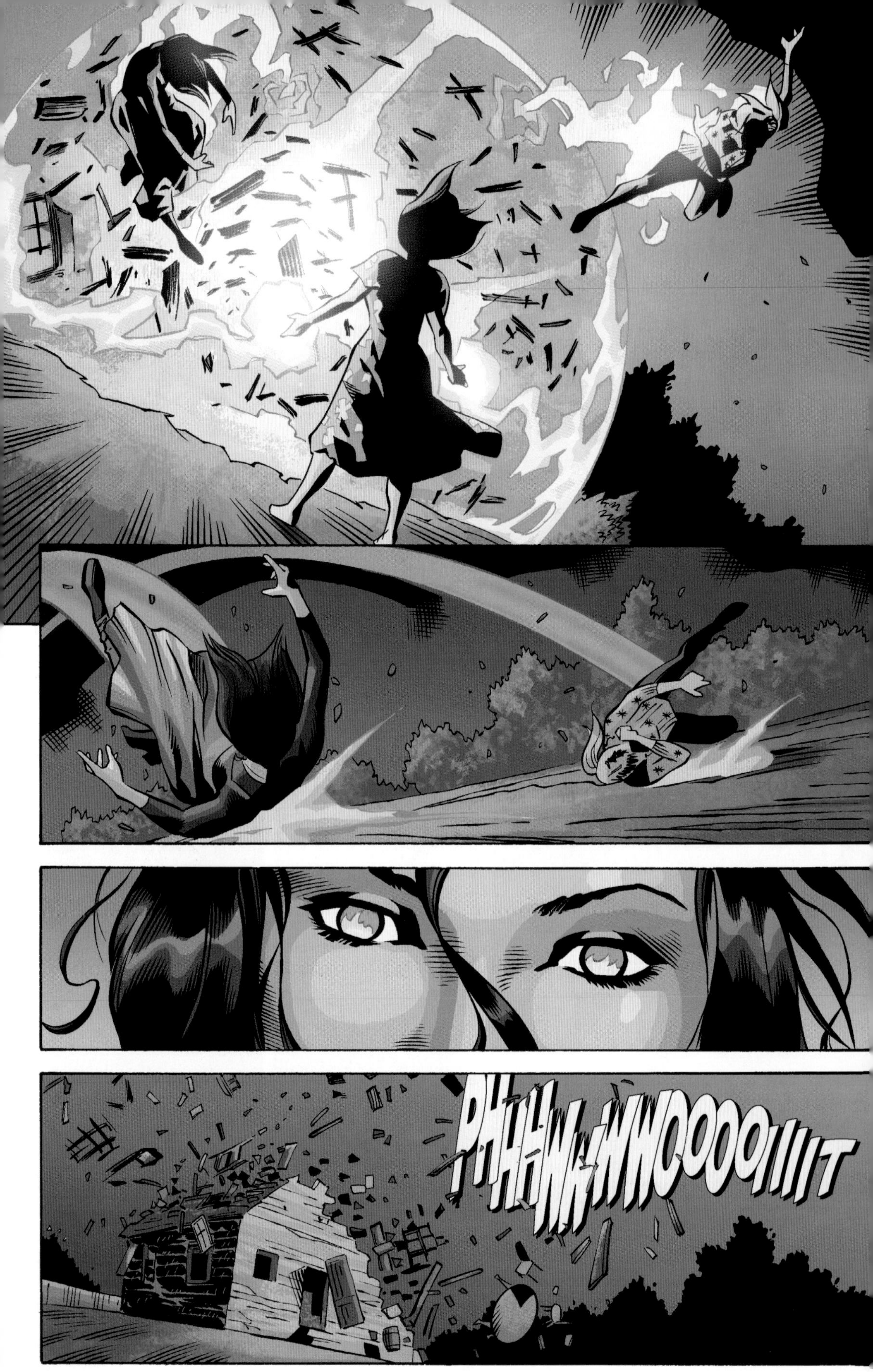
PHHHWAAWHOOOOIIIIIT

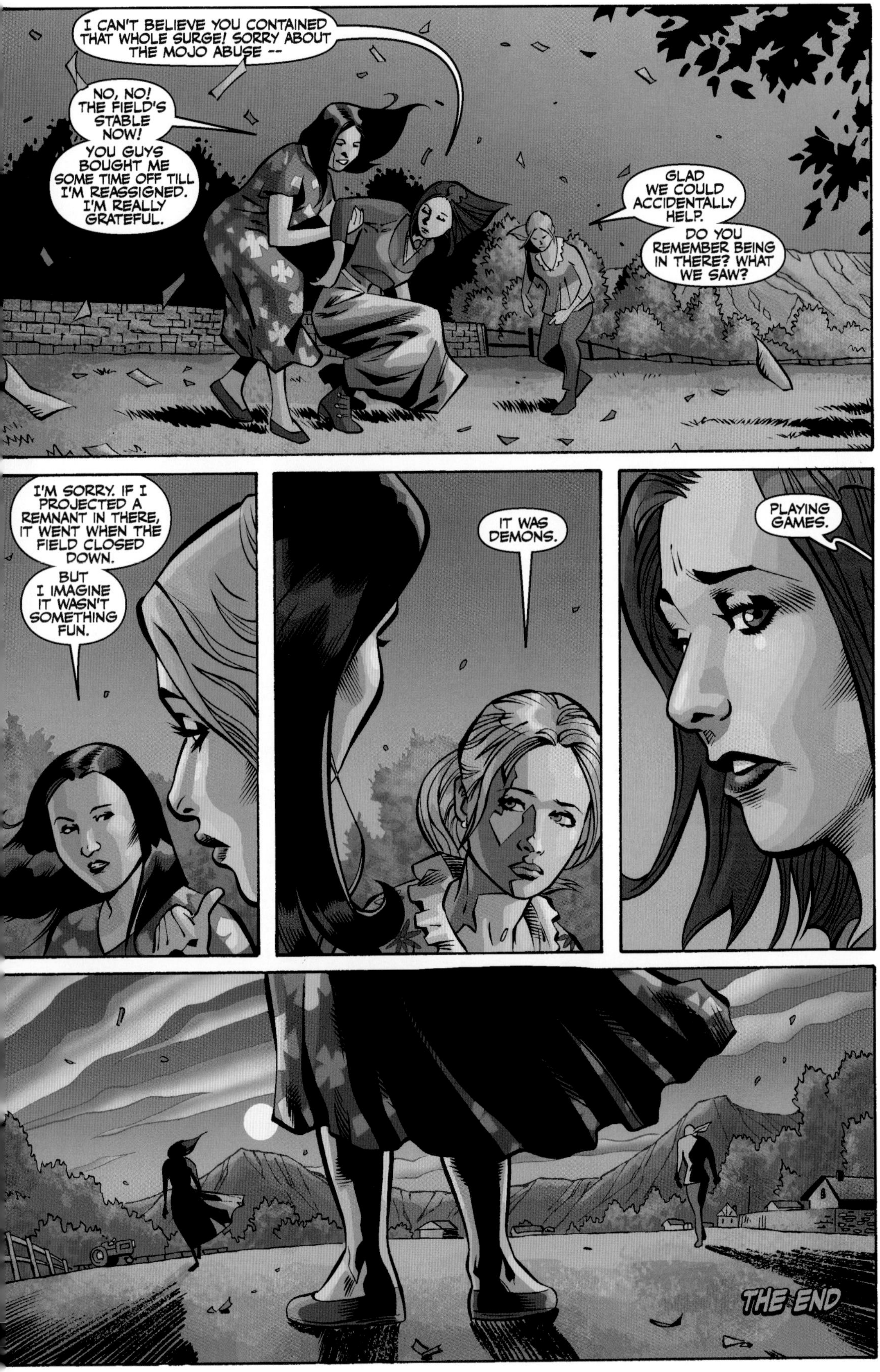

I CAN'T BELIEVE YOU CONTAINED THAT WHOLE SURGE! SORRY ABOUT THE MOJO ABUSE --
NO, NO! THE FIELD'S STABLE NOW!
YOU GUYS BOUGHT ME SOME TIME OFF TILL I'M REASSIGNED. I'M REALLY GRATEFUL.
GLAD WE COULD ACCIDENTALLY HELP.
DO YOU REMEMBER BEING IN THERE? WHAT WE SAW?
I'M SORRY. IF I PROJECTED A REMNANT IN THERE, IT WENT WHEN THE FIELD CLOSED DOWN.
BUT I IMAGINE IT WASN'T SOMETHING FUN.
IT WAS DEMONS.
PLAYING GAMES.
THE END

COVERS FROM

BUFFY THE VAMPIRE SLAYER

ISSUES #7–10

By

GEORGES JEANTY

with

DEXTER VINES

DAVE STEWART

& DAN JACKSON

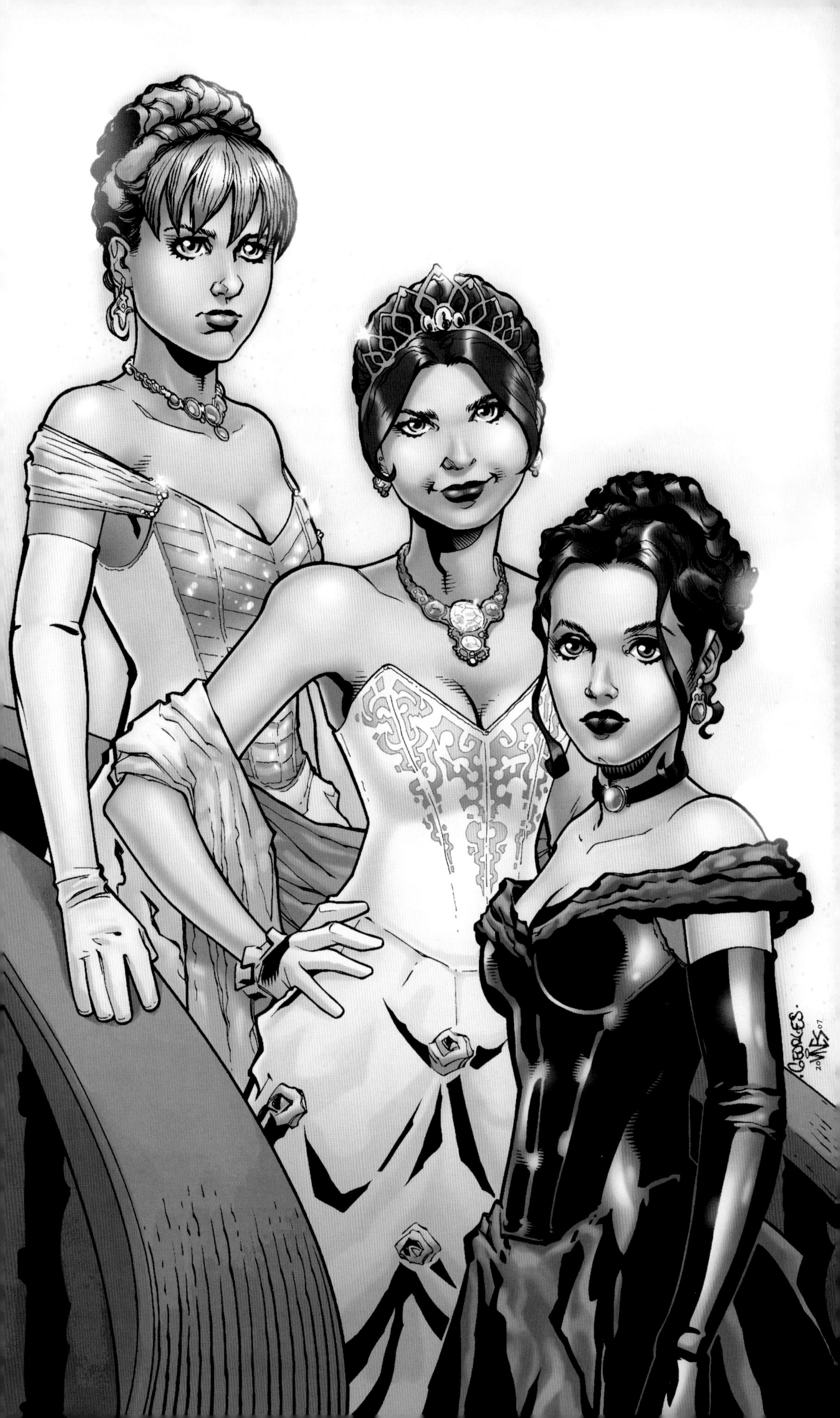

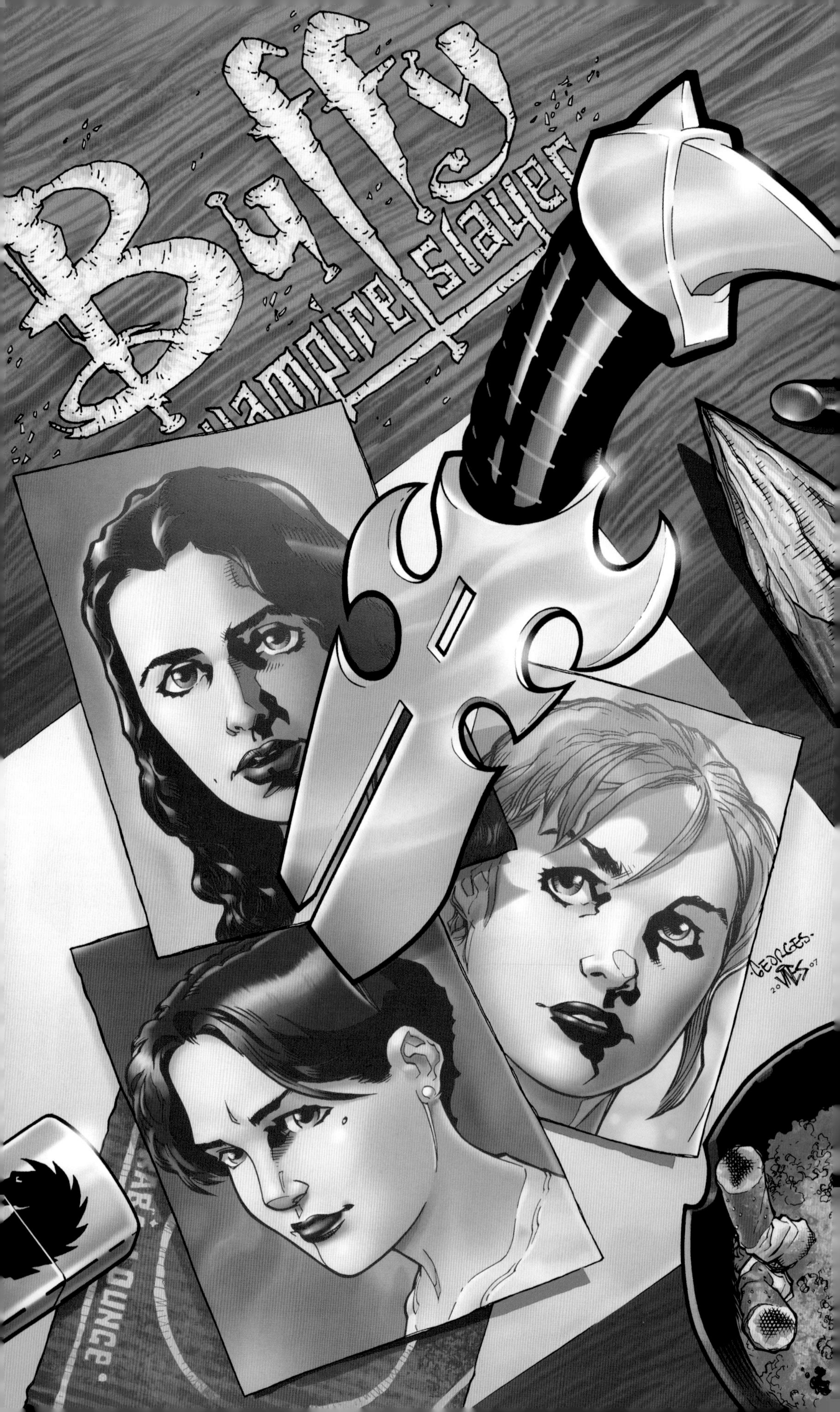
Buffy
vampire slayer
GEORGES JEANTY 2007

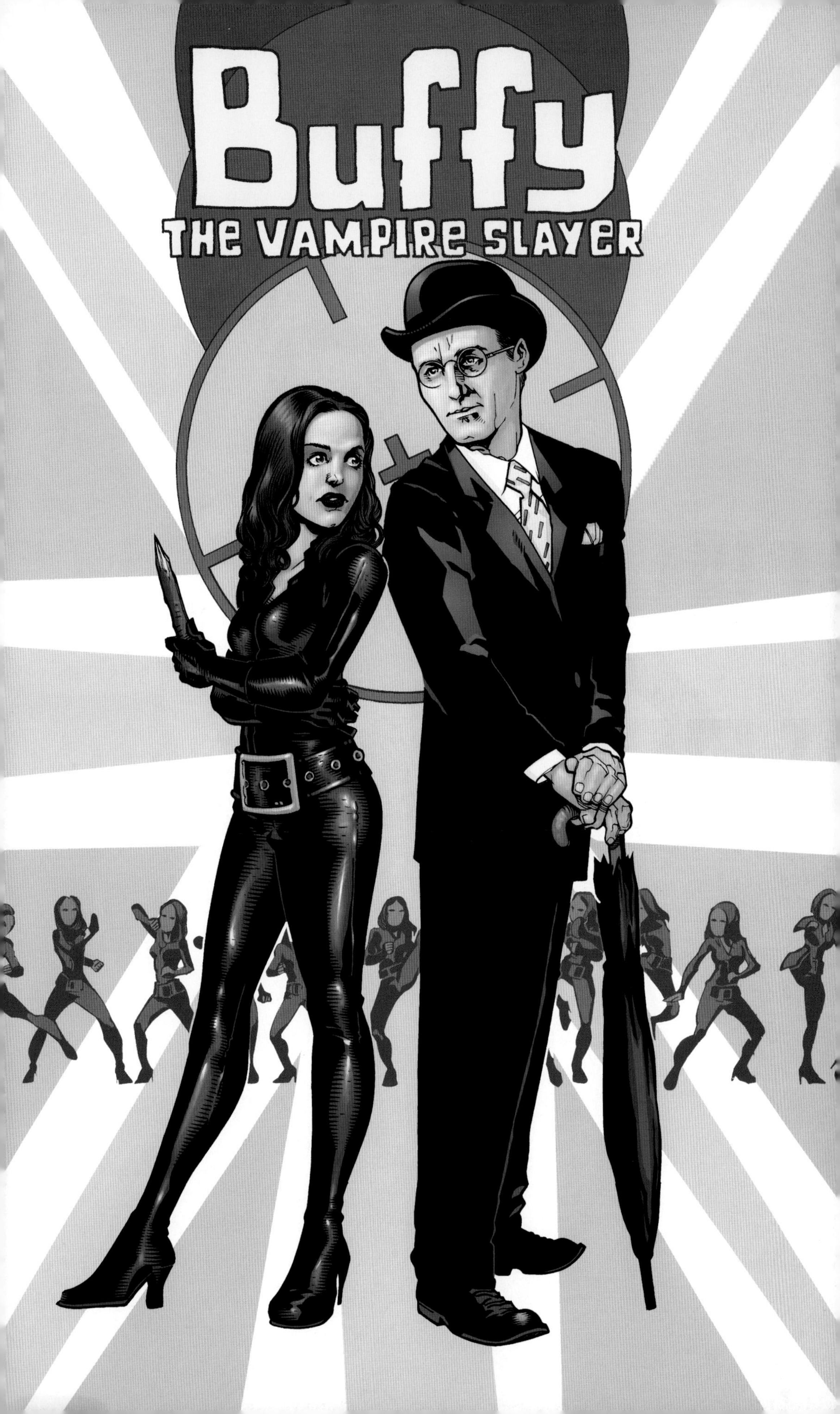
Buffy
THE VAMPIRE SLAYER

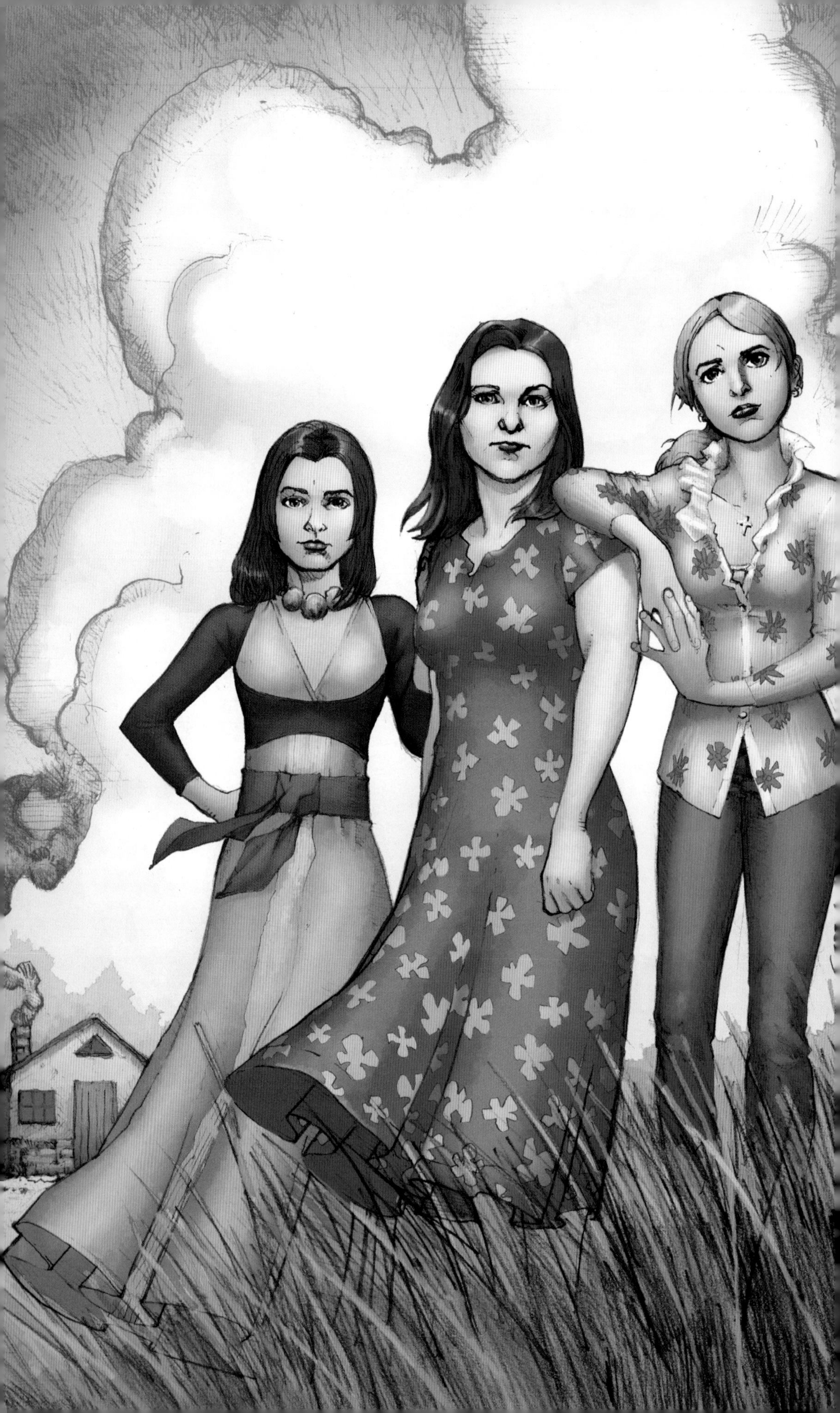